IDAHO

Real Estate

PRACTICE & LAW

Chuck Byers, GRI, CRB
Consulting Editor

ELEVENTH EDITION, UPDATE

Dearborn™
Real Estate Education

This publication is designed to provide accurate and authoritative information in regard to the subject matter covered. It is sold with the understanding that the publisher is not engaged in rendering legal, accounting, or other professional service. If legal advice or other expert assistance is required, the services of a competent professional person should be sought.

President: Roy Lipner
Vice President of Product Development and Publishing: Evan Butterfield
Managing Editor: Kate DeVivo
Senior Development Editor: Anne Huston
Director of Production: Dan Frey
Production Editor: Caitlin Ostrow
Typesetter: Janet Schroeder
Creative Director: Lucy Jenkins

Published by Dearborn™ Real Estate Education
30 South Wacker Drive
Chicago, IL 60606-7481
(312) 836-4400
http://www.dearbornRE.com

Printed in the United States of America.

06   07   10   9   8   7   6   5   4   3   2   1

Library of Congress Cataloging-in-Publication Data

Byers, Chuck.
  Idaho real estate : practice & law / Chuck Byers.–11th ed.
    p. cm.
  Rev. ed. of: Idaho real estate. 10th ed. c2002.
  Includes index.
  ISBN 1-4195-0312-X
  1. Real estate business—Law and legislation—Idaho 2. Vendors and purchasers—
Idaho. 3. Real property—Idaho. 4. Real estate business—Idaho. I. Dearborn Real Estate Education (Firm)
II. Idaho real estate. III. Title.
  KF2042.R4 G34 2005 Idaho 3
  346.79604′37--dc22   2005011987

CONTENTS

PREFACE

Real estate practice in any state is based on the state's constitution, laws, regulations, and court decisions in addition to fundamental federal laws and regulations. Each state's legislature, courts, and commissions make laws and regulations governing activities in that state. The Idaho legislature convenes each year on the second Monday in January. It also may be called into special session by order of the governor. In any of these sessions, new laws may be passed or changes may be made in existing laws that affect real estate practice. The practice of real estate in any specific location in Idaho may also be influenced by local agencies, bureaus, and organizations, including but not limited to county and city governments or local boards of REALTORS®, and by the controls and/or customs initiated by these organizations.

The purpose of *Idaho Real Estate: Practice & Law* is to discuss the body of laws and practices applicable to the state of Idaho. This text builds on basic information presented in Dearborn™ Real Estate Education's real estate principles texts. It is a good idea to first study the lesson in the main text, and then refer to the same subject area in this text. Online information can be accessed using the Web addresses available throughout the text and in Appendix A in the back of this book.

Following each chapter are questions drawn from material in the text. These tests can be both evaluative and educational. Be certain that you understand and are able to answer each question before you go on to the next chapter. An answer key for all of the tests is included at the back of the book.

Throughout your real estate course, you will be studying and taking tests in preparation for the Idaho Real Estate License Examination. All applicants for real estate licensing in Idaho must pass a standardized examination. In an additional section of the Idaho exam, the questions pertain to Idaho laws and rules. *Idaho Real Estate: Practice & Law*, 11th Edition Update, includes specific Idaho legislation as well as general information you will need to know in order to pass the examination.

■ HOW TO USE THIS BOOK

The conversion table on page viii provides a quick and easy reference for using *Idaho Real Estate: Practice & Law*, 11th Edition Update, in conjunction with various principles books. For instance, *Idaho Real Estate*'s Chapter 16, "Closing the Real Estate Transaction," may be read in conjunction with Chapter 22 in *Modern Real Estate Practice*, 17th Edition; Chapter 17 in *Real Estate Fundamentals*, 6th Edition; Chapter 12 in *Mastering Real Estate Principles*, 4th Edition; and Lesson 22 in *National Real Estate Principles* software.

Chapter Conversion Table

Idaho Real Estate: Practice & Law, 11th Edition Update	Modern Real Estate Practice, 17th Edition	Real Estate Fundamentals, 6th Edition	Mastering Real Estate Principles, 4th Edition	National Real Estate Principles Software, Ver. 2.0
1. Real Estate Brokerage	4, 5	9	13	4, 5
2. Buyer and Seller Representation Agreements	6	7, 9	15	6
3. Interests in Real Estate	7	3	7	7
4. How Ownership Is Held	8	5	9	8
5. Legal Descriptions	9	2	6	9
6. Real Estate Taxes and Other Liens	10	10	5, 25	10
7. Real Estate Contracts	11	7	14	11
8. Transfer of Title	12	4	10	12
9. Title Records	13	6	11	13
10. Real Estate License Law	—	—	16	—
11. Real Estate Financing	14, 15	12, 13	Unit VII	14, 15
12. Leases	16	8	8	16
13. Real Estate Appraisal	18	11	Unit VI	18
14. Environmental Issues and Control of Land Use	19, 21	14, 16	3	19, 21
15. Idaho Fair Housing	20	15	17	20
16. Closing the Real Estate Transaction	22	17	12	22

ACKNOWLEDGMENTS

The publisher would like to thank the following real estate professionals for their expertise, patience, and assistance in preparing this edition: Maris Cukurs, Realty Executives of Eastern Idaho; Jill Randall, Idaho Association of REALTORS®; Cynthia S. Thompson, ExecuTrain of Idaho; Pamela G. Trees, Idaho Real Estate Commission; and William R. "Bill" Zales, Tomlinson Black North Idaho, Inc.

Permission to use forms is given by the Idaho Association of REALTORS®, the Ada County Association of REALTORS®, Pioneer Title Company of Ada County, and the Code Commission of the State of Idaho. Forms reproduced here are for illustrative purposes only and may not be reproduced without the permission of the organization holding the copyright. Re-creation or unauthorized usage of the forms is a violation of trademark and copyright law, and will be prosecuted to the fullest extent of the law.

■ ABOUT THE CONSULTING EDITOR

Idaho Real Estate: Practice & Law, 11th Edition Update, was prepared by Consulting Editor Chuck Byers, GRI, CRB. Mr. Byers is Director of the Pioneer Real Estate School and has been a licensed owner/broker for over 30 years in Oregon and Idaho. Mr. Byers is past Regional Vice-President and past Board Director at the Real Estate Educators Association. He has twice been named REALTOR® of the Year by the Clatsop Board of REALTORS®, and was named the Instructor of the Year in 1999 by the Idaho Real Estate Commission. Mr. Byers holds a Bachelor of Science degree from the University of Oregon.

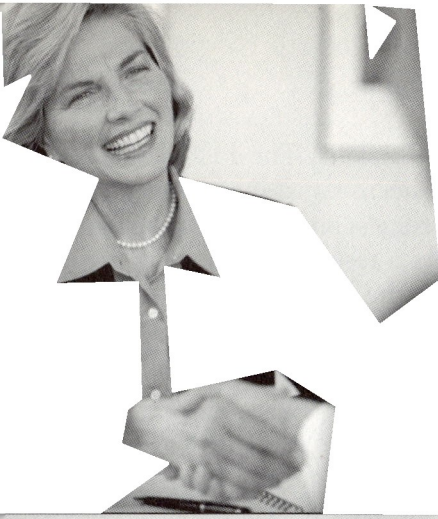

1

REAL ESTATE BROKERAGE

In Idaho, a person must be licensed to *engage* in the real estate business or *act* as a real estate broker, associate broker, or sales associate.

Activities requiring a real estate license include: while acting for another, for compensation or a promise or an expectation thereof engages in any of the following: "selling, listing, buying, negotiating, or offering to sell, list, buy, or negotiate the purchase, sale, option, or exchange of real estate or any interest therein or business opportunity or interest therein for others."

Idaho code also includes: "any person who directly or indirectly engages in, directs, or takes any part in the procuring of prospects, or in the negotiating or closing of any transactions which does or is calculated to result in any of the acts above set forth" [IC 54-2002 and IC 54-2004].

Exceptions: There are specific situations that *do not* require a real estate license including, but not limited to, the purchase, option, exchange, or sale of any interest in real property or business opportunity for a person's own account or use [IC 54-2003].

■ REAL ESTATE LICENSE LAW

Idaho real estate licenses are granted by the *Idaho Real Estate Commission* under the provisions of the *Idaho Real Estate License Law*. This law and the Commission's *Rules* regulate and place restrictions on the activities of brokers and salespeople. Many of the provisions were created to implement and enforce the law of agency with broker–client/customer relationships.

The status of Idaho's entire real estate industry has been elevated since the Real Estate License Law was first enacted in 1947. The law was initiated by the industry and is enforced by the industry at the licensee's expense. It places restrictions on the actions of people in the real estate business to protect the public they serve. In addition, the law requires licensed real estate salespeople to further their education if they wish to become brokers. The Idaho Real Estate Commission also encourages all real estate licensees to increase their education and knowledge to better serve their customers and clients through mandatory continuing education [IC 54-2023]. As a result of the improved services offered, the public has come to recognize the real estate broker or salesperson as a professional—a specialist in real estate.

Online Information

The Idaho Real Estate Commission Web site contains a complete set of the Idaho Real Estate License Law and Rules. It is a good idea for licensees to check this Web site for updated information at

WWWeb.Link

www.idahorealestatecommission.com
www.irec.idaho.gov

■ IDAHO'S AGENCY LAW

The Idaho Real Estate Brokerage Representation Act [IC 54-2082 through 54-2097] governs the legal relationships between brokers and the public in Idaho. The Act applies to all "regulated real estate transactions"—that is, transactions for which a real estate license is required by law. *The common law of agency, as it applies to real estate transactions, has been expressly abrogated (made null) by the statute.* A buyer or seller is not represented by a brokerage unless the buyer or seller and the brokerage have agreed, in writing, to such a client–brokerage relationship. Until that time, the buyer or seller is a customer.

A customer is not represented by a real estate professional but is owed certain legal services, as described below. *No type of agency representation may be assumed by a buyer or seller, or created orally or by implication.*

Customer-Level Duties [IC 54-2086]

If a buyer or seller is not represented by a brokerage in a regulated real estate transaction (in other words, he or she does not sign a listing agreement or a buyer-broker contract), he or she is a **customer**, for whom the brokerage and its associated licensees are *nonagents*—that is, there is no written agency representation between the parties. A customer is owed only the following legal duties and obligations by a nonagent brokerage and its licensees:

- To perform ministerial acts to assist the customer in the sale or purchase of real estate, with honesty, good faith, reasonable skill and care
- To properly account for monies or property placed in the care and responsibility of the brokerage
- To disclose to a buyer/customer all adverse material facts actually known or which reasonably should have been known by the licensee
- To disclose to a seller/customer all adverse material facts actually known or which reasonably should have been known by the licensee

Ministerial acts are defined by statute [IC 54-2083] as "reasonably necessary and customary acts typically performed by real estate licensees in assisting a transaction to its closing or conclusion."

A nonagent brokerage and its licensees owe no duty to a buyer/customer to conduct an independent inspection of property for the customer's benefit or to keep his or her bargaining information confidential. Similarly, no duty is owed to independently verify the accuracy or completeness of any statement or representation made by the seller or any source reasonably believed to be reliable by the licensee.

A nonagent brokerage and its licensees owe no duty to a seller/customer to conduct an independent investigation of a buyer's financial condition for the customer's benefit, to keep his or her bargaining information confidential, or to independently verify the accuracy or completeness of any statements made by the buyer or other reliable source.

Client-Level Duties [IC 54-2087]

If a buyer or seller enters into a written contract for representation in a regulated real estate transaction, that buyer or seller becomes a **client**, to whom the brokerage and its licensees owe the following agency duties and obligations:

- To perform the terms of the *written agreement* with the client.
- To exercise *reasonable skill and care*.
- To promote the best interests of the client in *good faith, honesty, and fair dealing, while using reasonable skill and care,* including
  - disclosing to the client all *adverse material facts* actually known or that reasonably should have been known by the licensee;
  - seeking a buyer to purchase the seller's property at a price and under terms and conditions acceptable to the seller and assisting in the negotiations for the property;
  - seeking a property for purchase at a price and under terms and conditions acceptable to the buyer and assisting in the negotiations for the property;
  - *for the benefit of the client/buyer:* when appropriate, advising the client to obtain professional inspections of the property or to seek appropriate tax, legal, and other professional advice or counsel;
  - *for the benefit of the client/seller:* upon written request by the client/seller, requesting reasonable proof of the prospective buyer's financial ability to purchase the real property that is the subject matter of the transaction. This duty may be satisfied by any appropriate method suitable to the transaction or, when deemed necessary by the real estate licensee, by advising the seller/client to consult with an accountant, lawyer, or other professional as dictated by the transaction.
- To maintain the *confidentiality* of specific client information, that is, information gained from a client (1) that is not a matter of public record; (2) that the client has not disclosed or authorized to be disclosed to third parties; (3) that if disclosed would be detrimental to the client; and (4) that the client would not be personally obligated to disclose to another party to the transaction.
- Duty to a client continues beyond the termination of representation only so long as the information continues to be considered confidential.
- To properly *account* for moneys or property placed in the care and responsibility of the brokerage.

■ Unless agreed to in writing, a brokerage or licensee owes no duty to a client to conduct an independent inspection of the property and owes no duty to independently verify the accuracy or completeness of any statement or representation made regarding a property.

Information that is required to be disclosed by law or that is generally disseminated in the marketplace (such as the "sold" prices of property), or that would constitute fraudulent misrepresentation if not disclosed, is *not* considered confidential client information [IC 54-2083].

Limited Dual Agency and Assigned Agency Duties [IC 54-2088]

Idaho's agency statute specifically permits a brokerage to act as a **limited disclosed dual agent.** A limited disclosed dual agency is defined as limited brokerage representation in which both a buyer and a seller are clients for the purposes of a regulated real estate transaction.

This situation comes up, for example, when a brokerage company has a home listed for sale and also represents the buyer. A brokerage may act as a limited disclosed dual agent only with the express written consent of all parties to the transaction. Both the buyer and the seller in this situation need to sign a written Consent for Limited Dual Representation and Assigned Agency agreement. The consent must be signed by all parties and include the following language:

The undersigned have received, read, and understood the Agency Disclosure Brochure. The undersigned understand that the brokerage involved in this transaction may be providing agency representation to both the buyer and the seller. The undersigned each understand that as an agent for both buyer/client and seller/client, a brokerage will be a limited dual agent of each client and cannot advocate on behalf of one client over another, and cannot legally disclose to either client certain confidential client information concerning price negotiations, terms, or factors motivating the buyer/client to buy or the seller/client to sell without specific written permission of the client to whom the information pertains. The specific duties, obligations, and limitations of a limited dual agent are contained in the Agency Disclosure Brochure as required by Section 54-2085, Idaho Code. The undersigned each understand that a limited dual agent does not have a duty of undivided loyalty to either client.

The undersigned further acknowledge that, to the extent the brokerage firm offers assigned agency as a type of agency representation, individual sales associates may be assigned to represent each client to act solely on behalf of the client consistent with applicable duties set forth in Section 54-2087, Idaho Code. In an assigned agency situation, the designated broker (the broker who supervises the sales associates) will remain a limited dual agent of the client and shall have the duty to supervise the assigned agents in the fulfillment of their duties to their respective clients, to refrain from advocating on behalf of any one client over another, and to refrain from disclosing or using, without permission, confidential information of any other client with whom the brokerage has an agency relationship.

All duties and obligations owed to a buyer or seller apply to limited dual agency relationships to the extent they do not unreasonably conflict with the duties and obligations owed to the other client.

However, without the express written consent of the client, a limited dual agent may not disclose

■ that a buyer is willing to pay more than the listing price of the property;
■ that a seller is willing to accept less than the listing price for the property;
■ the factors motivating the buyer to buy or the seller to sell; or
■ that a buyer or seller will agree to a price or financing terms other than those offered.

A limited dual agent does not have a duty of undivided loyalty to either client. By consenting to a limited dual agency, the buyer and seller agree to those limitations.

If a brokerage acts as a limited dual agent and assigns separate sales associates to act on behalf of the separate clients the designated broker will continue to act as a limited dual agent and is charged with the duty to

■ supervise the assigned agents in the fulfillment of their duties to their respective clients;
■ refrain from advocating on behalf of any one client over another; and
■ refrain from disclosing or using, without permission, confidential information of any other client with whom the brokerage has an agency relationship.

If a designated broker determines that confidential information of a client has been disclosed to another client in the transaction in violation of the code, the designated broker shall *promptly provide written notice of the disclosure to the affected client.*

Neither a buyer nor a seller has any cause of action against a limited dual agent who makes any of the disclosures required or permitted by law. *Making a required or permitted disclosure does not terminate a limited dual agency relationship.*

Each designated brokerage acting as a limited dual agent must obtain prior written consent of all parties to the transaction in statutory format. The required consent and disclosure form must be signed by each buyer and seller in the transaction. Receipt of the agency disclosure brochure and the signed Consent To Dual Representation and Assigned Agency by the buyer and the seller are sufficient informed legal consent to dual representation. A consent by the buyer and seller to possible dual representation in the future, such as a consent contained in a written marketing or representation agreement, also constitutes effective and informed legal consent to dual representation [IC 54-2088(4)].

■ DISCLOSURE REQUIREMENTS [IC 54-2085]

Agency Disclosure Brochure

Licensees are required by statute to provide prospective buyers or sellers (still customers at this time) with an **agency disclosure brochure** provided by the Idaho Real Estate Commission. The brochure must be provided at the time of the *first substantial business contact* [IC 54-2085].

The brochure lists the types of customer relationships and client representation options available to a buyer or seller as well as the legal duties and obligations owed to the buyer or seller in each type of relationship. The relationships outlined are the following:

- Customer—whether buyer or seller
- Single Agency—whether seller or buyer
- Limited Dual Agency
- Limited Dual Agency without Assigned Agents

The brochure clearly indicates the difference between a customer and a client, as described above, and contains conspicuous notices that no broker–client agency representation will exist in the absence of a written agreement between the client and the brokerage. Specifically, the brochure says, *"Remember! Unless or until you enter a written agreement for agency representation, you will NOT be represented at all."*

Representation Confirmation

After the Agency Disclosure Brochure is given to the customer, the brokerage's relationship with the buyer or seller as agent, nonagent, or limited dual agent with or without assigned agents must be determined, formalized, and disclosed. Once the buyer or seller has selected the preferred level of representation, the broker must formally confirm it in writing, using a *Representation Confirmation* notice. (See Figure 1.1 for a sample Representation Confirmation notice.) This Representation Confirmation must be attached to or included in any written brokerage representation agreement (listing or buyer–broker) and given to both parties to the transaction no later than the time a purchase and sale agreement is prepared or presented [IC 54-2085].

A licensee's failure to give the buyer or seller the agency disclosure brochure in a timely manner, or to properly obtain any required written agreement or confirmation, is a violation of the Idaho real estate license law and may subject the licensee to disciplinary action [IC 54-2060].

Written Brokerage Representation Agreement [IC 54-2050]

As mentioned above, the Representation Confirmation notice must be attached to or included in any written brokerage representation agreement. In addition, every brokerage representation agreement must include

- a conspicuous and definite expiration date;
- a legally enforceable description of the property, price, and terms;
- a statement of the fee or commission;
- proper signatures of the parties;
- all obligations of the buyer; and
- the manner in which any fee or commission will be paid.

Broker Compensation [IC 54-2089]

An agency relationship is not created by the payment of compensation or an agreement limited to the payment of compensation; it is only created when a client signs a written brokerage representation agreement—either a listing agreement or buyer-broker contract.

F I G U R E 1.1

Representation Confirmation Notice

REPRESENTATION CONFIRMATION AND ACKNOWLEDGMENT OF DISCLOSURE

Check one (1) box in Section 1 below and one (1) box in Section 2 below to confirm that in this transaction, the brokerage(s) involved had the following relationship(s) with the Buyer(s) and Seller(s).

Section 1:

A. ❑ The brokerage working with the BUYER(S) is acting as an AGENT for the BUYER(S)
B. ❑ The brokerage working with the BUYER(S) is acting as a LIMITED DUAL AGENT for the BUYER(S), without an ASSIGNED AGENT
C. ❑ The brokerage working with the BUYER(S) is acting as a LIMITED DUAL AGENT for the BUYER(S), and has an ASSIGNED AGENT acting solely on behalf of the BUYER(S)
D. ❑ The broker working with the BUYER(S) is acting as a NONAGENT for the BUYER(S)

Section 2:

A. ❑ The brokerage working with the SELLER(S) is acting as an AGENT for the SELLER(S)
B. ❑ The brokerage working with the SELLER(S) is acting as a LIMITED DUAL AGENT for the SELLER(S), without an ASSIGNED AGENT
C. ❑ The brokerage working with the SELLER(S) is acting as a LIMITED DUAL AGENT for the SELLER(S), and has an ASSIGNED AGENT acting solely on behalf of the SELLER(S)
D. ❑ The broker working with the SELLER(S) is acting as a NONAGENT for the SELLER(S)

Each party signing this document confirms that he has received, read, and understood the Agency Disclosure Brochure adopted or approved by the Idaho Real Estate Commission and has consented to the relationship confirmed above. In addition, each party confirms that the brokerage's agency office policy was made available for inspection and review. EACH PARTY UNDERSTANDS THAT HE IS A "CUSTOMER" AND IS NOT REPRESENTED BY A BROKERAGE UNLESS THERE IS A SIGNED WRITTEN AGREEMENT FOR AGENCY REPRESENTATION.

Idaho Code [IC 54-2050] outlines the required elements of a brokerage representation agreement. The amount of the broker's fee or commission and the manner in which it is to be paid is one of those required elements. *By itself, this provision for a broker's fee or commission to be paid does not create the agency relationship.*

Written Office Policy [IC 54-2090]

Each designated broker is responsible for adopting and maintaining a written policy in each office, including branch offices. The written office policy must identify and describe the types of representation in which that brokerage and its associated licensees may engage with any buyer or seller, or both, as part of that office's real estate brokerage services.

Duration of Express Representation [IC 54-2091]

A brokerage representation commences on the date indicated on the written agreement between the brokerage and the client. It shall end with whichever of the following events *occurs first:*

■ Performance or completion
■ Agreement by the parties
■ Expiration

The brokerage and the buyer or seller may change the legal nature of their relationship at any time during the course of the transaction. However, the brokerage is not relieved from meeting the disclosure requirements and obtaining the written agreements, consents, or confirmations required by the agency statute.

Post-Termination Obligations [IC 54-2092]

Except as the parties may otherwise agree in writing, a brokerage owes only the following two duties to a client after the termination of the representation agreement:

1. Accounting for all moneys and property received by the brokerage during the representation
2. Maintaining the confidentiality of all confidential client information

Other Changes from Common Law Agency

As mentioned previously, the Idaho Real Estate Brokerage Representation Act replaces the common law agency rules that once governed brokerage relationships in Idaho. The statute also *abolishes vicarious liability in real estate relationships* [IC 54-2093].

A client is not liable for any wrongful act, error, omission, or misrepresentation made by his or her broker/representative or subagent unless the client had actual knowledge (or reasonably should have known) of the wrongful act, error, omission, or misrepresentation. Similarly, a licensee or brokerage engaged in representing a client is not liable for the client's or any subagent's wrongful act, error, omission, or misrepresentation unless the brokerage had actual knowledge or should have known of the act or omission.

The act does not prohibit a brokerage from entering into a written agreement with a buyer or seller that creates an agency relationship in which the duties and obligations are greater than those provided for by the act. However, unless greater duties are specifically agreed to in writing, *the duties and obligations owed to a represented client are not fiduciary in nature* and are not subject to equitable remedies for the breach of a fiduciary duty [IC 54-2094].

The Idaho Real Estate Commission has the authority to promulgate rules to implement and enforce the Idaho Real Estate Brokerage Act.

■ REAL ESTATE BROKERAGE ISSUES

Compensation

The broker's commission, usually a specified percentage of the final sales price, is stated as one of the terms of the seller or buyer representation agreement. The amount or exact percentage the broker will receive is a matter to be decided by the broker and the principal in each transaction.

Idaho law and the Rules of the Idaho Real Estate Commission do not set uniform commission rates or approve of agreements to standardize rates [Rule 301].

Any agreement among competing brokers to set a fixed commission rate is considered *price fixing* and a violation of the Sherman Antitrust Act. All real estate commissions are strictly and fully negotiable between the principal/payer and the broker.

As mentioned earlier, Idaho statute [IC 54-2050] mandates essential elements to the brokerage representation agreement. One of these elements is that a listing agreement or buyer-broker contract must include any fee or commission to be paid to the broker as well as the manner in which it will be paid. The method of payment will also be included as a term of the agreement, although it is generally disbursed out of the purchase price.

Broker Liability

Gross negligence or reckless conduct in a regulated real estate transaction is grounds for disciplinary action. Conduct is grossly negligent or reckless when, taken as a whole, the conduct substantially fails to meet the generally accepted standard of care in the practice of real estate in Idaho [IC 54-2060].

Brokers make many statements or representations regarding the conditions of the property being offered for sale during the course of a real estate transaction. A conscientious licensee never intentionally misrepresents facts.

Statements openly made as opinions or predictions, statements or promises that become part of the contract, and honest mistakes fall into this category. The broker can, however, be held liable for false statements made or represented to be fact.

A statement made by a broker based on false information supplied by the principal is included in this category because deliberate misrepresentation was made by the principal, not by the broker. However, brokers and salespeople are held to a certain level of expertise as professionals, and they should know that any material statement should be verified.

A *negligent* misrepresentation is a misstatement of a material fact or a false statement that the speaker believes to be true, without having reasonable proof of its accuracy. Such statements are irresponsibly made, and a broker can be held liable for making them. However, the tort of negligent misrepresentation is *not* recognized in Idaho.

Calling the misstatement "negligent misrepresentation" puts a claimant in peril of having the action summarily dismissed. Claimants who have done their homework will find Idaho law doesn't recognize negligent misrepresentation (except as to accountants) as a viable theory of recovery.

Therefore, it is important that one understands the basics of the term "fraud."

Fraud is defined as

■ a deceitful practice or material misstatement of a material fact,
■ that is known to be false,
■ done with intent to deceive or with reckless indifference as to its truth, and
■ relied on by the injured party to his or her damage.

Fraudulent misrepresentation is a false statement regarding a material fact that is made by a person who knows the statement is false.

■ **EXAMPLE**   The owner tells the listing broker that the roof leaks when there's a moderately strong north wind during a rainstorm. The listing broker does not disclose this fact to a prospective purchaser. Deliberately or willfully *concealing* a material fact from a prospective purchaser is also misrepresentation.

Fraudulent acts may be "actual" or "constructive."

Actual fraud involves acts or omissions deliberately intended to deceive or to induce another to enter into a contract.

■ **EXAMPLE**   A selling broker produces an altered appraisal report on a particular property purporting the value of the property to be several thousand dollars higher than its true value. Based on the representations made, a buyer purchases the property.

Constructive fraud refers to acts or omissions not intended to be fraudulent but that in effect create a fraudulent situation. Constructive fraud by its recognized legal definition should be and usually is within the purview of coverage under professional errors and omissions (E&O) insurance policy definitions.

■ **EXAMPLE**   An owner of real estate gift deeds property to a "friend" for love and affection. Later, creditors who have a valid claim against the former owner find out about this transfer and request that the court disallow the transfer of title or have it "set aside" as an act of fraud. (There may not have been any *intent* to defraud the creditors, but in fact constructive fraud or fraud in law exists.)

A person found guilty of fraud may be subject to criminal as well as civil penalties, in addition to disciplinary action. Rarely, if ever, is intentional misrepresentation covered under errors and omissions insurance.

In summary, the key factor in defining fraud rests on the importance of the information being misrepresented and whether the other party has a right to rely on that information to make a decision and/or enter into a contract. In most real estate transactions, both seller and buyer have the right to assume a broker's statements are true.

Agreement Between Broker and Salesperson

The broker is advised to have a written agreement with each salesperson. The actual form of contract between a broker and a salesperson depends on whether the salesperson is to operate as the broker's employee or as an independent contractor. In Idaho, most brokers engage salespeople as independent contractors. To qualify as an independent contractor for federal tax purposes, as outlined in Section 3508 of the Internal Revenue Code (effective 1983), a real estate salesperson must meet the following three conditions:

1. The salesperson must be a licensed real estate agent.

2. Substantially all of the salesperson's compensation for services as a real estate agent must be directly related to sales or another performance output rather than to hours worked.
3. Services must be performed pursuant to a written contract that provides that the individual will not be treated as an employee for federal tax purposes.

The independent contractor arrangement does not protect the broker from tort and contract liability owing to the salesperson's actions. Any contract creating a broker–independent contractor relationship should include, but is not limited to, the following provisions:

■ The broker agrees to make current listings available to the salesperson and to provide advice, instruction, and full cooperation. Furthermore, the salesperson may share the broker's office facilities.

■ The salesperson agrees to work diligently to sell property listed with the broker and to solicit additional listings for the broker. The salesperson also agrees to conduct business and regulate his or her habits to enhance the broker's goodwill and reputation; to comply with all laws, rules, and codes of ethics that apply to real estate salespeople; and to conduct himself or herself in service to the public so that the public, broker, and salesperson receive the greatest possible benefit.

■ The contract should specify the exact amount of compensation to be paid the salesperson for both sales and listing commissions and describe how commissions on listings will be paid. The contract will usually provide that the salesperson's commission will not be due and payable until it is received in a certain agreed-upon form by the broker. There should be a provision authorizing the broker to deduct from the subagent's share of the commission any expenses incurred in collecting commissions, such as attorney's fees or court costs. The contract should stipulate how a dispute between two salespeople in the office over the division of a commission will be settled. This may be handled in one of two ways: (1) the contract could state that such a decision will be made by the supervising broker, or (2) (perhaps more fairly) the contract could provide that such disputes be submitted to arbitration.

■ The contract defines the relationship between the broker and the salesperson, who is a subagent only with respect to customers or clients for whom services are performed. In his or her relationship with the broker, the salesperson is an independent contractor and not a servant, employee, joint venturer, or partner of the broker.

■ The broker is authorized, when necessary, to take notes or security payment of commissions. In such instances, the salesperson's share of the commissions will be paid proportionately as the commissions are received by the broker.

■ The broker is authorized to make settlements of commission claims when he or she feels uncertain about the outcome of a legal suit to recover the commission and chooses a settlement as the best course of action. This clause also authorizes the broker to make a settlement with a purchaser who has forfeited earnest money.

■ The contract provides for a situation in which the purchaser's earnest money is forfeited and no settlement has been made. In this situation a broker cannot safely pay the salesperson's share of the commission out of the forfeited money because the possibility exists that the purchaser might later bring successful legal action against the broker for the return of the earnest money.

■ The salesperson agrees to furnish his or her own transportation and to carry liability insurance that protects the broker in the event the salesperson has an automobile accident in the course of his or her work for the broker.

■ Either party may terminate the relationship upon giving written notice to the other. However, some contracts specify that written notice must be given a certain number of days in advance. (The Rules require certain formalities when a real estate salesperson changes employment. It is recommended, but not necessary, that these also be incorporated into the contract.)

■ After the contract is terminated, the salesperson must not use any information gained from the broker's files or business to his or her advantage, or to the advantage of any other person or corporation. Further, the salesperson must return all listings, buyer's broker agreements, stationery, all legal papers, and any other of the broker's property. The contract also may provide for payment of commissions earned but not yet paid and for a future right to commissions on existing active listings that are sold after the salesperson's voluntary or involuntary termination.

In addition to these provisions, contracts often provide for the payment of a full or partial commission to the salesperson who sells his or her broker's own unlisted property. Under these circumstances the division of commissions earned could be other than normal. A provision in the contract also may allow associate licensees to purchase *in-house* listings. The broker may discount all or a portion of the office share of the commission. In addition, the contract may contain a reference to commissions owed the employing broker when associates sell their own real property through the office.

Other provisions might be added to this type of contract, depending on the nature of the relationship the parties wish to create. A broker should consult an attorney for assistance in drawing up the contracts to include any or all items suggested in this discussion.

■ BROKER SUPERVISION [IC 54-2038] AND RULE 304

The Idaho Code requires a real estate broker to adequately supervise the activities of licensees and unlicensed personnel for whom he or she is responsible. The following factors will be among those used to determine adequacy of supervision:

■ Was the designated broker physically available to supervise?
■ What was the experience level of the licensed associate?
■ Has the designated broker contracted to avoid supervisory responsibility?

■ In what types of activity were licensed sales associates or unlicensed personnel engaged?

■ Had the designated broker established written or oral policies and procedures?

■ Does the designated broker hold regular staff meetings and follow-up meetings to determine that policies and procedures are being implemented?

■ What corrective or remedial action does the designated broker take if a misdeed of a sales associate or unlicensed personnel is discovered?

While these factors will be among those used to determine adequacy of supervision, the Commission is not limited to making a determination on these factors alone but will examine all pertinent evidence.

The designated broker is responsible for the review and approval of all real estate agreements, including (but not limited to) those related to listing, buyer-brokerage, selling, or purchasing property. The broker has overall supervisory control and responsibility for the main office and all branch offices established under his or her license. The broker should be in attendance at the office on a regular basis and available to supervise the day-to-day operation of the office.

Absences and Changes [IC 54-2039]

If the designated broker will be absent from his or her main office for more than 21 consecutive days, he or she must appoint a designated broker of another office or an associate broker who is licensed and associated with the absent broker to manage, supervise, and oversee the regular office operations.

Whenever a designated broker or manager of a (licensed) branch office will be absent from his or her main office in which trust funds and original transaction files are maintained, for a period of more than 60 consecutive days, either (1) a new broker is designated or (2) all associated licenses are placed on an inactive status and the office shall be closed, and the broker's license is placed on an inactive status and all listings shall be terminated.

If the designated broker has his or her licensed revoked, suspended, or refused, the business entity shall have ten business days to designate another qualified individual to become the designated broker or all licensees shall be made inactive.

QUESTIONS

1. A brokerage's relationship with a buyer or seller as agent, nonagent, or limited dual agent must be confirmed, and all necessary agreements executed
   a. at any time after a purchase and sale agreement is executed by the parties.
   b. at the time of the first substantial business contact.
   c. no later than the time a purchase and sale agreement is prepared.
   d. no later than the closing.

2. Which of the following statements is *TRUE* of the amount of a broker's commission in a real estate sales transaction?
   a. It must be stated in the listing agreement.
   b. It is determined according to the standard rates set by agreement of local real estate brokers.
   c. If under dispute, it will be determined through arbitration by the Idaho Real Estate Commission.
   d. It must be paid with cash or a cashier's check upon closing.

3. A seller informs a broker that the house's basement has an inch or so of flooding in the spring. However, the broker doesn't advise the buyers. Two weeks after the buyers move in, there is a storm and the basement takes in about two inches of water. The broker is guilty of
   a. actual fraud.
   b. constructive fraud.
   c. innocent misrepresentation.
   d. fraudulent misrepresentation.

4. What brokerage representation relationship is required regardless of whether the consumer is a customer or client?
   a. Agreement of the parties
   b. Expiration of the terms of the agency
   c. The broker's disclosure of known adverse material facts to a customer
   d. Performance or completion of the representation

5. A buyer/customer is *NOT* protected with which of the following duties?
   a. Disclosure of all adverse material facts about the property known to the licensee
   b. Assistance in customary and necessary services in bringing the transaction to a close
   c. Confidentiality
   d. Proper accounting for money or property

6. Which of the following would *NOT* be included in a contract between a real estate broker and a salesperson who is an independent contractor?
   a. The salesperson is a subagent only with regard to the broker's clients; he or she is not an employee or partner of the broker.
   b. The broker will withhold state and federal taxes from the salesperson's pay.
   c. The salesperson will furnish his or her own automobile and take out an automobile insurance policy.
   d. The broker will pay a specified amount or percentage of compensation to the sales associate for both sales and listing commissions.

2

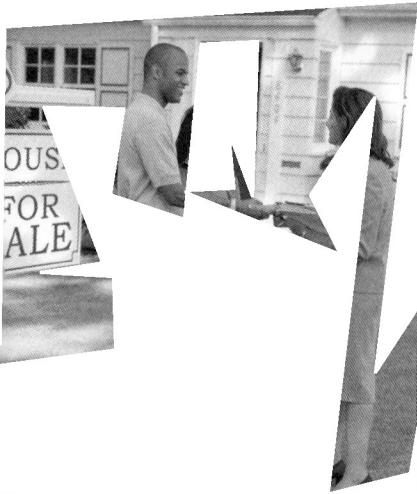

BUYER AND SELLER REPRESENTATION AGREEMENTS

■ WRITTEN BROKERAGE AGREEMENTS [IC 54-2050]

The Idaho Statute of Frauds, as applied to the real estate broker, sales associate, and associate broker, provides that *no contract for the payment of any sum of money or thing of value, as a commission or reward for the finding or procuring by one person of a purchaser of real estate of another, shall be valid unless the same shall be in writing, signed by the owner(s) of such real estate, or his or her legal, appointed, and duly qualified representative.* [See Figure 2.1 for a widely used Seller Representation agreement (listing agreement) and Figure 2.2 for a typical Buyer Representation agreement.]

Furthermore, the Idaho Real Estate Commission requires a broker or sales associate who obtains a listing or buyer-broker agreement to give the person or persons signing the agreement a legible, signed, true, and correct copy at the time the seller (listing) or buyer-brokerage agreement is signed. This will provide proof that the broker did not alter the contract after the buyer or seller signed it.

Every brokerage representation agreement, exclusive and nonexclusive (open), must state a definite expiration date, legally enforceable description of the property, price and terms, and fee or commission, and must be properly signed.

A brokerage representation agreement, whether designed to represent the seller (listing) or buyer-broker, may not contain a provision requiring the signing party to notify the broker of his or her intention to cancel the agreement after the expiration date. The principal needs to know exactly what the salesperson will do for the commission and what type of agency agreement is being entered into.

F I G U R E   2.1

Seller Representation Agreement

RE- 16 EXCLUSIVE SELLER REPRESENTATION AGREEMENT
THIS IS A LEGALLY BINDING CONTRACT. READ THE ENTIRE DOCUMENT INCLUDING ANY ATTACHMENTS. IF YOU HAVE ANY QUESTIONS, **CONSULT YOUR ATTORNEY AND/OR ACCOUNTANT** BEFORE SIGNING.

1 **DATE** _____   **AGENT:**_____
2   Acting as Agent for the Broker
3 **1. SELLER** _____
4 retains _____ Broker of _____ as
5 Exclusive SELLER'S Broker to sell, lease, or exchange the property described in Item #2 below, during the term of this agreement
6 and on any additional terms hereafter set forth.
7
8 **2. PROPERTY ADDRESS AND LEGAL DESCRIPTION.** The property address and the complete legal description of the property
9 are as set forth below.
10 Address_____
11 County_____ City _____ Zip _____
12 Legal Description_____
13 _____
14 or ☐ Legal Description Attached as addendum # _____. **(Addendum must accompany original listing)**
15
16 **3. TERM OF AGREEMENT.** The term of this Agreement shall commence on_____ and shall expire at
17 11:59 p.m. on _____ unless renewed or extended. If the SELLER accepts an offer to purchase or exchange,
18 the terms of this Agreement shall be extended through the closing of the transaction.
19
20 **4. PRICE.** SELLER agrees to sell the property for a total price of $ _____
21
22 **5. FINANCING.** SELLER agrees to consider the following types of financing: *(Complete all applicable provisions).*
23   ☐ FHA   ☐ VA   ☐ CONVENTIONAL   ☐ IHFA   ☐ RURAL DEVELOPMENT   ☐ Exchange
24   ☐ Cash   ☐ Cash to existing loan(s)   ☐ Assumption of existing loan(s)
25 ☐ SELLER will carry contract and accept a minimum down payment of $_____ and an acceptable
26 secured note for the balance to be paid as follows: _____
27 _____
28 Other acceptable terms _____
29 _____
30 Brokers are required by Idaho Real Estate Law to present all written offers.
31
32 **6. BROKERAGE FEE.**
33 (A) If Broker or any person, including SELLER, procures a purchaser ready, willing and able to purchase, transfer or exchange the
34 property on the terms stated herein or on any other price and terms agreed to in writing, the SELLER agrees to pay a total
35 brokerage fee of _____% of the contract or purchase price OR $_____ of which _____% of the contract or
36 purchase price OR $_____ will be shared with the cooperating brokerage unless otherwise agreed to in writing. The fee
37 shall be paid in cash at closing unless otherwise designated by the Broker in writing.
38 (B) Further, the brokerage fee is payable if the property or any portion thereof or any interest therein is, directly or indirectly, sold,
39 exchanged or optioned or agreed to be sold, exchanged or optioned within _____ days following expiration of the term
40 hereof to any person who has examined, been introduced to or been shown the property during the term hereof.
41 (C) If SELLER, upon termination of this Agreement, enters into an Exclusive Right to Sell Agreement to market said property with
42 another Broker, then the time period specified above in Section 6B, shall not apply and will be of no further force or effect.
43
44 **7. ADDITIONAL FEES:**_____
45 _____
46 _____
47

SELLER'S Initials (_____)(_____) _____Date

F I G U R E   2.1

Seller Representation Agreement (continued)

RE-16 EXCLUSIVE SELLER REPRESENTATION AGREEMENT JULY, 2006 EDITION   PAGE 2 OF 4

PROPERTY ADDRESS: _____

48 **8. INCLUDED ITEMS.** SELLER agrees to leave with the premises all attached floor coverings, attached television antennae, satellite dish and
49 receiving equipment, attached plumbing, bathroom and lighting fixtures, window screens, screen doors, storm doors, storm windows, window
50 coverings, garage door opener(s) and transmitter(s), exterior trees, plants or shrubbery, water heating apparatus and fixtures, attached fireplace
51 equipment, awnings, ventilating, cooling and heating systems, built in and "drop in" ranges (*but excluding all other ranges*), fuel tanks and
52 irrigation fixtures and equipment, and any and all, if any, water and water rights, and any and all, if any, ditches and ditch rights appurtenant
53 thereto that are now on or used in connection with the premises shall be included in the sale unless otherwise provided herein. Also included:
54 _____
55 _____
56 _____
57
58 **9. EXCLUDED ITEMS.** _____
59 _____
60 _____
61
62 **10. TITLE AND EXISTING ENCUMBRANCES.** Title to the property is to be conveyed by Warranty Deed unless otherwise provided herein, and
63 is to be marketable and insurable except for rights reserved in federal patents, federal, state or railroad deeds, building or use restrictions, building
64 and/or zoning regulations and ordinances of any governmental entity, and rights of way and easements established or of record. The individual
65 executing this Agreement warrant and represents that said individual either owns the property or has full power and right to enter into this
66 Agreement and to sell and convey the property on behalf of the SELLER and that to the best of said individual's knowledge the property is in
67 compliance with all applicable building and zoning regulations and with any applicable covenants and restrictions affecting the property except:
68 _____
69 _____
70 The SELLER agrees to provide good and marketable title to the property at the time of closing. The property is currently encumbered by the
71 following liens:
72 ☐   1st Mortgage ☐ 2nd Mortgage ☐ Home Equity Loan ☐ Other _____
73 ☐   The property is not encumbered by any mortgage, lien, or other security instrument.
74 Loan payments ☐ are ☐ are not current; loan ☐ is ☐ is not assumable. If loan is assumable, Buyer ☐ will ☐ will not be required to qualify and
75 ☐ will ☐ will not release SELLER'S liability.
76 SELLER is aware that some loans have a recapture provision or prepayment penalty and SELLER may be required to pay additional funds to
77 satisfy such **recapture or penalty.**
78
79 **11. MULTIPLE LISTING SERVICE AUTHORIZATION.** (Name of MLS) _____
80 _____/_____   By initialing this line, it is understood that Broker is a member of the above MLS. SELLER authorizes and directs
81 *(Initial)*   Broker to offer to cooperate with and compensate other Brokers, and to submit a Property Data Sheet and any
82 authorized changes to MLS as required in the Rules and Regulations of the above MLS. SELLER understands and
83 agrees that any MLS information regarding the above property will be made available to Buyer's Agents and/or Dual
84 Agents. SELLER acknowledges that it has been explained that any sales price information compiled as a result of this
85 Agreement may be provided to the County Assessor's office. SELLER agrees that any such disclosure is permissible.
86
87 **12. LOCKBOX AUTHORIZATION.**
88 _____/_____   By initialing this line, SELLER directs that a lockbox containing a key which gives MLS Keyholders access to the
89 *(Initial)*   property shall be placed on any building located on the property. SELLER authorizes MLS Keyholders to enter said
90 property to inspect or show the same. SELLER agrees to hold Broker harmless from any liability or loss.
91
92 **13. ADVERTISING AUTHORIZATION.**
93 SELLER ☐ does ☐ does not agree to allow Broker to advertise said property in print media.
94 SELLER ☐ does ☐ does not agree to allow Broker to advertise said property in internet advertising media.
95 SELLER ☐ does ☐ does not agree to allow Broker to advertise said property in other advertising media.
96 SELLER ☐ does ☐ does not agree to allow Broker to place the Broker's sign on above property.
97
98 **14. SELLER'S PROPERTY DISCLOSURE FORM.** If required by Title 55, Chapter 25 Idaho Code, SELLER shall within ten (10) days after
99 execution of a Purchase and Sale Agreement provide to Buyer "SELLER'S Property Disclosure Form" and Buyer shall have three (3) business
100 days from receipt of the disclosure report to rescind the offer in a written signed and dated document delivered to the SELLER or the SELLER'S
101 Agents. Buyer rescission must be based on a specific written objection to a disclosure made in the SELLER'S Property Disclosure Form.
102
103 SELLER'S Initials (_____)(_____) _____Date
104
105 **15. LEAD BASED PAINT DISCLOSURE.** SELLER has been advised of disclosure obligations regarding lead-based paint and lead-based paint

RE-16 EXCLUSIVE SELLER REPRESENTATION AGREEMENT JULY, 2006 EDITION PAGE 2 OF 4

F I G U R E   2.1

Seller Representation Agreement (continued)

PROPERTY ADDRESS: _____

106   hazards in the event property is a defined "Target Housing" under Federal Regulations. Said property ☐ **is** ☐ **is not** "Target Housing". If yes,
107   SELLER agrees to sign and complete the Information Disclosure and Acknowledgment Form provided to me and deliver to my agent all records,
108   test reports or other information related to the presence of lead-based paint or lead-based paint hazards, if any.
109

110   **17. TRANSACTION RELATED SERVICES DISCLAIMER:** SELLER understands that Broker is qualified to advise SELLER on general matters
111   concerning real estate, but is not an expert in matters of law, tax, financing, surveying, structural conditions, property inspections, hazardous
112   materials, or engineering. SELLER acknowledges that Broker advises SELLER to seek expert assistance for advice on such matters. The
113   Broker or Broker's agents may, during the course of the transaction, identify individuals or entities who perform services including **BUT NOT**
114   **LIMITED TO** the following; home inspections, service contracts, appraisals, environmental assessment inspection, code compliance inspection,
115   title insurance, closing and escrow services, loans and refinancing services, construction and repair, legal and accounting services, and/or
116   surveys. The SELLER understands that the identification of service providers is solely for SELLER'S convenience and that the Broker or their
117   agents is not guaranteeing or assuring that the service provider will perform its duties in accordance with the SELLER'S expectations. SELLER
118   has the right to make arrangements with any entity SELLER chooses to provide these services. SELLER hereby releases and holds harmless the
119   Broker and Broker's agents from any claims by the SELLER that service providers breached their agreement, were negligent, misrepresented
120   information, or otherwise failed to perform in accordance with the SELLER'S expectations. In the event the SELLER requests Broker to obtain
121   any products or services from outside sources, **SELLER agrees to pay for them immediately when payment is due.** For example: surveys or
122   engineering, environmental and/or soil tests, title reports, home or property inspections, appraisals, etc.
123

124   **18. CONSENT TO LIMITED DUAL REPRESENTATION AND ASSIGNED AGENCY:** The undersigned SELLERS(S) have received, read and
125   understand the Agency Disclosure Brochure (prepared by the Idaho Real Estate Commission). The undersigned SELLER(S) understand that the
126   brokerage involved in this transaction may be providing agency representation to both the SELLER(S) and the Buyer. The undersigned
127   SELLER(S) each understands that, as an agent for both SELLER/client and Buyer/client, a brokerage will be a limited dual agent of each client
128   and cannot advocate on behalf of one client over another, and cannot legally disclose to either client certain confidential client information
129   concerning price negotiations, terms or factors motivating the Buyer/client to buy or the SELLER/client to sell without specific written permission of
130   the client to whom the information pertains. The specific duties, obligations and limitations of a limited dual agent are contained in the Agency
131   Disclosure Brochure as required by Section 54-2085, Idaho Code. The undersigned SELLER(S) each understands that a limited dual agent does
132   not have a duty of undivided loyalty to either client.
133   The undersigned SELLER(S) further acknowledge that, to the extent the brokerage firm offers assigned agency as a type of agency
134   representation, individual sales associates may be assigned to represent each client to act solely on behalf of the client consistent with applicable
135   duties set forth in Section 54-2087, Idaho Code. In an assigned agency situation, the designated broker (the broker who supervises the sales
136   associates) will remain a limited dual agent of the client and shall have the duty to supervise the assigned agents in the fulfillment of their duties to
137   their respective clients, to refrain from advocating on behalf of any one client over another, and to refrain from disclosing or using, without
138   permission, confidential information of any other client with whom the brokerage has an agency relationship. SELLER ☐ **does** ☐ **does not**
139   consent to allow Buyer's Agents and/or Limited Dual Agents to show property and to allow the Broker to share brokerage fees as determined by
140   the Broker with Buyer's Agents and/or Limited Dual Agents.
141

142   **19. SELLER NOTIFICATION AND CONSENT TO RELEASE FROM CONFLICTING AGENCY DUTIES:** SELLER acknowledges that Broker as
143   named above has disclosed the fact that at times Broker acts as agent(s) for other Buyers and for SELLERS in the sale of the property. SELLER
144   has been advised and understands that it may create a conflict of interest for Broker to introduce Buyers to SELLER Client's property because
145   Broker could not satisfy all of its Client duties to both Buyer Client and SELLER Client in connection with such a showing or any transaction which
146   resulted.
147   **Based on the understandings acknowledged, SELLER makes the following election. (Make one selection only)**
148

149   _____ / _____   SELLER **does want** Broker to introduce any interested Client of Broker to Client SELLER'S property and
150   Initials   hereby agrees to relieve Broker of conflicting agency duties, including the duty to disclose confidential
151   **Limited Dual**   information known to the Broker at that time and the duty of loyalty to either party. Relieved of all conflicting
152   **Agency and/or**   agency duties, Broker will act in an unbiased manner to assist the SELLER and Buyer in the introduction of
153   **Assigned Agency**   Buyers to such SELLER Client's property and in the preparation of any contract of sale which may result.
154   SELLER authorizes Broker to act in a **limited dual agency** capacity. Further, SELLER agrees that Broker
155   **OR**   may offer, but is not obligated to offer, **assigned agency** representation, and if offered by the Broker,
156   SELLER authorizes Broker to act in such capacity.
157

158   _____ / _____   SELLER **does not want** Broker to introduce interested Buyer Clients to Client SELLER'S property
159   Initials   and hereby releases Broker from any responsibility or duty under the agency agreement to do so.
160   **Single Agency**   Broker shall be under no obligation or duty to introduce the Buyer to any Client SELLER'S property.
161
162   SELLER'S Initials (_____)(_____) _____ Date
163
164

F I G U R E 2.1

Seller Representation Agreement (continued)

RE-16 EXCLUSIVE SELLER REPRESENTATION AGREEMENT <u>JULY, 2006 EDITION</u> **PAGE 4 OF 4**

PROPERTY ADDRESS: _____

165   **20. INFORMATION WARRANTY.** SELLER warrants that all information provided by the SELLER herein and hereafter will be true and correct.
166

167   **21. DEPOSIT.** Brokers are authorized to receive a deposit from any prospective purchaser who offers to purchase or exchange the property and
168   shall notify SELLER of the receipt of any such deposit. Acceptance of such deposit by a Broker shall not constitute SELLER'S acceptance of any
169   such offer.
170

171   **22. GENERAL PROVISIONS.** In the event either party shall initiate any suit or action or appeal on any matter relating to this Agreement the
172   defaulting party shall pay the prevailing party all damages and expenses resulting from the default, including all reasonable attorneys' fees and all
173   court costs and other expenses incurred by the prevailing party. This Agreement is made in accordance with and shall be interpreted and
174   governed by the laws of the State of Idaho. All rights and obligations of the parties hereunder shall be binding upon and inure to the benefit of
175   their heirs, personal representatives, successors and assigns.
176

177   **23. NON-DISCRIMINATION.** The parties agree not to discriminate against any prospective SELLER or Lessor because of race, religion, creed,
178   color, sex, marital status, national origin, familial, or handicapped status of such person.
179

180   **24. SINGULAR AND PLURAL** terms each include the other, when appropriate.
181

182   **25. FACSIMILE TRANSMISSION.** Facsimile or electronic transmission of any signed original document and retransmission of any signed
183   facsimile or electronic transmission shall be the same as delivery of an original. At the request of either party or the Closing Agency, the parties
184   will confirm facsimile and electronic transmitted signatures by signing an original document.
185

186   **26. SEVERABILITY:** In the case that any one or more of the provisions contained in this Agreement, or any application thereof, shall be
187   invalid, illegal or unenforceable in any respect, the validity, legality or enforceability of the remaining provisions shall not in any way be
188   affected or impaired thereby.
189

190   **27. OTHER TERMS AND CONDITIONS:** _____

191   _____

192   _____

193   _____

194   _____

195   _____

196   _____

197   _____

198   **CONTRACTOR REGISTRATION # (if applicable)** _____

199   **Seller Signature:** _____   **Accepted:** _____
                                                                          (Broker)

200   **Seller Signature:** _____   **By:** _____
                                                                   (Agent)

201   **Date:** _____   **Date:** _____

202   **Address:** _____   **Address:** _____

203   **City:** _____ **State:** _____ **Zip:** _____   **City:** _____ **State:** ____ **Zip:** _____

204   **E-Mail:** _____   **E-Mail:** _____

205   **Phone(s):** _____   **Phone(s):** _____

206   **Fax:** _____   **Fax:** _____

207   THE PROVISIONS CONTAINED ON PAGES ONE, TWO AND THREE SHALL ALSO CONSTITUTE PART OF THE AGREEMENT OF THE PARTIES. EACH OF
208   THE PARTIES ACKNOWLEDGES READING THIS AGREEMENT IN FULL.

F I G U R E   2.2

Buyer Representation Agreement

RE-14 EXCLUSIVE BUYER REPRESENTATION AGREEMENT

THIS IS A LEGALLY BINDING CONTRACT. READ THE ENTIRE DOCUMENT INCLUDING
ANY ATTACHMENTS. IF YOU HAVE ANY QUESTIONS,
CONSULT YOUR ATTORNEY AND/OR ACCOUNTANT BEFORE SIGNING.

REALTOR®

EQUAL HOUSING OPPORTUNITY

DATE:_____   AGENT: _____
                                                    Acting as Agent for the Broker

1. BUYER _____

retains_____ Broker of _____**as**

Exclusive Buyer Broker (hereinafter referred to as Broker), where the BUYER is represented by one agent only for time herein set forth and for the express purpose of Representing BUYER in the purchase, lease, or optioning of real property. Further, BUYER agrees, warrants and acknowledges that BUYER has not and shall not enter into any exclusive buyer representation agreement with another broker in the state of Idaho as a broker for BUYER during the effective term of this agreement, unless otherwise agreed to in writing by BUYER and above-listed Broker. BUYER agrees to indemnify and hold the above-listed Broker harmless from any claim brought by any other broker or real estate salesperson for compensation claimed or owed during the effective term of this agreement. By appointing Broker as BUYER'S exclusive agent, BUYER agrees to conduct all negotiations for property through Broker, and to refer to Broker all inquiries received in any form from real estate brokers, salespersons, prospective sellers, or any other source, during the time this Exclusive Buyer Representation Agreement is in effect. BUYER desires to purchase, lease, or option the following real estate: Type of property:

☐ Residential   ☐ Residential Income   ☐ Commercial   ☐ Vacant Land   ☐ Other_____

Applicable City(s) _____, Idaho; Applicable Zip Codes _____

Applicable County(s) _____

Other Description: (i.e., geographical area, price, etc.)_____

2. TERM OF AGREEMENT: This EXCLUSIVE BUYER REPRESENTATION AGREEMENT (herein after referred to as Agreement) is in force from date _____ and will expire at 11:59 p. m. on date _____, or upon closing of escrow of such property purchased through this agreement.

3. BROKER REPRESENTATIONS AND SERVICES: The Broker and Broker's agents representing a BUYER are agents of the BUYER. Broker will use reasonable efforts as BUYER'S agent to locate property as described in Section One hereof from the information available in the Multiple Listing Service (MLS) and from other sources for unlisted property that the Broker may be aware of when applicable as set forth in Section One. The Broker's duty to locate property for the BUYER is limited to the properties that the Broker is aware of and does not include a duty to discover every unlisted property that may be privately advertised. Broker shall make submissions to BUYER describing and identifying properties that substantially meet the criteria set forth in Section One, for consideration of the BUYER and Broker agrees to negotiate acceptance of any offer to purchase or lease such property.

4. TRANSACTION RELATED SERVICES DISCLAIMER: BUYER understands that Broker is qualified to advise BUYER on general matters concerning real estate, but is not an expert in matters of law, tax, financing, surveying, structural conditions, property inspections, hazardous materials, or engineering. BUYER acknowledges that Broker advises BUYER to seek expert assistance for advice on such matters. Broker cannot warrant the condition of property to be acquired or guarantee that all material facts are disclosed by the Seller. Broker will not investigate the condition of any property including without limitation the status of permits, zoning, location of property lines, square footage, possible loss of views and/or compliance of the property with applicable laws, codes or ordinances and BUYER must satisfy themself concerning these issues by obtaining the appropriate expert advice. The Broker or Broker's agents may, during the course of the transaction, identify individuals or entities who perform services including **BUT NOT LIMITED TO** the following; home inspections, service contracts, appraisals, environmental assessment inspections, code compliance inspections, title insurance, closing and escrow services, loans and refinancing services, construction and repairs, legal and accounting services, and/or surveys. The BUYER understands that the identification of service providers is solely for BUYER'S convenience and that the Broker or their agents is not guaranteeing or assuring that the service provider will perform its duties in accordance with the BUYER'S expectations. BUYER has the right to make arrangements with any entity BUYER chooses to provide these services. BUYER hereby releases and holds harmless the Broker and Broker's agents from any claims by the BUYER that service providers breached their agreement, were negligent, misrepresented information, or otherwise failed to perform in accordance with the BUYER'S expectations. In the event the BUYER requests Broker to obtain any products or services from outside sources, **BUYER agrees to pay for them immediately when payment is due.** For example: surveys or engineering, environmental and/or soil tests, title reports, home or property inspections, appraisals, etc.

5. FINANCIAL INFORMATION: BUYER agrees to provide Broker and/or Broker's agents with certain pertinent financial information necessary to prove ability to purchase desired property.

BUYER'S Initials (_____) (_____) Date:_____

FIGURE 2.2

Buyer Representation Agreement (continued)

RE-14 EXCLUSIVE BUYER REPRESENTATION AGREEMENT, <u>JULY, 2006 EDITION</u>   PAGE 2 OF 3

BUYER'S NAME(S)_____

6. OTHER POTENTIAL BUYERS: BUYER understands that other potential buyers may consider, make offers on, or purchase through Broker the same or similar properties as BUYER is seeking to acquire. BUYER consents to Broker's representation of such other potential buyers before, during, and after the expiration of this Agreement and further releases Broker of any conflicting Agency duties.

7. LIMITS OF CONFIDENTIALITY OF OFFERS: BUYER understands that an offer submitted to a seller, and the terms thereof may not be held confidential by such seller or seller's representative unless such confidentiality is otherwise agreed to by the parties.

8. CONSENT TO LIMITED DUAL REPRESENTATION AND ASSIGNED AGENCY: The undersigned BUYER(S) have received, read and understand the Agency Disclosure Brochure (prepared by the Idaho Real Estate Commission). The undersigned BUYER(S) understand that the brokerage involved in this transaction may be providing agency representation to both the BUYER(S) and the Seller. The undersigned BUYER(S) each understands that, as an agent for both BUYER/client and Seller/client, a brokerage will be a limited dual agent of each client and cannot advocate on behalf of one client over another, and cannot legally disclose to either client certain confidential client information concerning price negotiations, terms or factors motivating the BUYER/client to buy or the Seller/client to sell without specific written permission of the client to whom the information pertains. The specific duties, obligations and limitations of a limited dual agent are contained in the Agency Disclosure Brochure as required by Section 54-2085, Idaho Code. The undersigned BUYER(S) each understands that a limited dual agent does not have a duty of undivided loyalty to either client.

    The undersigned BUYER(S) further acknowledge that, to the extent the brokerage firm offers assigned agency as a type of agency representation, individual sales associates may be assigned to represent each client to act solely on behalf of the client consistent with applicable duties set forth in Section 54-2087, Idaho Code. In an assigned agency situation, the designated broker (the broker who supervises the sales associates) will remain a limited dual agent of the client and shall have the duty to supervise the assigned agents in the fulfillment of their duties to their respective clients, to refrain from advocating on behalf of any one client over another, and to refrain from disclosing or using without permission, confidential information of any other client with whom the brokerage has an agency relationship.

    BUYER NOTIFICATION AND CONSENT TO RELEASE FROM CONFLICTING AGENCY DUTIES: BUYER acknowledges that Broker as named above has disclosed the fact that at times Broker acts as agent(s) for other BUYERS and for Sellers in the sale of the property. BUYER has been advised and understands that it may create a conflict of interest for Broker to introduce BUYER to a Seller Client's property because Broker could not satisfy all of its Client duties to both BUYER Client and Seller Client in connection with such a showing or any transaction which resulted.

Based on the understandings acknowledged, BUYER makes the following election.
(Make one election only)

_____/_____
Initials
**Limited Dual
Agency
and/or
Assigned Agency**

BUYER **DOES WANT** to be introduced to Seller's client's property and hereby agrees to relieve Broker of conflicting agency duties, including the duty to disclose confidential information known to the Broker at the time and the duty of loyalty to either party. Relieved of all conflicting agency duties, Broker will act in an unbiased manner to assist the BUYER and Seller in the introduction of BUYER to such Seller client's property and in the preparation of any contract of sale which may result. BUYER authorizes Broker to act in a **limited dual agency** capacity. Further, BUYER agrees that Broker may offer, but is not obligated to offer, **assigned agency** representation, and if offered by the Broker, BUYER authorizes Broker to act in such capacity.

OR

_____/_____
Initials
Single Agency

BUYER **DOES NOT WANT** to be introduced to Seller client's property and hereby releases Broker from any responsibility or duty under the agency agreement. Broker shall be under no obligation or duty to introduce the BUYER to any Seller client's property.

9. NON-DISCRIMINATION: The parties agree not to discriminate against any prospective Seller or Lessor because of race, religion, creed, color, sex, marital status, national origin, familial, or handicapped status of such person.

10. SEVERABILITY CLAUSE: In the case that any one or more of the provisions contained in this Agreement, or any application thereof, shall be invalid, illegal or unenforceable in any respect, the validity, legality or enforceability of the remaining provisions shall not in any way be affected or impaired thereby.

11. SINGULAR AND PLURAL terms each include the other, when appropriate.

12. DEFAULT / ATTORNEY'S FEES: In the event of default by BUYER under this Agreement, Broker shall be entitled to the Fee that Broker would have received had no default occurred, in addition to other available legal remedies. In the event of any suit or other proceeding arising out of this Agreement, the prevailing party shall be entitled to its reasonable attorney's fees and all costs incurred relative to such suit or proceeding. Venue of any action arising out of this Agreement shall be in the court of the county in which Broker's office is located.

BUYER'S Initials (_____) (_____) Date:_____

F I G U R E   2.2

Buyer Representation Agreement (continued)

141
142
143   **BUYER'S NAME(S)**_____

144   **13. COMPENSATION OF BROKER:** In consideration of the services to be performed by the Broker, BUYER agrees that broker may
145   be compensated in any of the following ways: <u>Check all that apply</u>.
146

147   ☐ A. **If the property is subject to a listing agreement with the Broker's Company or a cooperating Broker** through the
148   Multiple Listing Service (MLS) or otherwise, the fee will be the amount equal to the compensation offered by the aforementioned
149   Brokers but not less than _____% of the selling price. BUYER agrees to pay to the Broker any difference between the amount
150   received from the aforementioned Brokers and the stated minimum.
151

152   ☐ B. **If the property is not subject to a Listing Agreement,** such as a For Sale By Owner or a Custom Build Job, the BUYER
153   agrees that the Broker will be paid a fee of not less than ☐ _____% of selling price or ☐ $ _____. The Broker shall first
154   seek to obtain this fee through the transaction paid by the Seller. If the fee cannot be obtained through the Seller, the BUYER will
155   be responsible for such fee stated above.
156

157   ☐ C. **Retainer Fee.** BUYER will pay Broker a non-refundable retainer fee of $_____ due and payable upon signing of this
158   Agreement. Retainer fee ☐ shall ☐ shall not be credited against any compensation set forth in paragraph A or B.
159

160   ☐ D. **Hourly rate.** BUYER will pay Broker at the rate of $ _____ per hour for the time spent by Broker pursuant to this
161   Agreement to be paid when billed whether or not BUYER acquires or leases property. The fee ☐ shall ☐ shall not be credited
162   against any compensation as set forth in paragraph A, B, or C.
163

164   This compensation shall apply to transactions made for which BUYER enters into a contract during the original term of this Agreement
165   or during any extension of such original or extended term, and shall also apply to transactions for which BUYER enters into a contract
166   within _____ days after this Agreement expires or is terminated, if the property acquired by the BUYER was submitted in writing to the
167   BUYER by Broker pursuant to Section One hereof during the original term or extension of the term of this Agreement. Unless otherwise
168   indicated herein the Broker's fee shall be paid in cash at closing.

169   In the event BUYER chooses to purchase any property without using the representation of the Broker named above within the time this
170   agreement remains in force, above stated BUYER shall be liable to Broker for a cancellation fee equal to _____% of the contract or
171   purchase price of the property acquired or $ _____
172

173   **14. OTHER TERMS AND CONDITIONS:** _____
174   _____
175   _____
176   _____
177   _____
178

179   **15. AUTHORITY OF SIGNATORY:** If BUYER is a corporation, partnership, trust, estate, or other entity, the person executing this
180   agreement on its behalf warrants his or her authority to do so and to bind BUYER.

181   **16. TIME IS OF THE ESSENCE IN THIS AGREEMENT:** The terms hereof constitute the entire agreement and supersede all prior
182   agreements, negotiations and discussions between parties. This agreement may be modified only by a written agreement signed by
183   each of the parties.

184   **Buyer Signature:**_____   **Accepted:**_____
                                                                        (Broker)

185   **Buyer Signature:**_____   **By:**_____
                                                                        (Agent)

186   **Date:**_____   **Date:** _____

187   **Address:**_____   **Address:**_____

188   **City:**_____ **State:** _____ **Zip:**_____   **City:**_____ **State:** _____ **Zip:**_____

189   **E-Mail:** _____   **E-Mail:** _____

190   **Phone(s):**_____   **Phone(s):**_____

191   **Fax:**_____   **Fax:** _____

192

196
198

Open communication and discussion of the listing agreement always will help broker–principal, salesperson–principal, and broker–salesperson relationships.

The listing description should contain enough information so that the property can be located from the description alone. If the seller is married, the signatures of both spouses are *recommended* on all listings and are *required* if the seller is dealing with community property. The reason both signatures are recommended is that in a community property state, commingling of community property with separate property is very easy and often cannot be determined accurately without a court opinion.

The listing or buyer representation agreement should clarify certain other points. A listing agreement should include a provision that either authorizes or forbids the placement of a For Sale sign and a lockbox, if they are used, on the property. The agreement also should provide that the broker would have access to the property at reasonable times to show it to prospective purchasers. The agreement should set a date for the buyer's possession of the premises or, in other words, when the seller will be ready to move. In addition, the agreement should provide that, if an exchange of property is agreed on, the broker might represent and receive an additional commission from the other party to the exchange. No listing agreement may require the owner to pay any part of the broker's commission in advance without written permission.

■ MANUFACTURED HOUSING

The authority of real estate licensees to sell new and used manufactured housing is provided within Idaho code [IC 44-2102]. A real estate broker may offer for sale, list, buy for resale, or negotiate for a used manufactured housing unit that has been declared by the owner to be *real property*; however, a manufactured home salesperson or dealer may not.

A manufactured home salesperson may offer for sale, list, buy for resale, or negotiate for a used manufactured housing unit that is carried on the tax roll as *personal property*, but only to the extent the sale does not involve the purchase or sale of an interest in real estate. However, a real estate broker may engage in transactions involving manufactured housing that is considered personal property.

In addition, a licensed real estate broker or salesperson may participate in new manufactured home sales that include real estate if the real estate broker or salesperson has a valid, written agreement with a licensed manufactured home dealer to represent the interests of the manufactured home dealer in this type of transaction.

IC 63-304 states that a manufactured home may be considered real property under the following three conditions:

1. The running gear is removed.

2. The manufactured home becomes permanently affixed to a foundation on land owned or purchased by the owner or purchaser.
3. The owner or purchaser of a manufactured home records with the county recorder in the county in which the manufactured home will be situated a statement of intent to declare the manufactured home as real property.

The exercise of the declaration option requires all county assessors to treat those manufactured homes the same as any other site-built residence and permits lending institutions to treat the manufactured homes as real property or as any other residence.

A manufactured home may be considered real property for tax and financing purposes only and not for any other purposes. The fact that a new unit is sold to be placed on real property does *not* exempt a real estate professional from the need for licensure.

Revocation

Once a manufactured home has been converted to real property, it is considered to be a fixture and an improvement to the underlying land. It may not be physically removed from its site (except temporarily, for repairs or improvements) without the consent of all persons having an interest in the property to which the manufactured home has been affixed.

A homeowner who intends to remove a manufactured home that has been declared to be real property must give 30 days' written notice to the county assessor that a title report has been obtained identifying all interested persons, and that all parties have consented to the removal. Within five days of removal, the owner must obtain a certificate of title for the manufactured home, which then becomes personal property once again.

■ TYPES OF LISTINGS—BUYER AND SELLER REPRESENTATION AGREEMENTS

Idaho brokers use open, exclusive-agency, and exclusive-right-to-sell listing agreements. Net listings are prohibited by some states and not recommended by others. Although net listings are discouraged in Idaho by the requirement that listings state a fee or commission, Idaho law does not prohibit them.

Listing Considerations

Whereas a real estate listing is the broker's employment contract, it is also the means of securing merchandise or property to sell. The quantity and quality of the merchandise a broker has available for sale will determine to a great extent his or her success. Because a broker's public image is partly created by the merchandise or property offered by the agency, he or she has many factors to consider before taking a listing.

Terms.   The various factors involved in a real estate sale should be explained to the seller at the time the listing is taken. The seller undoubtedly will be required to pay certain financing and closing costs in connection with the sale and should consider these expenses when deciding on a selling price. Another consideration is the amount and type of loan the buyer will be able to obtain. If a seller makes unreasonable demands regarding price and/or terms after the broker has explained such factors, the broker may wish to decline the listing.

Potential.   The broker also must consider the buyer appeal that one property has over another. How will the property look to prospective purchasers? Will they realize the property's full potential when they see it? Is it neat and clean? Does it look as appealing as other properties in the neighborhood? Are there too many or too few furnishings? Will the property be accessible at reasonable times for licensees to preview and show it to prospective purchasers?

These are a few of the factors to consider when taking a listing. Remember the maxim: "A property well listed is half sold." The broker and each salesperson should seek only as many listings as the brokerage can effectively handle, taking the number of sales associates into consideration and emphasizing the quality and not the quantity of listing inventory. Recent court cases across the United States have held that the exclusive-right-to-sell listing creates an inherent duty of *due diligence* on the part of the real estate broker taking such a listing.

Inspecting the Premises

The broker should carefully inspect a property before accepting a listing. If possible, this inspection should be made in the owner's presence. The owner will be impressed with the broker's thoroughness, and the broker can discover any weaknesses in the property that should be considered when deciding on a selling price. The broker also should note any advantages in the property or the neighborhood that will make good selling points.

Familiarity with the property will enable the broker to discuss it more intelligently and sell it more quickly. Many sales have been delayed or lost because the broker had inadequate or incomplete information to answer all of the buyer's questions.

A record should be made of the size of the lot; size, style, and age of the house; condition of the home; number of rooms; type and condition of the heating system; and any other improvements on the property. Conditions of the existing loan and the amount of cash required by the owner from the sale also should be noted. In other words, the broker should learn as much as possible about the physical and financial aspects of the property. During the inspection the broker may note certain physical changes or improvements needed to affect an early sale. The broker may suggest that the owner make these changes before offering the property for sale.

Seller Disclosure [IC 55-2501]

Idaho Code requires sellers of residential property to complete a form detailing the condition of the property at the time of the sale. The disclosure is required of anyone who intends to transfer any residential real property by sale, exchange, installment sale contract, lease with option to purchase (or any other option to purchase), or ground lease coupled with improvements.

In addition, the disclosure requirement applies only to real property improved with or consisting of not less than one and not more than four dwelling units.

The disclosure form constitutes a statement of the condition of the property only as it is actually known by the transferor. Other than having lived at or owned the property, the disclosure form states that the transferor (seller) does not possess any greater knowledge than that which could be obtained by a careful inspection of the property. The statement is not a warranty of any kind, nor is it a substitute for inspections.

Idaho Code 55-2511 specifically states:

> . . . *neither the transferor or transferor's agents shall be liable for any error, inaccuracy or omission of any information [contained in the disclosure statement] if the error, inaccuracy or omission was not within the personal knowledge of the transferor or was based upon information timely provided by public agencies [or expert professionals hired to perform an inspection]. . . and ordinary care was exercised in obtaining and transmitting [the information].*

A sample of the statutory form and a form commonly used by REALTORS® (see Figure 2.3 and Figure 2.4) should be read and understood. Even though this disclosure is between a buyer and a seller, it should be remembered that a licensee could be held liable for failing to disclose adverse material facts about the condition of a property [IC 54-2086 (1) (e) and IC 54-2087 (3) (a)].

Disclosure exemptions.   Transfers of real property pursuant to a court order, such as those arising out of probate, bankruptcy, writs of execution, or eminent domain, are not subject to the mandatory disclosure law. Neither are transfers between spouses or former spouses arising out of a decree of or property settlement from a divorce, dissolution of marriage, annulment, or legal separation.

The following transfers are also exempt from mandatory disclosure:

- To a mortgagee by a mortgagor by deed in lieu of foreclosure or in satisfaction of a mortgage debt
- Transferors of newly constructed residential real property that has never been occupied

However, it should be noted that sellers (builders) of such newly constructed residential real property shall disclose information regarding annexation and city services:

- To a beneficiary of a deed of trust by a trustor in default
- By a foreclosure sale that follows a default in the satisfaction of an obligation secured by a mortgage
- Under a power of sale following a default in the satisfaction of an obligation secured by a deed of trust or other instrument within one year of foreclosure
- By a mortgagee or a beneficiary under a deed of trust who has acquired the residential real property at a sale conducted pursuant to a power of sale under a mortgage or deed of trust, or who has acquired the residential real property by deed in lieu of foreclosure

FIGURE 2.3

Seller's Disclosure [IC 55-5508]

Seller Property Disclosure Form

Seller's Name and Address_____

Section 55-2501, et seq., Idaho Code, requires Sellers of residential real property to complete a property condition disclosure form.

PURPOSE OF STATEMENT: This is a statement of the conditions and information concerning the property known by the Seller. Unless otherwise advised, the Seller does not possess any expertise in construction, architectural, engineering or any other specific areas related to the construction or condition of the improvements on the property. Other than having lived at or owning the property, the Seller possesses no greater knowledge than that which could be obtained upon a careful inspection of the property by the potential buyer. Unless otherwise advised, the Seller has not conducted any inspection of generally inaccessible areas such as the foundation or roof. It is not a warranty of any kind by the Seller or by any agent representing any Seller in this transaction. It is not a substitute for any inspections. Purchaser is encouraged to obtain his/her own professional inspections. Notwithstanding that transfer of newly constructed residential real property that previously has not been inhabited is exempt from disclosure pursuant to section 55-2505, Idaho Code, Seller of such newly constructed residential real property shall disclose information regarding annexation and city services in the form as prescribed in questions 1., 2., and 3.

(handwritten: Has to be completed)

1. Is the property located in an area of city impact, adjacent or contiguous to a city limits, and thus legally subject to annexation by the city?   _____Yes   _____No
2. Does the property, if not within city limits, receive any city services, thus making it legally subject to annexation by the city?
          _____Yes   _____No
3. Does the property have a written consent to annex recorded in the county recorder's office, thus making it legally subject to annexation by the city?   _____Yes   _____No
4. All appliances and services systems included in the sale, (such as refrigerator/freezer, range/oven, dishwasher, disposal, hood/fan, central vacuum, microwave oven, trash compactor, smoke detectors, tv antenna/dish, fireplace/wood stove, water heater, garage door opener, pool/hot tub, etc.) are functioning properly except: (please list and explain)
   _____
   _____
5. Specify problems with the following:
   Basement water _____
   Foundation _____
   Roof condition and age _____
   Well (type) _____ Problem _____
   Septic system (type)_____ Problem _____
   Plumbing _____
   Drainage _____
   Electrical _____
   Heating _____
6. Describe any conditions that may affect your ability to clear title (such as encroachments, easements, zoning violations, lot line disputes etc.) _____ _____
   _____
7. Are you aware of any hazardous materials or pest infestations on the property_____ _____
   _____
8. Have any substantial additions or alterations been made without a building permit? _____ _____
   _____
9. Any other problems, including legal, physical or other not listed above that you know concerning the property?
   _____

The Seller certifies that the information herein is true and correct to the best of Seller's knowledge as of the date signed by the Seller. The Seller is familiar with the residential real property and each act performed in making the disclosure of an item of information is made performed in good faith.

I/we acknowledge receipt of a copy of this statement.
Seller: Buyer:

Date:_____   Date: _____

Date: _____   Date: _____

Seller's Property Disclosure Form (REALTOR® RE 25 Form)

RE-25 SELLER'S PROPERTY DISCLOSURE <u>JULY, 2006 EDITION</u> PAGE 1 of 4

RE-25 SELLER'S PROPERTY DISCLOSURE FORM

Seller's Name(s): _____ **Date:** _____

Property Address: _____

Section 55-2501, et seq., Idaho Code, requires **SELLERS** of residential real property to complete a property condition disclosure form. "Residential Real Property" means real property that is improved by a building or other structure that has one (1) to four (4) dwelling units or an individually owned unit in a structure of any size. This also applies to real property which has a combined residential and commercial use. THE PURPOSE OF THE STATEMENT: This is a statement made by the **SELLER** of the conditions and information concerning the property known by the **SELLER**. <u>This is NOT a statement of any agent representing the **SELLER** and no agent is authorized to make representations, or verify representations, concerning the condition of the property.</u> Unless otherwise advised, the **SELLER** does not possess any expertise in construction, architectural, engineering or any other specific areas related to the construction or condition of the improvements on the property. Other than having lived at or owning the property, the **SELLER** possesses no greater knowledge than that which could be obtained upon careful inspection of the property by the potential **BUYER**. Unless otherwise advised, the **SELLER** has not conducted any inspection of generally inaccessible areas such as the foundation or roof. **This disclosure is not a warranty** of any kind by the **SELLER** or by any agent representing the **SELLER** in this transaction. It is not a substitute for any inspections. The **BUYER** is encouraged to obtain his/her own professional inspections.

Notwithstanding that transfer of newly constructed residential real property that previously has not been inhabited is exempt from disclosure pursuant to section 55-2505, Idaho Code, **SELLERS** of such newly constructed and existing residential real property shall disclose information regarding annexation and city services in the form as prescribed in questions **1, 2, and 3**.

1. *Is the property located in an area of city impact, adjacent or contiguous to a city limit, and thus legally subject to annexation by the city?*

    ☐ **Yes** ☐ **No** ☐ **Do Not Know** ☐ **The property is already within city limits**

2. *Does the property, if not within city limits, receive any city services, thus making it legally subject to annexation by the city?*

    ☐ **Yes** ☐ **No** ☐ **Do Not Know** ☐ **The property is already within city limits**

3. *Does the property have a written consent to annex recorded in the county recorder's office, thus making it legally subject to annexation by the city?*

    ☐ **Yes** ☐ **No** ☐ **Do Not Know** ☐ **The property is already within city limits**

THE FOLLOWING ARE IN THE CONDITIONS INDICATED:

APPLIANCES SECTION	None/Not Included	Working	Not Working	Do Not Know	Remarks
Built-in Vacuum System					
Clothes Dryer					
Clothes Washer					
Dishwasher					
Disposal					
Freezer					
Kitchen Vent Fan/Hood					
Microwave Oven					
Oven(s)/ Range(s)/Cook top(s)					
Trash Compactor					
Refrigerator					
ELECTRICAL SYSTEMS SECTION	None/Not Included	Working	Not Working	Do Not Know	Remarks
Air Purifier					
Security System(s)					
Ceiling Fan(s)					
Garage Door Opener(s)/Control(s)					
Inside Telephone Wiring/Jacks					
Aluminum Wiring					
Intercom System					
Light Fixtures					
Sauna					
Smoke Detector(s)/Fire Alarm(s)					
Bath Vent Fan(s)					
220 Volt Outlet(s)					
TV Antenna/Dish/Controls					
Switches and Outlets					

BUYER'S Initials (_____)(_____) Date _____   **SELLER'S** Initials (_____)(_____) Date _____

F I G U R E 2.4

Seller's Property Disclosure Form (REALTOR® RE 25 Form) (continued)

RE-25 SELLER'S PROPERTY DISCLOSURE <u>JULY, 2006 EDITION</u> PAGE 2 of 4

PROPERTY ADDRESS: _____

HEATING & COOLING SYSTEMS SECTION	None/Not Included	Working	Not Working	Do Not Know	Remarks
Attic Fan(s)					
Central Air Conditioning					
Room Air Conditioner(s)					
Evaporative Cooler(s)					
Fireplace(s)					
Fireplace Insert(s)					
Furnace/Heating System(s)					
Humidifier(s)					
Wood/Pellet Stove(s)					
Air Cleaner(s)					

MOISTURE & DRAINAGE CONDITIONS SECTION	Yes	No	Do Not Know	Remarks
Is the property located in a floodplain?				
Are you aware of any site drainage problems?				
Has there been any water intrusion or moisture related damage to any portion of the property, including, but not limited to, the crawlspace, floors, walls, ceilings, siding, or basement, based on flooding; moisture seepage, moisture condensation, sewer overflow/backup, or leaking pipes, plumbing fixtures, appliances, or moisture related damage from other causes?				
Have you had the property inspected for the existence of any types of mold?				
If the property has been inspected for mold, is a copy of the inspection report available?				
Are you aware of the existence of any mold-related problems on any interior portion of the property, including but not limited to, floors, walls, ceilings, basement, crawlspaces, and attics, or any mold-related structural damage?				
Have you ever had any water intrusion, moisture related damage, mold or mold-related problems on the property remediated, repaired, fixed or replaced?				

FUEL TANK SECTION	NA ( )	Propane ( )	Oil ( )	Diesel ( )	Gasoline ( )	Other ( )
Location:				Size:		
In Use: ( ) Not In Use: ( ) Above Ground: ( ) Buried: ( )						

WATER & SEWER SYSTEMS SECTION	None/Not Included	Working	Not Working	Do Not Know	Remarks
Hot Tub/Spa and Equipment					
Pool and Pool Equipment					
Plumbing System – Faucets and Fixtures					
Water Heater(s)					
Water Softener (owned)					
Water Softener (leased)					
Septic System					
Sump Pump/Lift Pump					
Landscape Sprinkler System					

WATER & SEWER SYSTEM TYPE SECTION	Public System	Community System	Private System	Cistern	Other
Domestic Water Provided By:					
Irrigation Water Provided By:					
Property Sewer Provided By:					
If Septic System, Date Last Pumped / /					

ROOF & SIDING SECTION: Age (If Known):	Yes	No	Do Not Know	Remarks
Is there present damage to the roof?				
Does the roof leak?				
Are there any problems with the siding?				

BUYER'S Initials (_____)(_____) Date _____   **SELLER'S** Initials (_____)(_____) Date _____

F I G U R E 2.4

Seller's Property Disclosure Form (REALTOR® RE 25 Form) (continued)

RE-25 SELLER'S PROPERTY DISCLOSURE **JULY, 2006 EDITION** PAGE 3 of 4

PROPERTY ADDRESS: _____

HAZARDOUS CONDITIONS SECTION	Yes	No	Do Not Know	Remarks
Are you aware of any asbestos or other toxic or hazardous materials on the property?				
Has the property ever been used as an illegal drug manufacturing site?				
Are you aware of any current or previous insect, rodent or other pest infestation(s) on the property?				
Have you ever had the property serviced by an exterminator or had the property otherwise remediated for insect, rodent or other pest infestation(s)?				
Is there any damage due to wind, fire, or flood?				
OTHER DISCLOSURES SECTION	Yes	No	Do Not Know	Remarks
Are there any conditions that may affect your ability to clear title such as encroachments, easements, zoning violations, lot line disputes, restrictive covenants, etc.?				
Has the property been surveyed since you owned it?				
Have you received any notices by any governmental or quasi-governmental entity affecting this property; i.e. local improvement district (LID) or zoning changes, etc?				
Are there any structural problems with the improvements?				
Are there any structural problems with the foundation?				
Have any substantial additions or alterations been made without a building permit?				
Has the fireplace/wood stove/chimney/flue been inspected?				
Has the fireplace/wood stove/chimney/flue been cleaned?				
Have you ever filed a homeowner's insurance claim on the property?				
ADDITIONAL REMARKS AND/OR EXPLANATIONS SECTION: Please list any other existing problems that you know of concerning the property including legal, physical, product defects or others that are not already listed. (Use additional pages if necessary.)				

The referenced property herein is exempt from the code because of Section 55-2505 for any of the following reasons:

☐ A transfer pursuant to court order including, but not limited to a transfer ordered by a probate court during the administration of the decedent's estate, a transfer pursuant to a writ of execution, a transfer by a trustee in bankruptcy, a transfer as a result of the exercise of the power of eminent domain, and a transfer that results from a decree for a specific performance of a contract or other agreement between persons:

☐ A transfer to a mortgagee by a mortgagor by deed in lieu of foreclosure or in satisfaction of the mortgage debt:

☐ A transfer to a beneficiary of a deed of trust by trustor in default:

☐ A transfer by a foreclosure sale that follows a default in the satisfaction of an obligation secured by a mortgage:

☐ A transfer by a sale under a power of sale following a default in the satisfaction of an obligation that is secured by a deed of trust or another instrument containing a power of sale occurring within one (1) year of foreclosure on the default:

☐ A transfer by a mortgagee, or beneficiary under a deed of trust, who has acquired the residential real property at a sale conducted pursuant to a power of sale under a mortgage or deed of trust or who has acquired the residential real property by a deed in lieu of foreclosure:

☐ A transfer by a fiduciary in the course of the administration of a decedent's estate, a guardianship, a conservatorship or a trust:

☐ A transfer from one (1) co-owner to one (1) or more other co-owners:

☐ A transfer made to the transferor's spouse or to one (1) or more persons in the lineal line of consanguinity of one (1) or more of the transferors:

☐ A transfer between spouses or former spouses as a result of a decree of divorce, dissolution of marriage, annulment or legal separation or as a result of a property settlement agreement incidental to a decree of divorce, dissolution of marriage, annulment or legal separation.

☐ A transfer to or from the state, a political subdivision of the state, or another governmental entity:

☐ A transfer that involved newly constructed residential real property, that previously has not been inhabited, except as required by questions 1, 2 and 3:

☐ A transfer to a transferee who has occupied the property as a personal residence for one (1) or more years immediately prior to the transfer:

☐ A transfer from a transferor who has both not occupied the property as a personal residence within one (1) year immediately prior to the transfer and has acquired the property through inheritance or devise:

☐ A transfer by a relocation company to a transferee within one (1) year from the date that the previous owner occupied the property:

☐ A transfer from a decedent's estate:

BUYER'S Initials (_____)(_____) Date _____   **SELLER'S** Initials (_____)(_____) Date _____

F I G U R E 2.4

Seller's Property Disclosure Form (Realtor® RE 25 Form) (continued)

RE-25 SELLER'S PROPERTY DISCLOSURE <u>JULY, 2006 EDITION</u> PAGE 4 of 4

PROPERTY ADDRESS: _____

The **SELLER** certifies that the information herein is true and correct to the best of the **SELLER'S** knowledge as of the date signed by the **SELLER**. The **SELLER** is familiar with the residential property and each act performed in making a disclosure of an item of information is made and performed in good faith.

SELLER and BUYER understand and acknowledge that the statements contained herein are the representations of the **SELLER** regarding the condition of the property. <u>No statement made herein is a statement of a **SELLER'S** agent or agents, and no agent is authorized to make any statement, or verify any statement, relating to the condition of the property.</u> **SELLER and BUYER** also understands and acknowledge that **SELLER** in no way warrants or guarantees the above information regarding the property. **SELLER and BUYER** also understand and acknowledge that, unless otherwise specifically set forth, no agent of the <u>**SELLER**</u> is an expert in environmental or other conditions which are or may be hazardous to human health, and which may exist on the property. **BUYER MAY, AT BUYER'S OPTION AND EXPENSE, CONSULT WITH ANY INDEPENDENT QUALIFIED INSPECTOR TO ASSESS OR DETECT THE PRESENCE OF SUCH KNOWN OR SUSPECTED HAZARDOUS CONDITIONS.**

SELLER and BUYER understand that Listing Broker and Selling Broker in no way warrants or guarantees the above information on the property.

SELLER hereby acknowledges receipt of a copy of this form:

_____ _____   _____ _____
SELLER   Date   **SELLER**   Date

BUYER hereby acknowledges receipt of a copy of this disclosure form and does hereby _____WAIVE _____NOT WAIVE the right to rescind the related purchase agreement within three (3) business days from the date of receipt of this form. **IF BUYER DOES NOT WAIVE THE RIGHT TO RECIND** as set forth above, **BUYER** may only rescind the purchase and sale agreement within three (3) business days following receipt of this disclosure statement, by a written, signed and dated document that is delivered to the seller or his agents by personal delivery, ordinary or certified mail, or facsimile transmission. BUYER's rescission must be based on a specific objection to a disclosure in the disclosure statement. The notice of rescission must specifically identify the disclosure objected to by the BUYER. If no signed notice of rescission is received by the SELLER within the three (3) business day period, BUYER's right to rescind is waived.

_____ _____   _____ _____
BUYER   Date   **BUYER**   Date

AMENDED DISCLOSURE FORM: Subsequent to the delivery of the initial **SELLER'S** Property Condition Disclosure Form previously acknowledged, **SELLER** hereby makes the following amendments. (Attach additional pages if necessary.) Other than those amendments made below, the **SELLER** states that there have been no changes to the information contained in the initial **SELLER'S** Property Condition Disclosure Form. **IF THERE ARE NO UPDATES, THERE IS NO NEED TO SIGN BELOW.**
_____
_____
_____

SELLER hereby acknowledges receipt of this <u>amended</u> form:

_____ _____   _____ _____
SELLER   Date   **SELLER**   Date

BUYER hereby acknowledges receipt of a copy of the <u>amended</u> disclosure form and does hereby _____WAIVE _____NOT WAIVE the right to rescind the related purchase agreement <u>based strictly on the amendments to the disclosure form</u> within three (3) business days from the date of receipt of this <u>amended</u> form. **IF BUYER DOES NOT WAIVE THE RIGHT TO RESCIND** as set forth above, **BUYER** may only rescind the purchase and sale agreement within three (3) business days following receipt of this <u>amended</u> disclosure statement, by a written, signed and dated document that is delivered to the SELLER or his agents by personal delivery, ordinary or certified mail, or facsimile transmission. BUYER's rescission must be based on a specific objection to a disclosure in the disclosure statement. The notice of rescission must specifically identify the disclosure objected to by the BUYER. If no signed notice of rescission is received by the SELLER within the three (3) business day period, BUYER's right to rescind is waived.

_____ _____   _____ _____
BUYER   Date   **BUYER**   Date

- By a fiduciary in the course of the administration of a decedent's estate, a guardianship, a conservatorship, or a trust
- From one co-owner to another
- To a transferor's spouse or a person in a transferor's line of consanguinity
- From or to the state, a political subdivision of the state, or another governmental entity
- To a transferee who has occupied the property as a personal residence for one or more years immediately prior to the transfer
- From a transferor who has *not* occupied the property as a personal residence for one or more years immediately prior to the transfer, and who acquired the property through an inheritance or devise
- By a relocation company to a transferee within one year from the date that the previous owner occupied the property
- From a decedent's estate

It should be remembered that even though the exemptions above may relieve the owner from disclosure, the licensee still needs to disclose any "adverse material facts known or which reasonably should have been known."

Psychologically Impacted Real Property [IC 55-2801, 2802, 2803]

For years licensees have been unsure about "psychologically impacted" property and whether the impact is material or not. Idaho statute defines psychologically impacted as certain circumstances surrounding the property regarding facts or suspicions.

Included would be an occupant or prior occupant who is or has been infected with a disease that is highly unlikely to be transmitted though occupancy of the dwelling.

Also, this category includes property where a suicide, homicide, or felony was committed or is suspected to have been committed but had no effect on the physical condition or its environment.

The third category addresses a registered or suspected sex offender occupying or residing near the property.

No cause of action. No cause of action shall arise against an owner of real property or a representative of the owner for failure to disclose that the property was psychologically impacted.

Request for disclosure. If a purchaser makes a written request for psychological impact disclosure, the seller is not obligated to make such disclosure. If the owner consents, the owner's representative shall advise the purchaser.

Taking the Listing [IC 54-2050]

When taking a listing, the real estate agent must get as much information as possible about the property so that all possible contingencies can be anticipated and provided for to eliminate confusion later on (see Figure 2.1).

A professional licensee should make two appointments with the potential seller; one to secure information to compare comparable properties similar to the subject property being listed. The second appointment is scheduled to present a competitive market analysis and to secure the actual listing.

During the first visit the following list suggests various subject areas that a real estate agent should explore and gather prior to actually listing a parcel of residential real estate:

- Street address
- Lot size
- Age and condition of the property
- Any real property to be removed from the premises and any personal property to be included in the sale (both the listing agreement and the subsequent sales contract should be specific on these points)
- Proposed possession date
- Amount of last year's taxes
- Amount of outstanding special assessments and whether they will be paid by the seller or assumed by the buyer
- Information on any existing loan, including name and address of lender, balance of loan, loan or account number, interest rate, total monthly payment, date the next payment is due, and whether the payment includes taxes and insurance
- Type of heating, air-conditioning, and kitchen equipment
- Type of title evidence
- Type of zoning
- Any information on utility costs and irrigation fees
- Membership in a homeowner's association and the related dues and regulations
- Any rented or leased equipment such as satellite dish or water softeners

Later the listing agent should check the county records and any existing mortgage, deed of trust, or contract to verify the information given by the seller.

Why does the seller want to sell?   Has the owner been transferred to another city? Has the family grown too large for the home? Does the owner have some extra money and want to buy a nicer home? Or do financial problems necessitate lower monthly payments? Are the owners divorcing and need to sell the house for the property settlement? Has there been friction with the neighbors? Perhaps the owner is simply speculating on the market, trying to make a profit.

The owner's reason for selling will determine the extent of his or her desire to sell. However, this information is considered confidential unless the seller authorizes the agent to disclose it to potential purchasers. In taking a listing, a broker also may identify a prospect that is willing to trade properties or purchase a different property.

Supply and demand.   How great is the market demand for a specific type of property? This is important to consider when comparing a parcel of real estate with similar properties. If the supply is great and the demand is low, the property may have to be offered at a reduced price to sell it within a reasonable time.

Price.   Real estate should be listed at a price that is close to the market value of comparable property. The buying public is well informed, and a broker will have a difficult time securing a higher price for the property. A seller's asking price is frequently above market value when it is based on his or her opinion of the property's value or on rumors of the price some other seller in the neighborhood obtained for similar property. The broker should advise the seller in this matter so that the seller can make an intelligent decision when a reasonable offer is made for the property. Many times sellers refuse legitimate offers only later to wish they had accepted.

Competitive market analysis (CMA).   To assist the seller in pricing their home based on current market conditions, the real estate professional may prepare a competitive (aka "comparative") market analysis (CMA). This analysis will compare similar properties that have recently sold; properties that are currently available; and possibly properties that were on the market but did not sell (expired).

Although most CMAs are computer generated, the licensee should advise the seller whether the licensee personally verified the information acquired for comparison by personally going to and seeing comparable properties to verify data or if the licensee just took information out of the MLS database or other data source without a personal verification.

CMAs without personal verification of information could lead to incorrect analysis of values and lead the owner to list at a price that does not equate to the actual market.

Obviously, a well-researched CMA can greatly assist the seller to determine a realistic market value.

If a broker elects to charge a fee for a price opinion, extra care should be taken to conform to the statutory requirements of Idaho Code 54-4105.

Sometimes a broker will take an exclusive listing for a property at the owner's inflated price and then make little effort to market the property. This often occurs because the sales associate or the broker

- has not learned that improperly priced listings can cause lost revenues, deteriorate company image, and give the public the wrong message about the real estate sales profession;
- is unable or unwilling to accept the responsibility of telling the seller that the property is priced too high and what marketing problems are created by overpricing;
- has the idea that later, when the property doesn't sell, the owner will willingly reduce the price;

■ wants to prevent another broker from obtaining the listing; and/or

■ believes that a listing at any price beats no listing at all.

A potential listing agent will earn the respect of the average seller who has a reason to sell by professionally presenting a well-organized and factual presentation of the realistic market value of the property regardless of whether the broker secures a listing.

■ BUYER REPRESENTATION AGREEMENT [IC 54-2050]

More and more buyers are becoming clients of the brokerage. This is due to buyers wanting to be represented by a licensee in the acquisition and negotiation on their behalf. On the agent's side, the licensee who has a buyer as a client will have more control to pursue the right property for the buyer (see Figure 2.2). With additional information from the buyer (may be confidential) the agent can fine-tune the search for the perfect property.

Unlike the Seller Representation (Listing) Agreement, a specific legal description is not available. Thus, the real estate professional should carefully interview the buyer and specifically identify the type of property sought as well as a geographical perimeter to search.

■ TERMINATION OF A LISTING OR BUYER REPRESENTATION CONTRACT

In Idaho, the buyer or seller can *always* terminate the agency relationship without good cause and the real estate agent then *must* cease to act in the buyer's or seller's behalf. Whether the buyer or seller is contractually liable for damages to the real estate broker is not the issue; that question may be answered through settlement or litigation.

**Duties Owed
After Termination
[IC 54-2092]**

Even though the contract has been terminated, the brokerage still has to account for all monies and property received. Care must be taken when working with new construction. Often there are remaining weather-related items that still need to be installed. If monies are withheld prior to or upon closing prior to the project being completed, the brokerage is still responsible for accounting for this money.

Also, during the course of the transaction, the licensee may acquire defined confidential information [IC 54-2083 and IC 54-2087]. This confidential information may need to remain confidential forever!

■ CANCELLATION OR WITHDRAWAL OF A LISTING OR BUYER REPRESENTATION CONTRACT

The relative rights of a seller or buyer principal or a broker to withdraw or cancel an agreement are determined by contract law and court decisions, and the facts in each case bear heavily on the result.

The term *withdrawal* of a listing agreement means that the contract remains in full force and effect, but the property is no longer marketed or offered for sale by the broker.

The term *cancellation* of a listing shall mean that the contract is fully terminated, either with or without the broker's consent and with or without *good cause* on the part of the buyer or seller.

As a general proposition, an owner may, at any time, *withdraw* from the broker the *authority to sell* the property (i.e., stop offering the property for sale). Some listing agreements specify a penalty for early, unilateral withdrawal of the property from sale by the owner.

When a principal *cancels* a listing or buyer representation agreement (as opposed to withdrawing), the buyer or seller is essentially breaking the contract, even though it may be upheld in court as justifiable. If an agreement cannot be reached between the parties, it would be up to the courts to determine what damages (if any) should be awarded to the broker for early, unilateral *cancellation* of the listing agreement by an owner or buyer.

The Idaho Real Estate Commission has no legal authority to determine whether a buyer's or seller's unilateral cancellation is appropriate, and the Commission usually will not become involved in listing cancellation disputes. However, the Idaho Real Estate Commission does offer a good explanation about the differences between cancellation and withdrawal with their Guideline #1 available at

WWWeb.Link   *www.idahorealestatecommission.com*
www.irec.idaho.gov

■ LICENSEES DEALING WITH THEIR OWN PROPERTY [IC 54-2055]

An active licensee shall disclose in writing to any buyer or seller that he or she holds an active Idaho real estate license when buying or selling property for his or her own account.

In addition, each actively licensed person buying or selling real property, or any interest therein, must conduct the transaction through the broker with whom he or she is licensed, *whether or not the property is listed.*

■ ADVERTISING [IC 54-2053]

The Idaho Real Estate Commission has enacted a series of rules concerning the advertising of real property by real estate licensees. An actively licensed broker or sales associate, dealing with property owned wholly or in part by the licensee and not listed with a broker, shall disclose clearly in all advertising the fact that the person responsible for the advertising is a real estate licensee.

All advertising of listed property must show the listing broker's business name. No other business name may be used until a proper notice of the change in the business name has been received at the office of the Idaho Real Estate Commission. No advertising may provide any information to the public or to prospective clients that is misleading in nature.

It should also be noted that any unsolicited advertisements sent by facsimile or other electronic device without permission of the receiver would be in violation of Title 47, USC Section 227 and could cost the offender $500.

Information is *misleading* when, taken as a whole, a distinct probability exists that it will deceive the persons whom it is intended to influence. All advertising of branch offices must show the same business name as the main office of the broker. An Idaho reciprocal licensed broker in any advertising of Idaho real property may name only licensees who are actively licensed by reciprocity in Idaho.

As these rules indicate, it is very important for a real estate licensee to check all advertising to ensure that the ads are in compliance with the Rules as well as the federal Truth-in-Lending Law, which includes Regulation Z as well as Fair Housing Laws.

■ REPAIR AND INSPECTION REQUIREMENTS

At the time a property is listed, the seller should be made aware that in certain financing situations a buyer's lender may require inspections of some or all of the following: roof; plumbing; heating system; electrical system; foundation; pests; crawlspaces; street access; wells and water system; sewer and septic system; water heaters; smoke alarms; handrails; venting; peeling paint; wood stoves; fireplaces; and fireplace inserts.

Many of these systems, problems, and features are covered by a comprehensive property inspection report. If a buyer has any questions regarding these systems, the licensee should suggest that he or she contact a professional home inspection service or an expert in the particular field.

QUESTIONS

1. Which of the following provisions is *NOT* included in the Idaho Real Estate Commission's rules regarding listing agreements?

   a. A listing agreement must state the exact fee the broker will earn.

   b. A listing agreement must be accompanied by a qualified expert's report of the property's condition.

   c. A listing agreement must be in writing and signed by both broker and seller.

   d. The seller must receive a true copy of the listing agreement after signing it.

2. When deciding whether or not to take a listing, the broker or listing agent should

   a. consider the local demand for the type of property being offered and whether the property has sufficient appeal to attract buyers in the current market.

   b. take as many listings as possible to build up a large inventory.

   c. list the property at any price the seller desires.

   d. accept a listing without inspecting the property.

3. Which of the following is *TRUE* of advertisements for real property placed by real estate licensees?

   a. They may state only the licensee's box number or street address.

   b. They may simply give a telephone number to call for more information.

   c. They must indicate that they were placed in the name of a licensed real estate broker.

   d. They must identify the owner of the property.

4. Upon obtaining a listing, a broker or licensed salesperson is obligated to

   a. set up a listing file and issue it a number in compliance with Idaho Real Estate License Law and Rules.

   b. place advertisements in the local newspapers.

   c. cooperate with every real estate office wishing to participate in the marketing of the listed property.

   d. give the person or persons signing the listing a legible, signed, true, and correct copy.

5. Rob listed his house for sale with Broker Ben on February 1. The listing agreement was to last five months. In April, Rob decided that the house was no longer for sale. Which of the following statements is *TRUE*?

   a. Rob has canceled the agreement.

   b. Rob has withdrawn Ben's authority to sell the property and may be subject to a penalty.

   c. Rob is required by law to leave his house on the market until June.

   d. The Idaho Real Estate Commission will decide if Rob's action is justifiable.

6. If Tom, a real estate salesperson, decides to sell his own house without using a broker, which of the following is *TRUE* of any advertisement for the property?

   a. Tom must disclose the name, address, and phone number of his employing broker.

   b. Tom must disclose the fact that he is a real estate licensee.

   c. If Tom is acting as a private citizen, he does not need to disclose his status.

   d. The License Law prohibits Tom from selling his own home in this manner.

7. Recently a sex offender moved into the neighborhood where a home is for sale. A buyer, not familiar with the neighborhood, buys the home. Later, he finds out about the sex offender and threatens to sue the agent for failure to disclose an adverse material fact. Does the buyer have cause of action?

    a. Yes, because the agent should have known a material fact; it was in the newspaper.
    b. No, because sex offenders are protected under the Fair Housing Act.
    c. Yes, this is an adverse material fact; the buyer would not have purchased had it been known a sex offender resided in the neighborhood.
    d. No, this situation is not a material fact and no cause of action shall be brought against the seller or representative of the seller.

8. What type of manufactured housing can a real estate licensee market?

    a. A licensee cannot market any manufactured housing unless he or she has a dealer's license.
    b. A licensee must have a dealer's license to market manufactured housing.
    c. A licensee can only sell used manufactured homes on leased land.
    d. A licensee can market used and new manufactured housing providing there is a marketing agreement with a dealer.

9. After a listing has been terminated, what duties does the listing agent owe in the future?

    a. The agent owes none because the agency relationship has ended and all duties are automatically terminated.
    b. The agent must follow up after termination to make sure everyone is happy.
    c. The agent must maintain confidentiality from a client after the listing has expired.
    d. The agent can disclose the motivation of the seller after the listing has terminated.

10. A licensee co-owns a property with his daughter in order to secure financing. The daughter later decides to sell the property as a "for sale by owner." The licensee must

    a. do nothing because his daughter is the owner and he co-owns only as a condition of financing.
    b. disclose he is her parent to any prospective buyer.
    c. disclose he is a licensee and run the transaction through the broker with whom he is licensed.
    d. disclose co-ownership to the Idaho Real Estate Commission.

3

INTERESTS IN REAL ESTATE

■ ESTATES IN FEE

Freehold estates are recognized in Idaho. *Idaho law presumes that a fee simple interest is being conveyed unless expressly stated to the contrary.*

A *defeasible fee estate*, also referred to as a *fee simple qualified*, is also recognized in Idaho. *Defeasible* means it is capable of being annulled. Qualifications of ownership are placed on the property by the grantor, who uses language such as "so long as," "while," "during the period," "provided that," "on the condition that," or "if." The type of defeasible fee estate created depends on the particular phrase used.

Defeasible estates can be divided into two types: a *determinable fee estate* and a *fee simple subject to a condition subsequent* or *precedent*. The owner of the defeasible fee holds the same interest as the owner of the fee simple absolute estate, but the defeasible fee holder's interest may be annulled at some later date if certain events should happen.

The determinable estate carries the limitation that the interest will terminate *automatically* upon the happening of a specific event, and title will revert to the original grantor or that grantor's heirs. (In the case of the *determinable fee subject to an executory limitation*, the ownership automatically transfers to a designated third party.) The continued ownership of a fee simple determinable estate is predicated upon certain conditions that are usually expressed by the words "so long as," "while," or "during the period." Because the courts frown on automatic reversions, they require the use of the above language or a clear expression of intent that the interest would trigger the reversion.

■ **EXAMPLE** Hank conveys land "to the city of Boise *so long as* it is used for a park, and when it is no longer used for a park it shall revert back to Hank or his heirs."

The fee simple subject to a condition subsequent, on the other hand, is a grant that is to be used for a specific purpose and contains the words "provided that," "on the condition that," or "if." It is similar in that should a breach of the condition occur, the property can revert to the original grantor or the grantor's heirs; however, the reversion is not automatic. The grantor or the grantor's heirs must physically retake possession of the property or exercise their power of termination within a reasonable period of time after the breach. The estate remains with the grantee until the grantor exercises these powers through court action.

■ **EXAMPLE** Jackie deeds her property to the city of Sandpoint, Idaho, *on the condition that* the city use the property for a public park. A fee simple subject to a condition subsequent has been created, and if the condition is violated, Jackie may exercise her power of termination and end the city of Sandpoint's estate.

Jackie could also have created *a fee simple subject to a condition precedent*, and she probably would have had she required the city to appropriate the money to build a park in a certain period of time (for example, two years). The transfer of the title to the property would occur only when the condition had been met, even though the document had been prepared and recorded previously.

■ LIFE ESTATES

The degree, quantity, nature, and extent of ownership interest that a person has in real or personal property that is limited in duration to the life of its owner or the life of some other designated party is called a *life estate*.

Future Interests

Under Idaho law, a *future interest* (such as that held by a *remainderman*) passes by succession, will, and transfer in the same way as a present interest. A mere *possibility* (such as an heir's expectancy) is not a transferable interest, however.

Legal Life Estates

Curtesy and *dower* has been abolished in Idaho. Idaho has *community property laws*. Community property is discussed in Chapter 4 of this text.

Homestead

In Idaho, a *homestead* is an *exemption allowed by law to protect a homeowner against unsecured creditors* and has nothing to do with the "homestead" as a legal life estate that is recognized by many states.

The homestead consists of the house or manufactured home in which the owner resides or intends to reside and the land on which the dwelling unit is situated. The property actually must be used or intended to be used as a principal home for the owner. If the owner is married, the homestead may consist of the community or jointly owned property of the couple or the sole and separate property of either spouse—if it is a principal residence.

The amount of the homestead exemption was increased from $50,000 to $100,000 in 2006. This amount is after payment of any real estate taxes or special assessments, mortgages, deeds of trust, or liens that have an appropriate priority claim. Stated in a different way, homestead exemption would be "equity" not to exceed $100,000 (the difference between the market value less valid liens, or financial claims, against the property).

There are two ways to create the homestead exemption. The first is the automatic nature of the homestead under Idaho Code that occurs when the property is occupied as a principal residence by the owner (for not less than six months a year).

The second way occurs when the owner selects a homestead from unimproved or improved land that is not yet occupied as a homestead. To create the homestead exemption in the second situation, the owner must execute and file a declaration of homestead in the office of the county recorder in which the land is located. The conveyance or encumbrance of a homestead of a married person cannot occur unless the instrument by which it is conveyed or encumbered is executed and acknowledged by both husband and wife.

The homestead is exempt from attachment and from execution or forced sale for the debts of the owner up to $100,000. Also exempt are proceeds from the voluntary sale of the homestead, in good faith, for the purpose of acquiring a new homestead and the insurance receipts covering destruction of homestead property held for use in restoring or replacing the homestead.

A homestead is presumed abandoned if the owner vacates the property for a continuous period of at least *six months*. If an owner will be absent from the homestead for more than six months, but does not intend to abandon the homestead and has no other principal residence, the owner may execute and acknowledge a Declaration of Nonabandonment.

■ EASEMENTS

An easement is a *nonpossessory right to use* or enjoy the land owned by another person for a specific purpose and in a specific manner. The easement rights do not include the right to possess or remove any part of the land, below or on its surface. The various types of easements discussed in the main text are all applicable in Idaho. An *easement by necessity*, as described in the text, is also known as an *easement by operation of law* in Idaho.

The creation of many of the different types of easements in Idaho is covered by the Idaho Code. The rules concerning *implied grants of easements* are contained in the Idaho Code (Section 55-603), which provides that "a transfer of real property passes all easements attached thereto and creates in favor thereof an easement to use other real property of the person whose estate is transferred in the same manner and the same extent as such property was obviously and permanently used by the person whose estate is transferred, for the benefit thereof, at the time when the transfer was agreed upon or completed." Thus, an easement is transferable from one easement holder to another.

Implied easements by reservation are also recognized in Idaho. If an owner conveys the portion of his or her land that is burdened by a use for the benefit of the land retained by him or her, an easement by implied reservation arises in favor of the grantor if all conditions that are indispensable to the creation of an implied easement are met.

An *easement by necessity* exists only in cases of strict necessity—that is, where the property would otherwise be *landlocked*, having no means whatsoever for passage to a public road. The doctrine does not apply where the grantee has another means of access, even though it may be extremely inconvenient.

An *easement by prescription* may be acquired in Idaho by adverse use for a continuous period of five years. The interest so acquired is as effectual as one obtained by conveyance, but it is not a marketable title until established on record by appropriate court proceedings against the owner of the burdened land.

The essential elements that must be shown in order to establish an easement by prescription are: open and notorious use, continuous and uninterrupted use for a period of five years, hostile to the true owner, exclusive, and under some claim of right.

Payment of taxes is not required to obtain an easement by prescription. The easement acquired by prescription is limited to the exact nature of the hostile use placed on the property by the party establishing the easement right.

The Idaho Code also recognizes two additional types of easements: the solar easement and the conservation easement.

Solar Easement [IC 55-615]

An easement obtained for the purpose of exposure of a solar energy device to sunlight is known as a *solar easement*. Such an easement shall be created in writing and shall be subject to the same conveyance and instrument recording requirements as other easements. Any document creating a solar easement shall include, but not be limited to

■ the vertical and horizontal angles, expressed in degrees, at which the solar easement extends over the real property subject to the solar easement;
■ any terms or conditions or both under which the solar easement is granted or will be terminated; and
■ any provisions for compensation of the owner of the property benefitting from the solar easement in the event of interference with the enjoyment of the solar easement or compensation of the owner of the property subject to the solar easement for maintaining the solar easement.

A solar easement shall be presumed to be attached to the real property on which it was first created and shall be deemed to pass with the property when title is transferred to another owner, as prescribed under the Idaho Code (Section 55-603).

Conservation Easement [IC 55-2101]

The second easement described under the Idaho Code is the *conservation easement*. The Idaho Code defines a *conservation easement* as a nonpossessory interest of a holder in real property imposing limitations or affirmative obligations, the purposes of which include

■ retaining or protecting natural, scenic, or open-space values of real property;

■ ensuring its availability for agricultural, forest, recreational, or open-space use;

■ protecting natural resources;

■ maintaining or enhancing air or water quality; and

■ preserving the historical, architectural, archaeological, or cultural aspects of real property.

■ BOUNDARY BY AGREEMENT

The doctrine known as *agreed boundary, practically located boundary,* or *boundary by acquiescence* is recognized by Idaho law. This doctrine permits neighbors, under certain circumstances, to fix a boundary that will, from that time forward, operate as the boundary line, even though a subsequent survey may reveal that the true property line is located elsewhere. Adjoining landowners frequently have difficulty in setting the precise location of their boundary line versus their legal lot line.

Although the boundary description contained in a deed or other legal document may be easy to understand, it may nevertheless be difficult to specifically mark on the ground without the help of a surveyor. Unless an owner employs a surveyor to mark out property lines and corners, there may be only an approximate idea of where the boundaries are.

The boundary by agreement can be an express agreement. It can also be proven by the conduct of the parties, which is known as *acquiescence*. Idaho law requires that the actual boundary line be unknown to the parties or in dispute.

The consensual erection or establishment of a line of separation between the two adjoining properties establishes a new boundary line. The doctrine will generally be held to operate only when the new boundary line results from a disagreement or uncertainty between the neighbors as to the legal property line. It does not apply if the neighbors were either certain or mistaken as to the old line when they established the new line.

This theory, as is found in many situations, is obviously of a factual nature and subject to litigation. Once established, a boundary by agreement binds not merely the parties but their successors as well, even though there may be nothing in the records to warn successors of such a change. Because the theory of boundary by agreement is based on consent (and not on hostility, as is adverse possession), a real estate agent, broker, or a property owner who is having a property boundary dispute should seek competent legal assistance.

**Water Rights
[IC 42-101 through
42-107]**

Ownership of water rights in Idaho is determined by the *doctrine of prior appropriation*, not the doctrine of riparian rights.

Idaho water law is called the *appropriation doctrine* because water rights in Idaho are based on diversion and beneficial use of water. The appropriation doctrine has also been called *first in time is first in right* because the priority date determines who gets water when there is not enough to go around. The water right is also called an *appropriation,* and someone who has a water right is said to have appropriated water. A water right under the law of the state of Idaho can be established only by appropriation, and, once established, it can be lost if it is not used.

Under the doctrine of prior appropriation, all waters of the state, when flowing in their natural channels, including the waters of all natural springs and lakes within the boundaries of the state, are declared to be the property of the state.

The state supervises the appropriation and allotment of water through the Idaho Department of Water Resources (IDWR). The right to use water for useful or beneficial purposes is recognized and confirmed.

The right to use public waters is not considered a property right in itself, but the right becomes appurtenant to the land or other use to which, through necessity, the water is being applied.

The right to continue the water use can be denied only for failure on the part of the user to pay the ordinary charges or assessments that may be made to cover the expenses for the delivery of the water, or for failing to apply the water to a beneficial use for a period of five consecutive years.

Prerequisites to appropriation of water are putting the water to a beneficial use and diverting the water from its natural channel or location to the property.

What Is a Water Right?   The constitution and statutes of the state of Idaho declare all the waters of the state, when flowing in their natural channels, including the waters of all natural springs and lakes within the boundaries of the state, and ground waters of the state, to be *public waters.* The constitution and statutes of the state *guarantee the right* to appropriate the unappropriated public waters of the state of Idaho. When a right to the use of public waters is established by appropriation, a water right is established that is a real property right, much like property rights in land.

A water right is the right to *divert the public waters* of the state of Idaho and put them to a *beneficial use,* in accordance with one's *priority date.* A *priority date* is the date the water right was established. How this date is determined will be described in a later section of this chapter. The priority date is important because it determines who gets water when there is a shortage. If there is not enough water available to satisfy all of the water rights, those with the oldest (or senior) water rights get their water rights satisfied first and so on in order until there is no water left. It is the persons with the new (or junior) water rights who do not get water when there is not enough to satisfy all the water rights.

Beneficial uses include such uses as domestic use, irrigation, stock watering, manufacturing, mining, hydropower, municipal use, aquaculture, recreation, and fish and wildlife, among others. The amount of the water right is only that amount of water put to beneficial use. Due to the *beneficial use requirement,* a water right (or a portion of a water right) *may be lost if not used within a continuous five-year period.*

A *diversion* is a structure for capturing the water before it is put to use. Typical diversion structures include pumps, headgates, ditches, pipelines, and dams, or some combination. A diversion is generally required to establish a water right. Some public agencies are authorized to acquire water rights without diversions. These water rights, called *instream flow* water rights, are typically authorized for purposes of protecting some public interest in a natural stream or lake, such as recreation, wildlife, or natural beauty. A water right may also be acquired to water livestock directly from the stream. This is called an *instream livestock* water right.

What is a claim?　There are two types of filings that are often called *claims*. The first is a *statutory claim* that was filed with the IDWR to make a record of an *existing* beneficial use right. In 1978, a statute was enacted requiring persons with beneficial rights (other than water rights used solely for domestic purposes) to record their water rights with the IDWR. The purpose of the statute was to provide some means of recording water rights for which there were no previous records. However, these records are merely affidavits of the water users and do not result in licenses, decrees, or other confirmations of the water rights.

The other type of claim is a *notice of claim* to a water right that is filed with the IDWR in water rights adjudications. An adjudication is a court action for the determination of *existing* water rights, which results in a decree that confirms and defines each water right. When an adjudication of a particular source is commenced, the IDWR is required to notify the water users of the commencement of the adjudication and to notify them that they are required to file notices of claims with the IDWR for their water rights. The IDWR then investigates the notices of claims and prepares a report that is filed with the court.

Private waters are covered under Idaho Code (Section 42-212):

> *The Department of Water Resources is hereby prohibited from issuing or granting permits to divert or appropriate the waters of any lake not exceeding five (5) acres in surface area at highwater mark, pond, pool or spring in this state that is located or situated wholly or entirely on the lands of a person or corporation, except to the person or corporation owning said land, or with his or its written permission, executed and acknowledged as required for the conveyance of real estate.*

Surface Water　Prior to 1903, Idaho had a "posted notice" statute that provided for posting a notice at the point of diversion and recording the notice at the county recorder's office, followed by actual diversion and beneficial use of water. If the statutory requirements were met, the priority date for a water right established under the posted notice statute was the date of posting the notice.

Prior to May 20, 1971, there were two ways in which a right to surface water could be established. The first way was to simply divert water and apply it to beneficial use. This is called a *beneficial use, historic use,* or *constitutional* water right. The priority date for a water right established by this method is the date water was first put to beneficial use. The second way to establish a right to surface water was to comply with the statutory method in effect at the time the water right was established.

Since May 20, 1971, there is only one way to establish a right to surface water: by following the application/permit/license procedure described later in this chapter. The priority date for a water right established by this method is the date of filing the application with the IDWR. This priority date is shown on the license that is issued when the process is completed. (The one exception to this rule is for water rights used solely for instream watering of livestock.)

Ground Water

Prior to March 25, 1963, there were two ways to establish rights to ground water, which are the same methods described for establishing rights to surface water. Since March 25, 1963, there is only one way to establish a right to ground water, and that is by following the procedure described later in this chapter.

There is one exception to this rule. A beneficial use right to ground water may still be established for domestic purposes. *Domestic purposes* is defined by statute as "water for homes, organization camps, public campgrounds, livestock, and for any other purpose(s). . . including irrigation of up to one-half (½) acre of land, if the total use is not in excess of thirteen thousand (13,000) gallons per day [this is not a misprint]; or any other uses if the total use does not exceed a diversion rate of 0.04 cubic feet per second and a diversion volume of 2,500 gallons per day." *Domestic purposes* does not include "water for multiple ownership subdivisions, mobile [manufactured] home parks, or commercial or business establishments." The rules and regulations of the IDWR interpret the exception as limited to single-family domestic purposes.

Ground water recharge.   The appropriation and underground storage of water for the purpose of recharging ground water basins constitute a beneficial use under Idaho law. As a result, the IDWR is empowered to issue permits for the ground water recharge uses. However, where "incidental ground water recharge" results from the diversion and use of water for other beneficial purposes, the user is not entitled to an additional permit.

Projects designed to recharge ground water basins are subject to review by the IDWR and an aquifer recharge district board of directors composed of representatives of commercial, agricultural, industrial, municipal, and private water users. The director of the IDWR is directed by statute to ensure that no other water rights are injured by a ground water recharge project and to regulate and reduce the amount of water diverted for recharge.

Procedure for Establishing a Water Right [IC 42-201 through 42-250]

If you are currently diverting the public waters of the state and putting the water to beneficial use, you may already have a valid water right established either by the statutory method or by beneficial use. If water was used on your property before you acquired it, and the person you acquired the property from did not "reserve" the water right in the deed conveying the property to you, and you continued the use of water, you may have acquired a valid water right along with your land. Also, some water rights (including water rights established by both the statutory method and by beneficial use) have been confirmed by a decree of a state or federal court. The IDWR keeps records of water right decrees and licenses, and these records are available for public inspection.

A property owner may have the right to use water from a water right held by someone else, such as a municipal provider, a homeowner's association, an irrigation district, or a canal company.

You may need a new water right for an existing use of water if a water right was not properly established for the existing use. An example is a use of surface water that was initiated after 1971 without application to the IDWR for a permit. A new water right is also needed for a new use of water. If you wish to establish a new water right, there are certain procedures you will need to follow.

First, an application for a permit must be filed with the IDWR. Application forms are available from the IDWR. The information that must be included in the application is described by statute and in the rules and regulations of the IDWR. The IDWR is required to publish notice of the application, and other persons may file protests to the application with the IDWR. If protests are filed, the IDWR must hold a hearing.

The IDWR must then review the application (including any hearing record), and if the application meets the requirements of the statute and the rules and regulations, a permit is issued. The permit describes the appropriation to be made and the deadline within which the appropriation must be completed. Prior to the end of the period in which the appropriation must be completed, the IDWR sends the permit holder a notice that the deadline is approaching and that the permit holder must submit proof of beneficial use. "Proof of beneficial use" is a form sent to the permit holder by the IDWR that the permit holder fills out and returns to the IDWR. In the proof form, the permit holder states that he or she has completed the appropriation.

After the permit holder files the proof form, a field examination must be made. The permit holder may request that the field examination be made by the IDWR, in which case an examination fee is required to be paid to the IDWR.

The permit holder may instead have the field examination completed by a certified water right examiner not associated with the IDWR. The examiner submits a report to the IDWR after the examination is completed. The purpose of the field examination is to ensure that water is in fact being used as described in the permit. If so, the IDWR issues a license that describes the appropriation that has been completed.

A water right permit is considered personal property and does not automatically transfer with the land, although a fully perfected right will.

Snake River Basin Adjudication

The purpose of the general adjudication of water rights in the Snake River Basin is to make a complete and accurate record of all existing water rights. The largest part of the state is covered by the adjudication.

The term *adjudicate* means to settle judicially. A water right adjudication can be described as a "fair, comprehensive, technically correct, and legally sufficient determination of existing water rights." Despite an agreement with the federal government that domestic and stockwater users may waive or defer filing a notice of claim of water rights in the Snake River Basin Adjudication (SRBA), David Shaw, former chief of the adjudication bureau of the IDWR, urged water users to allow previously filed notices of claims to be decreed by the court.

Mr. Shaw explained, "It is our best judgment that domestic and stockwater filings are prudent, and we are still encouraging people to file on their domestic and stockwater uses for several reasons. An SRBA-decreed water right will become legally appurtenant to the property. An SRBA-decreed water right is a valuable asset to property. Further, an SRBA-decreed water right will have the best form of legal security that exists for a water right under Idaho law."

A Commencement Notice informed members of the general public that if they had an existing water right, it was necessary for them to file a Notice of Claim to that water right with the IDWR. Filing is required whether or not they have previously recorded their water rights with the IDWR.

Upon filing, the claim will be checked for accuracy and reported to the court to be decreed by the judge. The first reports to the court were filed in 1992; final reports were submitted in June 2005.

Water rights may be lost by not filing a Notice of Claim in the SRBA. Idaho Code (Section 42-1409) requires claimants of water rights to inform the IDWR *in writing of changes in ownership or of any change in mailing address.*

Each purchaser of a water right from within the boundaries of the SRBA must provide the IDWR written notice of any change in ownership or mailing address. Purchasers must also ask the IDWR whether a water rights claim has been filed, and if one needs to be filed, they must do so immediately.

While a real estate licensee or lawyer may assist an owner, it is the owner's responsibility to check with the IDWR to see whether any water rights to the property have been claimed in the SRBA and to make any required filing.

At the closing of any real estate transaction, buyer and seller should sign a form (No. 42-1409) that notifies the IDWR who the buyer and seller are, what the legal description of the property is, and what is known about the water rights. This form must be mailed to the IDWR after it has been completed and signed. Following are four important things to remember regarding the SRBA and the sale or exchange of property:

1. Purchasers of property with appurtenant water rights after the adjudication process begins, and for which a notice of claim has been filed, will have the duty to notify the department in writing of the name and address of the new owner.
2. A notice of change in ownership must be accompanied by some evidence of the change in ownership or the signature of the original claimant. Purchasers who fail to file a change in ownership will be considered to have been served by notices sent to the previous owner, even if the notices are not in fact received by the purchasers.
3. No new fee is required to record the new owner of the property with the IDWR.
4. If a water right exists on the property being purchased and was not claimed by the prior owner, the purchaser must file a claim for the water use in the SRBA.

Filing a Drilling Permit [IC 42-238]

The drilling permit describes general conditions of approval and provides for specific conditions that may be applicable in a particular locality or situation. The drilling permit authorizes the construction or modification of a well and does not authorize water use or diversion.

Restrictions for issuance of a drilling permit include the following four:

1. The well shall be constructed by a driller currently licensed in the state of Idaho who must maintain a copy of the drilling permit at the drilling site.
2. Drilling permits to construct single-family domestic wells, including irrigation (less than one-half acre) and stockwater wells, utilizing fewer than 13,000 gallons of water per day, generally may be obtained without other prior approvals from the IDWR. Only a licensed well driller may obtain a verbal approval from the IDWR to drill domestic wells. When such authorizations are verbal, the driller is responsible for submitting a completed drilling permit application with the fee and the verbally issued permit number.
3. Irrigation of more than one-half acre and commercial, injection, or other wells require a water right permit, an injection well permit, or other approvals prior to issuance of a drilling permit. No verbal approval will be issued for those uses.
4. Monitoring wells require a well bore schematic and a map or plat showing the location of each well prior to issuance of drilling permits. All applications for monitor wells must be submitted by a professional engineer or geologist registered in the state of Idaho.

Abandonment of a well in Idaho may only be performed by a person who has first obtained a drilling permit from the IDWR. Authorization is required from the director of the IDWR prior to the abandonment, and the person abandoning the well must submit a report describing the abandonment to the director.

Measurement of Water [IC 42-102]

The measurement of water is as follows: "A cubic foot of water per second of time shall be the legal standard for the measurement of water in this state, and it shall be the duty of the Idaho Department of Water Resources to devise a simple, uniform system for the measurement and distribution of water."

Legal advice.   Perfecting, maintaining, and using water rights often present complex legal questions. Whenever water rights issues arise in a real estate transaction, the broker or salesperson should advise clients to seek professional legal advice.

WWWeb.Link

The Idaho Department of Water Resources (IDWR) can be found on the Web at *www.idwr.state.id.us*

■ GEOTHERMAL ENERGY [IC 42-4001]

The Idaho Geothermal Resources Act states: "It is hereby declared that the State of Idaho claims the right to regulate the development and use of all the geothermal resources within this state and that geothermal resources are natural resources of limited quantity and of a unique value to all of the people of the state."

Under Idaho Code (Section 42-4002[c]), a *geothermal resource* is the natural heat energy of the earth. It is the energy, in whatever form, that may be found in any position and at any depth below the surface of the earth present in, resulting from, or created by, or that may be extracted from natural heat. It includes all minerals in solution or other products obtained from the material medium of any geothermal resource. Ground water having a temperature of 212 degrees Fahrenheit or more in the bottom of a well is classified as a geothermal resource.

Under Idaho statute, geothermal resources are considered *sui generis*, that is, unique, being neither a mineral resource nor a water resource. But they are regulated because they are closely related to and possibly affect or are affected by water and mineral resources in many instances.

QUESTIONS

1. When Quentin's son got married, Quentin deeded the newlyweds a house free and clear of any financial liens. The conveyance included a stipulation that if they should ever divorce, their ownership of the property would terminate automatically and title to the property would pass to Quentin's daughter Martha. Their ownership interest in the property is a fee simple
   a. subject to a life estate with an estate in remainder to Martha.
   b. determinable estate subject to an executory limitation.
   c. defeasible subject to a condition precedent.
   d. defeasible subject to a condition subsequent.

2. Joan conveyed a small farm to her mother for the rest of her mother's life. Upon her mother's death, title to the property will pass back to Joan. Joan's interest in the farm while her mother is still alive is known as a(n)
   a. dower.
   b. remainder.
   c. executory limitation.
   d. reversion.

3. The homestead exemption granted by Idaho law to a homeowner is
   a. $25,000.
   b. $27,000.
   c. $50,000. 100,000
   d. $55,000.

4. Which of the following is NOT true regarding the abandonment of a well in Idaho?
   a. The well must be declared an unbeneficial use before it can be abandoned.
   b. The abandonment may only be performed by a person who has first obtained a drilling permit from the IDWR.
   c. Authorization is required from the director of the IDWR prior to the abandonment.
   d. The person abandoning the well must submit a report describing the abandonment to the director of the IDWR.

5. A homestead is presumed abandoned if the owner vacates the property for a continuous period of at least how many months?
   a. 3   c. 9
   b. 6   d. 12

6. In Idaho, a person may lose his or her water rights, no matter how these rights were obtained, by not putting the water to beneficial use for a period of how many years?
   a. 3   c. 10
   b. 5   d. 15

7. Geothermal resources are the natural heat energy of the earth, in whatever form, and are classified as
   a. mineral resources.
   b. discrete resources.
   c. water resources.
   d. neither water nor mineral resources.

8. Which of the following are NOT automatically transferred when the property is sold?
   a. Water rights obtained under a water permit
   b. Mineral rights received, but not reserved
   c. An appurtenant easement
   d. An incorporeal hereditament

HOW OWNERSHIP IS HELD

■ FORMS OF OWNERSHIP

Chapter 3 in this text described *what* estates or interests in real estate may be owned. Chapter 4 discusses *how* real estate may be owned. Idaho recognizes the following three different forms of ownership:

1. Ownership in severalty (sole ownership)
2. Co-ownership (tenancy in common, joint tenancy, and community property)
3. Ownership in trust

Ownership in severalty and ownership in trusts are self-defined. However, the uniqueness of co-ownership issues that are specific to Idaho will be addressed in the following paragraphs.

Co-ownership

According to Idaho law, a deed of conveyance granting title to a parcel of real estate to two or more persons automatically creates a tenancy in common unless the wording of the deed expressly states the intention to create a joint tenancy or unless the property is acquired as a partnership or community property. Joint tenancy in Idaho does feature the right of survivorship; unity of title, time, interest, and possession must be present.

Tenancy by the entirety. Because of the complexity of Idaho's community property laws, this form of co-ownership cannot be used on real estate owned by a husband and wife as part of their community property. It can, however, be used on property that either spouse owns separately. The owner-spouse can convey the property to both of them on the same instrument with words of conveyance that express the intention of creating a tenancy by the entirety with the right of survivorship and not as community property or some other form of co-ownership.

Tenancy by the entirety form of ownership is seldom used in Idaho due to potential conflicts with Idaho community property statutes.

Partition.   Any joint tenant or tenant in common may file a suit for partition. If the land involved cannot be partitioned or divided fairly among the co-owners, the court may order the property sold and the proceeds distributed to the former co-owners.

Community Property

In Idaho, all property owned by a married person is presumed to be community property until proven that it is being held as separate property. A person's separate property consists of all money and other property owned by him or her before the marriage as well as any such property acquired by gift or inheritance after the marriage.

In regard to separate property, each spouse is responsible for his or her own debts. A separate property cannot be appropriated for payment of a spouse's debts. However, community property may be taken to satisfy either spouse's separate debts. In Idaho, net income from all separate property during a marriage is considered a community asset.

At any time either before or during a marriage, either spouse may purchase and own property as sole and separate. The purchaser must declare and place in the public record the intention to own this property as sole and separate, so that the law will recognize it as such.

Community property consists of all property and earnings from personal services (in other words, salary) acquired by a husband and wife during a *valid marriage*. Rents and profits from the separate property of either spouse become part of the community property, especially if commingled or resulting from community effort.

Note.   Effective January 1, 1996, *common-law marriage is no longer recognized in the state of Idaho*. A common-law marriage entered into prior to January 1, 1996, remains valid. The revised statute, IC 32-201, defines marriage as *a personal relation arising out of a civil contract between a man and a woman, to which consent of parties capable of making it is necessary. Consent alone will not constitute marriage; it must be followed by the issuance of a license and a solemnization as authorized and provided by law. Marriage created by a mutual assumption of marital rights, duties and obligations shall not be recognized as a lawful marriage.*

In effect, each spouse owns one-half of the community property. Under Idaho law either the husband or the wife has the right to manage and control the community property and either may bind community property, other than real estate, by contract. Neither spouse may convey or encumber real estate held as community property unless the other spouse also joins in (signs) any contract or document involved.

Upon the death of either spouse, one-half of the community property automatically belongs to the survivor and the other half is distributed according to the deceased's will. If the deceased left no will, the other half of the community property passes to the surviving spouse—subject to Idaho law regarding descent and distribution.

Maintaining separate property. Idaho law includes strict regulations on how sole ownership of property can be maintained and legal complications avoided. For example, using community funds to pay the taxes, insurance payments, or loan payments for a parcel of separate property could damage that property's sole and separate status. Any licensee who takes a listing for separately owned property should make certain that it is in fact separate property. A licensee who neglects to check on this fact could be liable for misrepresentation.

Most title companies require a release of any possible interest by the spouse. If one spouse resides in the sole and separate property of the other, a homestead may exist. The title company will require both spouses to sign a deed or release before it will insure the title.

QUESTIONS

1. A deed grants title to a parcel of real estate "to Bob and Renee." If the real estate is not being acquired as partnership property and Bob and Renee are not married, Bob and Renee will acquire title as

   a. joint tenants.
   b. trustees.
   c. part of their community property.
   d. tenants in common.

2. A married couple's community property includes

   a. proceeds received as a beneficiary from a nonpartnership life insurance policy.
   b. property inherited by either spouse.
   c. wages earned by either spouse.
   d. real estate acquired by either spouse as a gift.

3. Which of the following statements is *TRUE* concerning community property in Idaho?

   a. Upon the death of either spouse, and if the deceased left a will, all the community property automatically belongs to the surviving spouse, and the deceased's separate property is distributed according to his or her will.
   b. Any real estate that is part of a married couple's community property is held by the husband and wife in a tenancy by the entirety.
   c. Neither spouse may sell any real estate owned as part of their community property unless both spouses sign the sales contract and deed.
   d. Technically, a husband owns two-thirds of a couple's community property, whereas his wife owns only one-third.

4. If a newly married spouse died and left no will, to whom does the remaining half of the community property pass to?

   a. The children of the deceased spouse
   b. The children of the remaining spouse
   c. The parents of the deceased spouse
   d. The remaining spouse

5

LEGAL DESCRIPTIONS

■ LEGAL DESCRIPTIONS IN IDAHO

The following three types of legal descriptions are used in Idaho:

1. Government Rectangular Survey System
2. Recorded plat
3. Metes-and-bounds

An acceptable description must use one of the three systems. It should be noted that a *street address is not an acceptable legal description*. A proper legal description must allow for the determination of the exact size, shape, and location of the property. The government Rectangular Survey System is the base system to which all legal descriptions refer.

■ GOVERNMENT RECTANGULAR SURVEY SYSTEM

All measurements in Idaho are made from an initial point, which is south of the city of Meridian and east of the Kuna Caves. This initial point is approximately 36 miles east, 95 miles north of Idaho's southwestern border (see Figure 5.1).

The Boise Principal Meridian runs north and south at a longitude of 116°24'15". At the Canadian border on the north, you would be at Township 65 North (T 65 N); Township 16 South (T 16 S) is at the southern border of Idaho. The Boise Principal Meridian passes through the city of Meridian as it goes north from the initial point.

The base line, running east and west, passes just south of Boise in the western part of the state and south of Idaho Falls in the eastern part of the state. As you travel across the state in counties like Blaine County, you find a road that is built along the base line and is called Base Line Road. (See Figure 5.1 for the location of the initial point, the Boise Principal Meridian, and the base line as they cross the state.)

FIGURE 5.1

Boise Principal Meridian

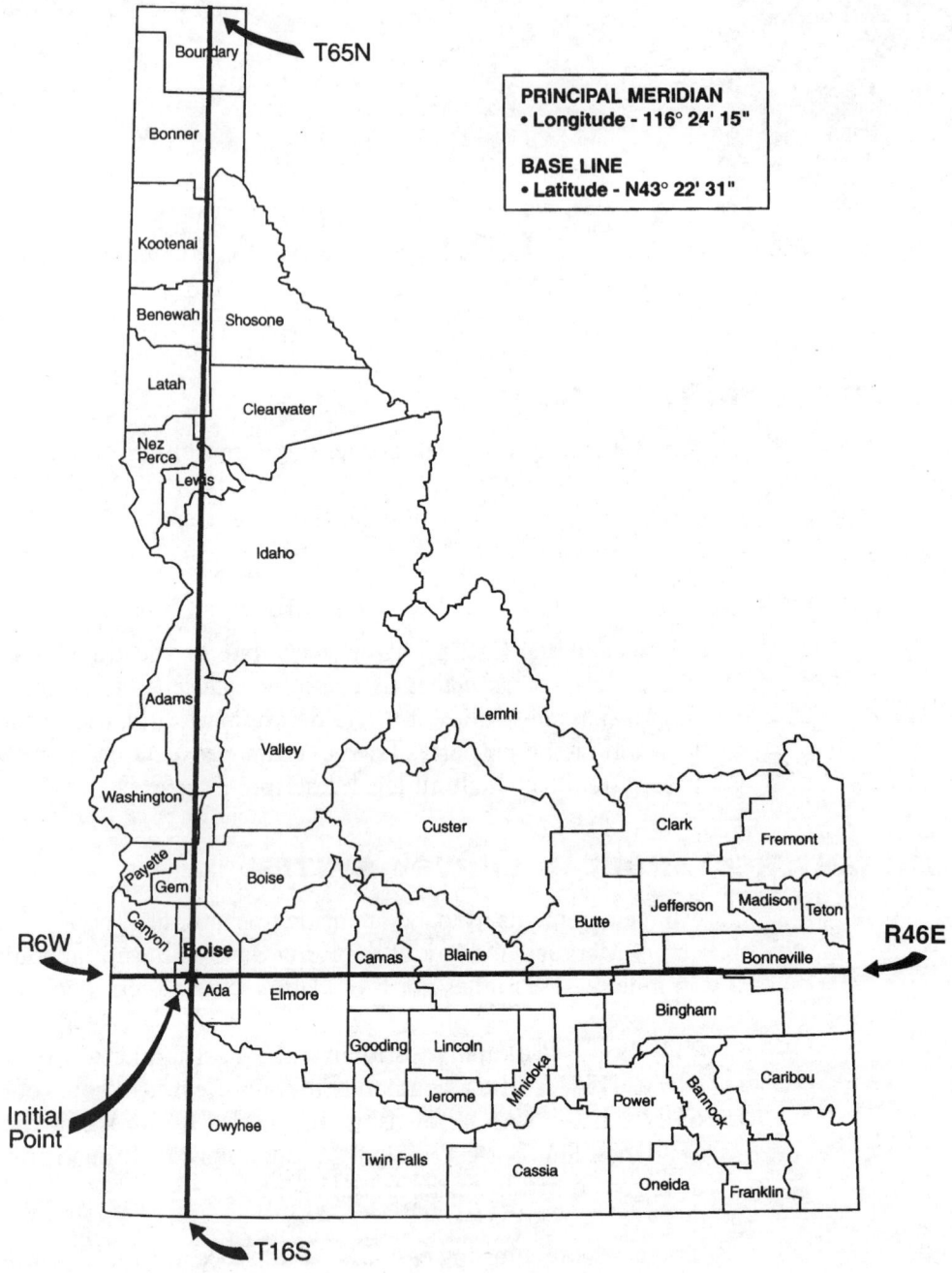

PRINCIPAL MERIDIAN
• Longitude - 116° 24' 15"

BASE LINE
• Latitude - N43° 22' 31"

■ RECORDED PLATS

Most of the parcels of land within the urban areas of the state are described using recorded plats. Under Idaho Code, if a tract of land is divided into five or more lots, parcels, or sites for the purpose of immediate or future sale or building development (except for agricultural purposes), a formal subdivision

F I G U R E 5.2

Discovery Creek Subdivision No. 1

plat must be approved by the local jurisdiction and recorded by the county recorder. (See Chapter 14 of this book for a detailed discussion of this process.)

After the subdivision has been formally approved and recorded, a property then can be described as "Lot 5, Block 2 of Summer Wind Subdivision, Ada County, Idaho," for instance. (An example of a formally platted subdivision is shown as Figure 5.2.) On the plat you will find metes-and-bounds descriptions as the lot lines and streets are measured and described. In addition you will find a reference to the township, range, and section shown on the face of the plat just under the formal name of the subdivision.

Coordinate System of Land Description

The Idaho Code [IC 55-1701] permits land descriptions made after January 1, 1996, to be made according to the National Ocean Service's National Geodetic Survey (NGS), a system of plane coordinates known as the "Idaho coordinate system of 1983." The system divides Idaho into three zones—clusters of counties in the eastern, central, and western parts of the state. The use of a coordinate description, however, is supplemental to other surveys and descriptions and must include the property by reference to the government description discussed above.

Air Lots— Condominiums

Idaho, like all other states, has enacted a Condominium Property Act. A licensed surveyor will prepare a plat that shows the elevations of floor and ceiling surfaces and the boundaries of the condominium units. These elevations will refer to an official *datum*. Most cities will have an established local official datum that will be used by most surveyors. After the plats have been prepared and approved, they will be officially recorded.

■ METES-AND-BOUNDS LEGAL DESCRIPTION

If a property is irregular in shape and is located in an area where formal platting has not occurred, the property probably will be described using a metes-and-bounds legal description. A survey of the property will be done by a licensed surveyor and a legal description prepared from this survey. The point of beginning (POB) normally will be a section corner or township corner that directly ties the metes-and-bounds legal description to the government rectangular survey system. All metes-and-bounds descriptions must begin and end at the POB.

■ RECORDING OF SURVEYS

Idaho Code [IC 55-1901] renders a method for preserving evidence of land surveys by providing for public record of surveys. After making a survey in conformity with established principles of land surveying, a surveyor shall file a record of survey with the county recorder in the county or counties wherein the lands surveyed are situated. A record of survey shall be filed within 90 days after completing any survey that

■ discloses a material discrepancy with previous surveys of record;
■ establishes boundary lines or corners not previously existing or of record; or

■   produces evidence or information that varies from, or is not contained in, surveys of record relating to the public land survey, lost public land corners, or obliterated land survey corners.

Idaho Code [IC 54-1227] was amended to require that in order for survey monuments to be "permanent" and "reliable" they must be steel or iron rods of not less than one-half inch in diameter, a minimum of 24 inches long, and permanently marked with the registration mark of the surveyor. Idaho Code [IC 55-1905 through IC 55-1910] provides the details of how the records will be kept, what must be included, when a survey does not have to be recorded, the filing fee, and the duties of the county recorder.

QUESTIONS

1. Which of the following legal descriptions is/are used in Idaho?
   a. Metes-and-bounds
   b. Government Rectangular Survey System
   c. Recorded plats
   d. All of the above

2. A property located in the NW 1/4 of Section 10, Township 10 North, and Range 2 West of the Boise Principal Meridian (BPM) would be located where in relationship to the initial point?
   a. Northwest of it
   b. Northeast of it
   c. Southwest of it
   d. Southeast of it

3. Which of the following does *NOT* constitute a proper legal description of a parcel of real estate in Idaho?
   a. Section 12 of T 3 N, R 4 E, Boise Principal Meridian
   b. 6510 Robertson Drive, Boise, Idaho
   c. Lot 5, Block 2 of Summerwind Subdivision, Ada County, Idaho
   d. A metes-and-bounds description that has as its point of beginning the northwest corner of Section 4, T 2 N, R 2 W, Boise Principal Meridian

4. The initial point is located
   a. approximately 36 miles east of Idaho's western border.
   b. approximately 95 miles north of Idaho's southern border.
   c. south of the city of Meridian and east of the Kuna Caves in Ada County.
   d. near all of the above.

5. If you were standing at the Canadian border in northern Idaho, the township would be numbered
   a. T 65 N.   c. T 65 W.
   b. T 65 S.   d. T 16 S.

6. The range number along the eastern border of Idaho would be approximately
   a. R 26 W.   c. R 46 N.
   b. R 46 W.   d. R 46 E.

6

REAL ESTATE TAXES AND OTHER LIENS

■ REAL ESTATE TAXES

Idaho, like most other states, collects property taxes in order to pay for the costs of local government services based on the value of the property being taxed.

Assessment
[IC 63-003]

The process of property taxation starts on January 1 of each year. On this date the current taxes for the year become an accruing lien on the property although the actual amount of the tax has not been determined. The county assessor in each county is charged with the responsibility of determining the value of real and personal property for tax purposes.

The State Tax Commission has an important responsibility to the county assessors and the county commissioners. The tax commission provides supervision and technical assistance through guidelines and rules that prescribe the methods used by the county assessor in determining market values for tax purposes.

Each year the tax commission does a ratio study that is based on the actual sales prices of real property compared to the market values of real property determined by the county assessor. This study helps establish guidelines for the county assessor.

At least 20 percent of the taxable properties in the county shall be included in each year's appraisal, resulting in a complete appraisal of all taxable property every five years.

The board of county commissioners may request that the Idaho state tax commission grant an extension of the five-year reappraisal deadline. The request shall be in writing and shall set forth the reason(s) that the county is unable to complete the reappraisal process due to extraordinary circumstances.

Extraordinary circumstances may include, but are not limited to, natural disasters or unforeseen circumstances that result in extreme financial hardship to the county. In no case shall an extension exceed two years.

Annually, all taxable property, not actually appraised each year, shall be indexed to reflect current market value for assessment purposes using market value property transactions and results of the annual appraisal of 20 percent of the taxable property. The county assessor shall maintain in the respective offices sufficient records to show when each parcel or item of property was last appraised.

Between the first day of January and the fourth Monday of June, the county assessor is required to complete all current assessments. Any real property that has been omitted may later be added to the assessment roll.

The estimated value must be calculated using the three recognized approaches to value: the *cost approach*, the *market approach*, and the *income approach*. If all three approaches are not applicable to the property being valued, then as many of the approaches as possible will be used.

When a property owner believes his or her property has been assessed (valued) unfairly, the assessed value can be appealed to the county board of equalization. The county commissioners sit as the county board of equalization and must meet at least once a month through the fourth Monday of June for the specific purpose of equalizing the assessed value of real property.

The terms *market value* and *assessed value* are synonymous. In Idaho, the county assessor is required to determine the fair market cash value as of January 1 of each year for tax purposes. The assessor also is required to separate values of the land and improvements. Thus, the total combined assessment value will be the value of the land plus the value of the improvements.

■ OCCUPANCY TAX [IC 63-317]

Idaho's *occupancy tax* provides for a tax on all newly constructed and occupied residential and commercial buildings, except additions to existing improvements, during their first year of occupancy.

Likewise, improvements subject to the occupancy tax are prorated for the portion of the year for which the improvement was occupied. Owners must notify the county assessor at the time they occupy a new property. The failure to report first occupancy will result in a penalty of five percent of the tax per month, to a maximum of 25 percent of the tax.

■ **EXAMPLE** Dan is building a house and completes the structure on June 4, at which time Dan moves in. The structure now becomes subject to *occupancy tax* that will be prorated for the length of time the structure is occupied (June 4 through December 31 of the current year).

The assessor must notify the owner of the assessed value of the construction and of the owner's right to apply for a *homeowner's exemption*. With new construction the owner must apply within 30 days of notification and must meet the statutory requirements. The homeowner's exemption is the lesser of 50 percent of the value of the new construction or $50,000.

Manufactured Home Occupancy Tax [IC 63-317]

New manufactured housing shall not be subject to property taxation during the first year of occupancy if occupied after January 1. For the purposes of this section, *new manufactured housing* means manufactured housing, whether real or personal, never previously occupied.

The owner of any new manufactured housing upon which no occupancy tax has been charged shall report to the county assessor that the new manufactured housing has been occupied. As soon as practical after receiving such a report, the county assessor shall appraise and determine the market value for assessment purposes.

Property Tax Relief

Limitation on budget requests and tax charges.   Idaho law protects the public from exceptional property tax increases by limiting budget requests and tax charges. Unless a majority of the voters in a particular taxing district vote for an increase in property taxes for a specific purpose, that taxing district may not certify an annual budget request that increases property taxes exceeding the limitations set forth in IC 63-802.

Exemption for personal residence [IC 63-602G].   The first $75,000 or 50 percent (whichever is less) of the combined market value of residential improvements and the land is exempt from property taxation if

- the property is the primary residence and occupied by the individual applying for the exemption after January 1 but before April 15;
- the State Tax Commission has certified to the county commissioners that all the property in the county has been assessed by the assessor; and
- the owner applies to the county assessor for the exemption by April 15 for the current year.

It should be noted that a cosigner of a loan in which the cosigner is named on the deed does not negate the ability of the owner to apply for and receive 100 percent eligibility for homeowner exemption.

Idaho also allows for certain hardship exemptions and tax reductions. An ordinary exemption for the current year's taxes may be applied for to the board of equalization by a person whose ability to pay the property taxes is affected by unusual circumstances. In addition, a person can apply for an extraordinary exemption for delinquent taxes.

"Circuit breaker."   A reduction in real property taxes for a personal residence may be available if the claimant

- was domiciled in Idaho the year before a claim is filed;
- is older than 65 years of age;
- is younger than 18 years of age and orphaned;

■   is a widow or widower;

■   is disabled and meets certain disability requirements;

■   is a disabled veteran of an American war and meets certain disability requirements;

■   is a certified prisoner of war or hostage (certification comes from a federal agency); or

■   is blind.

A claimant's spouse who resides in a medical care facility is deemed to be part of the household. Unreimbursed medical expenses are deductible from household income, and a widow or widower can file on behalf of his or her deceased spouse.

Tax Rate

The property tax rate is stated as a percentage of the taxable market value of the property. Every property has a particular tax code area that is made up of the cumulative tax levies for all the appropriate tax jurisdictions. For example, if the total levies of the specific tax code area are 0.014875 (1.4875 percent) and the property's taxable market value is $100,000, the taxes would be as follows:

$$\text{Tax rate} \times \text{Market value} = \text{Taxes}$$
$$0.014875 \times \$100,000 = \$1,487.50$$

Tax Statements [IC 63-903]

The county treasurer is required to send out tax statements prior to the fourth Monday in November each year. All taxes are paid to the county treasurer and can be paid in either one payment or two equal installments. Payment made as a single payment must be made on or before December 20. If the taxpayer elects to pay the taxes in two equal installments, the first payment is due on December 20, and the second payment is due and payable on or before June 20 of the following year.

Property taxpayers who cannot afford to pay their taxes may be subject to penalties and interest charges. Penalty and interest provisions are applicable only to the unpaid portion of the tax due on the half-year payment dates of December 20 for the current year and June 20 of the following year for the second half of the current year's taxes.

Delinquency

If the first half of tax payment is not made by the due date, the taxes become delinquent. A penalty fee of two percent and an interest charge of 12 percent per annum is added to the taxes owed. On January 1 of each year, the tax collector enters the first-half delinquencies on the assessment roll. This entry has the effect of a sale to the tax collector as grantee in trust. If the second-half tax payment is not made on or before June 20, the taxes become delinquent, and the penalty of two percent and interest of 12 percent are backdated to the previous January 1. On or before July 1, the second-half delinquency entries are made (backdated to January 1 in the year the taxes fall delinquent on the roll).

Tax Sale [IC 63-1005]

When property taxes are past due for three years, the county gives notice in the local papers and issues a deed to the property to itself. The property owner may redeem the property after the delinquency and prior to the tax sale by paying all past-due taxes, accumulated interest, penalties, and costs. The county will have a tax sale and sell the property to the highest bidder. The county issues a deed to the new owner.

WWWeb.Link   The Idaho State Tax Commission can be found on the Web at
http://tax.idaho.gov/propertytax/propertytax.htm

■ OTHER LIENS

Special Assessments

Special assessments are taxes levied on real estate to fund public improvements to the property. Payments of Local Improvement District (LID) installments are made to the local municipality or taxing district. Under current Idaho law, all LIDs are required to be recorded with the county recorder, making them part of the public record. This was not true for many years, and there may be some LIDs that are still not recorded.

Mechanics' Liens

Mechanics' liens statutes are provided for those persons who perform labor (including professional services such as surveying and engineering) or who provide materials to use in the improvement of an owner's land or buildings. These groups are entitled to file liens against the property for an amount equal to the value of the labor and/or materials provided.

The law also includes persons who rent, lease, or otherwise supply equipment for the improvement of a lot to be able to file a mechanic's lien [IC 45-501].

A claim of lien must be filed within 90 days after labor or services are completed or materials are furnished or after cessation of labor, services, or furnishing of materials for any cause [IC 45-507]. Idaho Code [IC 45-511] allows the lien claimant to collect other amounts besides the terms of contract as may be found by the court pursuant to IC 45-522.

The owner of the property must be notified prior to the filing of the mechanic's lien. Within 5 business days of the filing of a mechanic's lien claim, a copy of the lien must be delivered personally or sent by certified mail to the owner.

Mechanics' liens have priority over liens that are recorded after work began on the project. The date of filing of the mechanic's lien does not establish the lien date. The lien date is the date the mechanic started work on the project.

Under Idaho's Mechanics' Labor Law Statute, if there are claims by more than one mechanic or materialman and the proceeds are insufficient to pay all claimants, the liens are paid in the following priority:

1. All laborers, other than contractors or subcontractors
2. All materialmen, other than contractors or subcontractors
3. Subcontractors
4. Original contractor
5. Professional engineers and licensed surveyors

In addition, if the proceeds are not sufficient to pay everyone the total amount owed, each group will share on a pro rata basis. (Idaho does not have a "first in time, first in right" requirement regarding mechanics' liens.) The lienholder then must file suit to foreclose the lien within six months after filing the notice. If the foreclosure is not filed within this period, the lien will expire.

Judgments

Judgments are effective after they are issued by a court and have been docketed and filed with a county recorder. The judgment becomes a lien only within the county in which it is filed, but a judgment can be recorded in any county in the state. The judgment lien remains a lien against the property for a five-year period. The lien then can be extended for successive five-year periods until action has been taken to collect or enforce the lien.

QUESTIONS

1. In Idaho, real estate taxes become a lien on the property on
   a. January 1.
   b. June 20.
   c. December 20.
   d. July 1.

2. Juanita plans to pay the current year's real estate taxes in one payment. To guard against paying a penalty and interest on the taxes, the taxes must be paid by
   a. June 20 of the next year.
   b. December 20 of the current year.
   c. January 1 of the next year.
   d. July 1 of the next year.

3. Larry will pay the current year's real estate tax in two equal installments. The second-half payment must be made by
   a. July 1 of the current year.
   b. December 20 of the current year.
   c. January 1 of the next year.
   d. June 20 of the next year.

4. Property taxes in Idaho become delinquent on
   a. January 1 and December 21.
   b. January 1 and July 1.
   c. December 21 and June 21.
   d. January 1 and June 21.

5. To claim a mechanic's lien for materials supplied, a supplier must file a notice of the lien in the public record within
   a. 90 days after the material is supplied.
   b. 6 months after the material is supplied.
   c. 60 days after the material is supplied.
   d. 90 days after the work is started.

6. The market value of a home is $250,000. Of this amount, $50,000 is the value given to the land, and $200,000 is considered "improvements." The owners have filed for their $75,000 or 50 percent homeowner's exemption, and it has been granted. The total tax levy on the property will be 0.009945. How much is the real estate tax?
   a. $1,740.38
   b. $1,989.00
   c. $2,686.25
   d. $1,243.13

7. In question 6, if the owners decide to pay the taxes in two equal installments, the first payment will be
   a. $994.50.
   b. $1,343.13.
   c. $870.19.
   d. $621.57.

8. In Idaho, a parcel of real estate may be sold for the unpaid real estate taxes when such taxes are delinquent for
   a. six months.
   b. one year.
   c. two years.
   d. three years.

9. To claim a mechanic's lien, original contractors, engineers, and surveyors must file a notice of the lien in the public record within
   a. 90 days after the work is completed.
   b. 6 months after the work is completed.
   c. 60 days after the work is completed.
   d. 90 days after the work is started.

10. After a judgment lien is filed with the county recorder, for how long is it effective?
    a. No set time
    b. Indefinitely
    c. One year
    d. Five years

11. Judgment liens can be extended for how long?
    a. Cannot be extended
    b. One year
    c. Five years
    d. Indefinitely, five years at a time

12. A reduction in real property taxes for a personal residence may be available to all but which of the following individuals?
    a. Juan, a 78-year-old retiree
    b. Peter, a 26-year-old single parent
    c. Zoa, a 34-year-old widower
    d. Lorie, a 41-year-old disabled veteran

13. To qualify for a homeowner's exemption, the property must
    a. be occupied by owner or tenant.
    b. be owned and occupied by the owner as of January 1.
    c. be owned and occupied by the owner no later than April 15.
    d. be owned and occupied by a tenant no later than April 15.

14. If proceeds are insufficient to pay all claimants who have filed mechanics' liens, who has the highest priority?
    a. Original contractor
    b. Subcontractors
    c. All materialmen, other than contractors or subcontractors
    d. All laborers, other than contractors or subcontractors

7

REAL ESTATE CONTRACTS

■ BROKER'S AUTHORITY TO PREPARE DOCUMENTS

In Idaho it has long been a practice for real estate brokers to prepare some documents by completing or filling in preprinted contract forms, specifically earnest money agreements, purchase and sale agreements, and property listing agreements. When other types of documents are needed, an attorney should be consulted.

The Idaho Real Estate Commission's policy is to prohibit licensees from providing legal advice to either party in a real estate transaction and to encourage licensees to recommend that clients consult an attorney when legal assistance is desired or necessary. The Idaho Real Estate Commission's rules specifically prohibit a licensee from discouraging any party to a transaction from seeking an attorney's advice.

■ CONTRACTS IN GENERAL

A *contract* is a voluntary agreement between legally competent parties to perform or refrain from performing certain acts for a consideration.

Statute of Limitations

The law allows a specific time limit during which parties to a contract may bring a legal suit to enforce their rights. Any party who does not take steps to enforce his or her rights within this time period may lose the right to do so. In Idaho, an injured party must bring a suit for performance *within five years after the breach of a written contract* and *within four years after the breach of a verbal contract*, as shown below:

Idaho Statute of Limitations

Written contract	5 *years*
Judgment lien	5 *years*
Adverse possession	5 *years*
Easements by prescription	5 *years*

Verbal contract   *4 years*
Mechanic's or materialman's lien   *6 months*

■ IDAHO REQUIREMENTS FOR A VALID REAL ESTATE CONTRACT

The following are the six essential elements of a valid real estate contract that are applicable to Idaho:

1. Legally competent parties
2. An offer and acceptance or mutual assent that includes meeting of the minds
3. A legal object
4. A legal consideration
5. An enforceable legal description
6. A written document, signed by all parties to the contract

Capacity to Contract

Under Idaho law a person becomes of age and has the legal capacity to enter into a valid contract at the *age of 18.* Persons younger than this age are referred to as infants or minors.

Although a minor does not have the legal capacity to contract, he or she may make a contract and live up to it. A *minor's contracts are not void, but they are voidable:* the minor may disaffirm any such contract within a reasonable time after reaching *majority* (the legal age of 18).

A minor who is not under the care of a parent or guardian, however, generally is held responsible for contracts to purchase items considered necessities. A married minor may enter into contractual agreements and can sue or be sued. A contract entered into by such a person, however, could be ruled invalid by the courts if it is contested (challenged).

Married women.   Under common law, married women did not have the capacity to enter into contracts, and their contracts were void. In Idaho, as in all other states, this limitation no longer exists. A married woman can enter into a valid contract and may sue or be sued.

Insane persons.   Any contract is void if made by a person who has been declared by a court to be of unsound mind. Such persons must be sufficiently deranged so that they do not comprehend that they are making a contract or what the resultant consequences or obligations will be.

Felons.   Under Idaho law a contract entered into by a person who is imprisoned for committing a serious crime (felony) is void unless such a person has obtained express permission from the state parole board.

Statute of Frauds [IC 9-503]

The Idaho Statute of Frauds, as defined by the Idaho Supreme Court as it pertains to real estate transactions, provides that *agreements for the sale of real property or of an interest therein and leases of real property for a period of more than one year are unenforceable unless the sale or lease agreement, or some note or memorandum thereof, is in writing and signed by both parties.*

The Idaho Statute of Frauds likewise limits the effective transfer of any interest in real property, such as liens, easements, or rights-of-way, other than by operation of law. Disputes involving the statute of frauds are almost always complex.

The above general description of the law is cited so that real estate licensees will be aware of its provisions. In reality, certain exceptions may take a particular transaction out of the operation of the statute of frauds. An attorney should be consulted when a broker or salesperson suspects that a statute of frauds problem may exist.

A listing agreement to pay a broker money or other valuable consideration for finding a purchaser for another person's property is not valid and enforceable unless the agreement is in writing and signed by the owner of the real estate or his or her legal representative.

■ CONTRACTS FOR THE SALE OF REAL ESTATE

In Idaho, a contract for the sale of real estate is known as a *Real Estate Purchase and Sale Agreement*. Figure 7.1 contains the provisions of the sale in addition to a receipt for the purchaser's earnest money deposit. The Idaho Real Estate Commission requires that the actual amount of money received by the broker as a deposit and the form of payment (check, note, car title, etc.) be specifically stated in the agreement.

Clauses in the Contract   The actual contents of a real estate purchase and sale agreement and receipt for earnest money may vary from office to office and form to form. The Idaho Real Estate Commission does not require that any particular form be used; however, it does recommend the use of good current standard forms that have been especially designed for selling specific types of property.

A standardized form in general use by REALTORS® in Idaho for residential real estate has been developed by the Idaho Association of REALTORS®, Inc./Ada County Association of REALTORS®, Inc. (see Figure 7.1). Members of this trade organization also have use of additional forms for specialized practice, including Pre-Sold New Construction, Commercial Investment Real Estate, and Vacant Land.

As you read the following discussion on the divisions or clauses in a real estate purchase and sale agreement and receipt for earnest money, try to locate the various provisions in the actual contract form (see Figure 7.1).

Date.   Every contract must indicate the actual date of the offer.

Purchasers' names.   The purchasers' names must be written as they will appear on all legal documents. If the purchasers are husband and wife, that fact should be noted. If there is only one purchaser, his or her marital status should be indicated.

F I G U R E 7.1

Real Estate Purchase and Sale Agreement and Receipt for Earnest Money

RE-21 REAL ESTATE PURCHASE AND SALE AGREEMENT

REALTOR® THIS IS A LEGALLY BINDING CONTRACT. READ THE ENTIRE DOCUMENT INCLUDING ANY ATTACHMENTS. IF YOU HAVE ANY QUESTIONS, **CONSULT YOUR ATTORNEY AND/OR ACCOUNTANT** BEFORE SIGNING.

EQUAL HOUSING OPPORTUNITY

1   ID#_____   DATE _____
2
3   **LISTING AGENCY**_____ Office Phone # _____ Fax #_____
4   Listing Agent _____ E-Mail _____ Phone # _____
5   **SELLING AGENCY**_____ Office Phone # _____ Fax #_____
6   Selling Agent _____ E-Mail _____ Phone # _____
7
8   **1. BUYER:**_____(Hereinafter called
9   "**BUYER**") agrees to purchase, and the undersigned SELLER agrees to sell the following described real estate hereinafter referred to as "PREMISES"
10   **COMMONLY KNOWN AS**_____City_____
11   _____County, ID, Zip_____ legally described as:_____
12   _____
13   **OR** Legal Description Attached as addendum # _____   **(Addendum must accompany original offer.)**
14
15   **2. $**_____   **PURCHASE PRICE:**_____**DOLLARS,**
16   payable upon the following **TERMS AND CONDITIONS** (not including closing costs) :
17
18   **3. FINANCIAL TERMS: Note: A+C+D+E must add up to total purchase price.**
19
20   $_____   **(A).   EARNEST MONEY:** BUYER hereby deposits _____ DOLLARS as
21   Earnest Money evidenced by: ☐cash ☐personal check ☐cashier's check ☐note (due date):_____
22   ☐other _____ and a receipt is hereby acknowledged. Earnest Money to be deposited
23   in trust account ☐upon receipt, or ☐ upon acceptance by all parties and shall be held by: ☐Listing Broker ☐Selling Broker
24   ☐other_____ for the benefit of the parties hereto. The responsible Broker shall be _____.
25
26   **(B).   ALL CASH OFFER:** ☐NO ☐YES If this is an all cash offer do not complete lines 32 through 61, fill blanks with N/A
27   **(Not** Applicable).   **IF CASH OFFER, BUYER'S OBLIGATION TO CLOSE SHALL NOT BE SUBJECT TO ANY FINANCIAL CONTINGENCY.**
28   BUYER agrees to provide SELLER within_____business days from the date of acceptance of this agreement by all parties, evidence of
29   sufficient funds and/or proceeds necessary to close transaction. Acceptable documentation includes, but is not limited to, a copy of a recent bank or
30   financial statement or contract(s) for the sale of BUYER'S current residence or other property to be sold.
31
32   $_____   **(C).   NEW LOAN PROCEEDS:** This Agreement is contingent upon BUYER obtaining the following financing:
33   ☐ **FIRST LOAN** of $_____ not including mortgage insurance, through ☐FHA, ☐VA, ☐CONVENTIONAL, ☐IHFA,
34   ☐RURAL DEVELOPMENT, ☐OTHER_____ with interest not to exceed _____ % for a period of _____ year(s) at: ☐Fixed Rate
35   ☐Other_____ BUYER shall pay no more than_____ point(s) plus origination fee if any. SELLER shall pay no more than_____point(s).
36   Any reduction in points shall first accrue to the benefit of the ☐BUYER ☐SELLER ☐Divided Equally ☐N/A.
37
38   ☐ **SECOND LOAN** of $_____ with interest not to exceed _____ % for a period of _____ year(s) at: ☐Fixed Rate
39   ☐Other_____ BUYER shall pay no more than_____ point(s) plus origination fee if any. SELLER shall pay no more than_____point(s). Any
40   reduction in points shall first accrue to the benefit of the ☐BUYER ☐SELLER ☐Divided Equally ☐N/A.
41
42   **LOAN APPLICATION:** BUYER ☐has applied ☐ shall apply for such loan(s) within_____ business day(s) of SELLER'S acceptance. Within_____
43   business days of final acceptance of all parties, BUYER agrees to furnish SELLER with **a written confirmation showing lender approval of**
44   **credit report, income verification, debt ratios in a manner acceptable to the SELLER(S) and subject only to satisfactory appraisal and final lender**
45   **underwriting.** If such written confirmation is not received by SELLER(S) within the strict time allotted, SELLER(S) may at their option cancel this
46   agreement by notifying BUYER(S) in writing of such cancellation within _____ business day(s) after written confirmation was required. If SELLER does
47   not cancel within the strict time period specified as set forth herein, SELLER shall be deemed to have accepted such written confirmation of lender approval
48   and shall be deemed to have elected to proceed with the transaction. SELLER'S approval shall not be unreasonably withheld. **If an appraisal is required**
49   **by lender, the property must appraise at not less than purchase price** or BUYER'S Earnest Money may be returned at BUYER'S request. *BUYER*
50   *may also apply for a loan with different conditions and costs and close transaction provided all other terms and conditions of this Agreement are*
51   *fulfilled, and the new loan does not increase the costs or requirements to the SELLER.*
52   **FHA / VA:** If applicable, it is expressly agreed that notwithstanding any other provisions of this contract, BUYER shall not be obligated to complete the
53   purchase of the property described herein or to incur any penalty or forfeiture of Earnest Money deposits or otherwise unless BUYER has been given in
54   accordance with HUD/FHA or VA requirements a written statement by the Federal Housing Commissioner, Veterans Administration or a Direct
55   Endorsement lender setting forth the appraised value of the property of not less than the sales price as stated in the contract. SELLER agrees to pay fees
56   required by FHA or VA.
57
58   $_____   **(D).   ADDITIONAL FINANCIAL TERMS:**
59   ☐ Additional financial terms are specified under the heading "OTHER TERMS AND/OR CONDITIONS" (Section 4).
60   ☐ Additional financial terms are contained in a **FINANCING ADDENDUM** of same date, attached hereto, signed by both parties.
61
62   $_____   **(E).   APPROXIMATE FUNDS DUE FROM BUYERS AT CLOSING** *(Not including closing costs)*: **Cash at closing**
63   to be paid by BUYER at closing in GOOD FUNDS, includes: **cash, electronic transfer funds, certified check or cashier's check. NOTE:** *If any*
64   *of above loans being Assumed or taken "subject to", any net differences between the approximate balances and the actual balance of said loan(s)*
65   *shall be adjusted at closing of escrow in:* ☐Cash ☐Other:_____
66
67   **BUYER'S** Initials (_____)(_____) Date _____   **SELLER'S** Initials (_____)(_____) Date _____
68

71   RE-21 RESIDENTIAL PURCHASE AND SALE AGREEMENT PAGE 1 of 6 JULY, 2006 EDITION

F I G U R E   7.1

Real Estate Purchase and Sale Agreement and Receipt for Earnest Money (continued)

72   RE-21 RESIDENTIAL PURCHASE AND SALE AGREEMENT PAGE 2 of 6 <u>JULY, 2006 EDITION</u>
73
74   **PROPERTY ADDRESS:**_____ **ID#:**_____
75
76   **4. OTHER TERMS AND/OR CONDITIONS:** This Agreement is made subject to the following special terms, considerations and/or contingencies
77   which must be satisfied prior to closing _____
78   _____
79   _____
80   _____
81   _____
82   _____
83   _____
84   _____
85   _____
86   _____
87
88   **5. ITEMS INCLUDED & EXCLUDED IN THIS SALE**: All existing fixtures and fittings that are attached to the property are **INCLUDED IN THE PURCHASE**
89   **PRICE** (unless excluded below), and shall be transferred free of liens. These include, but are not limited to, all attached floor coverings, attached television
90   antennae, satellite dish and receiving equipment, attached plumbing, bathroom and lighting fixtures, window screens, screen doors, storm windows, storm doors,
91   all window coverings, garage door opener(s) and transmitter(s), exterior trees, plants or shrubbery, water heating apparatus and fixtures, attached fireplace
92   equipment, awnings, ventilating, cooling and heating systems, all ranges , ovens, built-in dishwashers, fuel tanks and irrigation fixtures and equipment, all water
93   systems, wells, springs, water, water rights, ditches and ditch rights, if any, that are appurtenant thereto that are now on or used in connection with the premises
94   and shall be included in the sale unless otherwise provided herein. BUYER should satisfy himself/herself that the condition of the included items is acceptable. It
95   is agreed that any item included in this section is of nominal value less than $100.
96
97   **(A). ADDITIONAL ITEMS SPECIFICALLY INCLUDED IN THIS SALE:** _____
98   _____
99   _____
100
101   **(B). ITEMS SPECIFICALLY EXCLUDED IN THIS SALE:** _____
102   _____
103
104   **6. TITLE CONVEYANCE:** Title of SELLER is to be conveyed by warranty deed, unless otherwise provided, and is to be marketable and insurable except for
105   rights reserved in federal patents, state or railroad deeds, building or use restrictions, building and zoning regulations and ordinances of any governmental unit,
106   and rights of way and easements established or of record. Liens, encumbrances or defects to be discharged by SELLER may be paid out of purchase money at
107   date of closing. No liens, encumbrances or defects which are to be discharged or assumed by BUYER or to which title is taken subject to, exist unless otherwise
108   specified in this Agreement.
109
110   **7. TITLE INSURANCE: There may be types of title insurance coverages available other than those listed below and parties to this**
111   **agreement are advised to talk to a title company about any other coverages available that will give the BUYER additional coverage.**
112
113   **(A). PRELIMINARY TITLE COMMITMENT:** Prior to closing the transaction, ☐ SELLER or ☐ BUYER shall furnish to BUYER a preliminary commitment of a
114   title insurance policy showing the condition of the title to said premises. BUYER shall have ____ business day(s) from receipt of the preliminary commitment or
115   not fewer than twenty-four (24) hours prior to closing, within which to object in writing to the condition of the title as set forth in the preliminary commitment. If
116   BUYER does not so object, BUYER shall be deemed to have accepted the conditions of the title. It is agreed that if the title of said premises is not marketable,
117   or cannot be made so within _____ business day(s) after notice containing a written statement of defect is delivered to SELLER, BUYER'S Earnest Money
118   deposit will be returned to BUYER and SELLER shall pay for the cost of title insurance cancellation fee, escrow and legal fees, if any.
119
120   **(B). TITLE COMPANY: The parties agree that** _____ **Title Company**
121   located at_____ shall provide the title policy and preliminary report of commitment.
122
123   **(C). STANDARD COVERAGE OWNER'S POLICY**: SELLER shall within a reasonable time after closing furnish to BUYER a title insurance policy in the
124   amount of the purchase price of the premises showing marketable and insurable title subject to the liens, encumbrances and defects elsewhere set out in this
125   Agreement to be discharged or assumed by BUYER unless otherwise provided herein. **The risk assumed by the title company in the standard coverage**
126   **policy is limited to matters of public record.** BUYER shall receive a ILTA/ALTA Owner's Policy of Title Insurance. A title company, at BUYER's request, can
127   provide information about the availability, desirability, coverage and cost of various title insurance coverages and endorsements. If BUYER desires title
128   coverage other than that required by this paragraph, BUYER shall instruct Closing Agency in writing and pay any increase in cost unless otherwise provided
129   herein.
130
131   **(D). EXTENDED COVERAGE LENDER'S POLICY (Mortgagee policy):** The lender may require that BUYER (Borrower) furnish an Extended Coverage
132   Lender's Policy. This extended coverage lender's policy considers matters of public record and additionally insures against certain matters not shown in the
133   public record. **This extended coverage lender's policy is solely for the benefit of the lender and only protects the lender.**
134
135   **8. MECHANIC'S LIENS - GENERAL CONTRACTOR DISCLOSURE STATEMENT NOTICE:** BUYER and SELLER are hereby notified that,
136   subject to Idaho Code §45-525 *et seq.*, a "General Contractor" must provide a Disclosure Statement to a homeowner that describes certain rights afforded
137   to the homeowner (e.g. lien waivers, general liability insurance, extended policies of title insurance, surety bonds, and sub-contractor information). The
138   Disclosure Statement must be given to a homeowner prior to the General Contractor entering into any contract in an amount exceeding $2,000 with a
139   homeowner for construction, alteration, repair, or other improvements to real property, or with a residential real property purchaser for the purchase and
140   sale of newly constructed property. Such disclosure is the responsibility of the General Contractor and it is not the duty of your agent to obtain this
141   information on your behalf. You are advised to consult with any General Contractor subject to Idaho Code §45-525 *et seq.* regarding the General
142   Contractor Disclosure Statement.
143
144   **BUYER'S** Initials (_____)(_____) Date _____   **SELLER'S** Initials (_____)(_____) Date _____
145
146   This form is printed and distributed by the Idaho Association of REALTORS®, Inc. This form has been designed for and is provided only for use by real estate professionals who are members of the
147   National Association of REALTORS®. **USE BY ANY OTHER PERSON IS PROHIBITED.**
148   Copyright Idaho Association of REALTORS®, Inc. All rights reserved.
149
150   RE-21 RESIDENTIAL PURCHASE AND SALE AGREEMENT PAGE 2 of 6 <u>JULY, 2006 EDITION</u>

F I G U R E   **7.1**

Real Estate Purchase and Sale Agreement and Receipt for Earnest Money (continued)

152   RE-21 RESIDENTIAL PURCHASE AND SALE AGREEMENT PAGE 3 of 6 <u>JULY, 2006 EDITION</u>

153   PROPERTY ADDRESS:_____ ID#:_____

155   **9. INSPECTION:**

156   **(A). BUYER chooses** ☐to have inspection ☐not to have inspection. If BUYER chooses not to have inspection skip section 9C. BUYER shall

157   have the right to conduct inspections, investigations, tests, surveys and other studies at **BUYER'S expense**. BUYER shall, within _____ business

158   day(s) of acceptance, complete these inspections and give to SELLER written notice of disapproved of items. BUYER is strongly advised to exercise

159   these rights and to make BUYER'S own selection of professionals with appropriate qualifications to conduct inspections of the entire property.

161   **(B). FHA INSPECTION REQUIREMENT, If applicable:** "For Your Protection: Get a Home Inspection", HUD 92564-CN must be signed on or

162   before execution of this agreement.

164   **(C). SATISFACTION/REMOVAL OF INSPECTION CONTINGENCIES:**

165   **1).** If BUYER **does not** within the strict time period specified give to SELLER written notice of disapproved items, BUYER shall conclusively

166   be deemed to have: (a) completed all inspections, investigations, review of applicable documents and disclosures; (b) elected to proceed with the

167   transaction and (c) assumed all liability, responsibility and expense for repairs or corrections other than for items which SELLER has otherwise agreed in

168   writing to repair or correct.

170   **2).** If BUYER **does** within the strict time period specified give to SELLER written notice of disapproved items, **BUYER shall provide to**

171   **SELLER pertinent section(s) of written inspection reports**. SELLER shall have _____business day(s) in which to **respond in writing.** The

172   SELLER, at their option, may correct the items as specified by the BUYERS in their letter or may elect not to do so. If the SELLER agrees to correct the

173   items asked for in the BUYERS letter, then both parties agree that they will continue with the transaction and proceed to closing. **This will remove the**

174   **BUYER'S inspection contingency.**

176   **3).**If the SELLER elects not to correct the disapproved items, or does not respond in writing within the strict time period specified, then the

177   BUYER(S) have the option of either continuing the transaction without the SELLER being responsible for correcting these deficiencies or giving the

178   SELLER written notice within _____ business days that they will not continue with the transaction and will receive their Earnest Money back.

180   **4).** If BUYER **does not** give such written notice of cancellation within the strict time periods specified, BUYER shall conclusively be deemed

181   to have elected to proceed with the transaction without repairs or corrections other than for items which SELLER has otherwise agreed in writing to

182   repair or correct. SELLER shall make the property available for all inspections. BUYER shall keep the property free and clear of liens; indemnify and

183   hold SELLER harmless from all liability, claims, demands, damages and costs; and repair any damages arising from the inspections. No inspections

184   may be made by any governmental building or zoning inspector or government employee without the prior consent of SELLER unless required by local

185   law.

187   **10. LEAD PAINT DISCLOSURE:** The subject property ☐is ☐is not defined as "Target Housing" regarding lead-based paint or lead-based paint

188   hazards. If yes, BUYER hereby acknowledges the following: (a) BUYER has been provided an EPA approved lead-based paint hazard information

189   pamphlet, "Protect Your Family From Lead in Your Home", (b) receipt of SELLER'S Disclosure of Information and Acknowledgment Form and have

190   been provided with all records, test reports or other information, if any, related to the presence of lead-based paint hazards on said property, (c) that

191   this contract is contingent upon BUYERS right to have the property tested for lead-based paint hazards to be completed no later than

192   _____ or the contingency will terminate, (d) that BUYER hereby ☐waives ☐does not waive this right, (e) that if test results show

193   unacceptable amounts of lead-based paint on the premises, BUYER has the right to cancel the contract subject to the option of the SELLER (to be given

194   in writing) to elect to remove the lead-based paint and correct the problem which must be accomplished before closing, (f) that if the contract is

195   canceled under this clause, BUYER'S earnest money deposit will be returned to BUYER.

197   **11. SQUARE FOOTAGE VERIFICATION:** BUYER IS AWARE THAT ANY REFERENCE TO THE SQUARE FOOTAGE OF THE REAL PROPERTY OR

198   IMPROVEMENTS IS APPROXIMATE. IF SQUARE FOOTAGE IS MATERIAL TO THE BUYER, IT MUST BE VERIFIED DURING THE INSPECTION PERIOD.

200   **12. SELLER'S PROPERTY DISCLOSURE FORM:** If required by Title 55, Chapter 25 Idaho Code SELLER shall within ten (10) days after execution

201   of this Agreement provide to BUYER "SELLER'S Property Disclosure Form" or other acceptable form. BUYER has received the "SELLER'S Property

202   Disclosure Form" or other acceptable form prior to signing this Agreement: ☐Yes ☐No ☐N/A

204   **13. COVENANTS, CONDITIONS AND RESTRICTIONS (CC& R'S):** BUYER is responsible to obtain and review a copy of the CC& R's (if

205   applicable). BUYER has reviewed CC& R's. ☐Yes ☐No

207   **14. SUBDIVISION HOMEOWNER'S ASSOCIATION:** BUYER is aware that membership in a Home Owner's Association may be required and

208   BUYER agrees to abide by the Articles of Incorporation, By-Laws and rules and regulations of the Association. BUYER is further aware that the

209   Property may be subject to assessments levied by the Association described in full in the Declaration of Covenants, Conditions and Restrictions,

210   BUYER has reviewed Homeowner's Association Documents: ☐Yes ☐No ☐N/A Association fees/dues are $_____

212   per _____☐BUYER ☐SELLER ☐N/A to pay Homeowner's Association **SET UP FEE of $**_____ **and/or property**

213   **TRANSFER FEES of** $_____ at closing.

215   **15. "NOT APPLICABLE DEFINED:"** The letters "n/a," "N/A," "n.a.," and "N.A." as used herein are abbreviations of the term "not applicable." Where

216   this agreement uses the term "not applicable" or an abbreviation thereof, it shall be evidence that the parties have contemplated certain facts or

217   conditions and have determined that such facts or conditions do not apply to the agreement or transaction herein.

219   **BUYER'S** Initials (_____)(_____) Date _____   **SELLER'S** Initials (_____)(_____) Date _____

222   RE-21 RESIDENTIAL PURCHASE AND SALE AGREEMENT PAGE 3 of 6 <u>JULY, 2006 EDITION</u>

F I G U R E   7.1

Real Estate Purchase and Sale Agreement and Receipt for Earnest Money (continued)

223 RE-21 RESIDENTIAL PURCHASE AND SALE AGREEMENT PAGE 4 of 6 JULY, 2006 EDITION
224 **PROPERTY ADDRESS:**_____ ID#:_____
225

226 **16. COSTS PAID BY:** Costs in addition to those listed below may be incurred by BUYER and SELLER unless otherwise agreed herein, or provided by
227 law or required by lender, or otherwise stated herein. The below costs will be paid as indicated. Some costs are subject to loan program requirements.
228 **SELLER agrees to pay up to $_____ of lender required repair costs only.**
229 BUYER or SELLER has the option to pay any lender required repair costs in excess of this amount.
230

	BUYER	SELLER	Shared Equally	N/A		BUYER	SELLER	Shared Equally	N/A
Appraisal Fee					Title Ins. Standard Coverage Owner's Policy				
Appraisal Re-Inspection Fee					Title Ins. Extended Coverage **Lender's** Policy – Mortgagee Policy				
Closing Escrow Fee					Additional Title Coverage				
Lender Document Preparation Fee					Fuel in Tank – Amount to be Determined by Supplier				
Tax Service Fee					Well Inspection				
Flood Certification/Tracking Fee					Septic Inspections				
Lender Required Inspections					Septic Pumping				
Attorney Contract Preparation or Review Fee					Survey				

231
232 **17. OCCUPANCY:** BUYER ☐ does ☐ does not intend to occupy property as BUYER'S primary residence.
233
234 **18. FINAL WALK THROUGH:** The SELLER grants BUYER and any representative of BUYER reasonable access to conduct a final walk
235 through inspection of the premises approximately _____ calendar day(s) prior to close of escrow, NOT AS A CONTINGENCY OF THE SALE, but
236 for purposes of satisfying BUYER that any repairs agreed to in writing by BUYER and SELLER have been completed and premises are in
237 substantially the same condition as on acceptance date of this contract. SELLER shall make premises available for the final walk through and
238 agrees to accept the responsibility and expense for making sure all the utilities are turned on for the walk through except for phone and cable. If
239 BUYER does not conduct a final walk through, BUYER specifically releases the SELLER and Broker(s) of any liability.
240
241 **19. RISK OF LOSS: Prior to closing of this sale, all risk of loss shall remain with SELLER. In addition, should the premises be materially**
242 **damaged by fire or other destructive cause prior to closing, this agreement shall be void at the option of the BUYER.**
243
244 **20. CLOSING**: On or before the closing date, BUYER and SELLER shall deposit with the closing agency all funds and instruments necessary to
245 complete this transaction. **Closing means the date on which all documents are either recorded or accepted by an escrow agent and the sale**
246 **proceeds are available to SELLER.** The closing shall be no later than (Date)_____.
247 The parties agree that the **CLOSING AGENCY** for this transaction shall be _____
248 located at_____.
249 If a long-term escrow / collection is involved, then the long-term escrow holder shall be _____.
250
251 **21. POSSESSION:** BUYER shall be entitled to possession ☐upon closing or ☐date _____ time _____ ☐A.M. ☐ P.M.
252 Property taxes and water assessments (using the last available assessment as a basis), rents, interest and reserves, liens, encumbrances or obligations
253 assumed and utilities shall be pro-rated as of _____.
254
255 **22. SALES PRICE INFORMATION:** SELLER and BUYER hereby grant permission to the brokers and either party to this Agreement, to disclose
256 sale data from this transaction, including selling price and property address to the local Association / Board of REALTORS®, multiple listing service, its
257 members, its members' prospects, appraisers and other professional users of real estate sales data. The parties to this Agreement acknowledge that
258 sales price information compiled as a result of this Agreement may be provided to the County Assessor Office by either party or by either party's Broker.
259
260 **23. FACSIMILE TRANSMISSION:** Facsimile or electronic transmission of any signed original document, and retransmission of any signed facsimile
261 or electronic transmission shall be the same as delivery of an original. At the request of either party or the Closing Agency, the parties will confirm
262 facsimile and electronic transmitted signatures by signing an original document.
263
264 **BUYER'S** Initials (_____)(_____) Date _____   **SELLER'S** Initials (_____)(_____) Date _____
265

269
270 RE-21 RESIDENTIAL PURCHASE AND SALE AGREEMENT PAGE 4 of 6 JULY, 2006 EDITION
271
272

F I G U R E **7.1**

Real Estate Purchase and Sale Agreement and Receipt for Earnest Money (continued)

275 PROPERTY ADDRESS:_____ ID#:_____

276 **24. SINGULAR AND PLURAL** terms each include the other, when appropriate.

277

278 **25. BUSINESS DAYS & HOURS** A business day is herein defined as Monday through Friday, 8:00 A.M. to 5:00 P.M. in the local time zone
279 where the subject real property is physically located. A business day shall not include any Saturday or Sunday, nor shall a business day include
280 any legal holiday recognized by the state of Idaho as found in Idaho Code § 73-108. The time in which any act required under this agreement is to
281 be performed shall be computed by excluding the date of execution and including the last day. The first day shall be the day after the date of
282 execution. If the last day is a legal holiday, then the time for performance shall be the next subsequent business day.

283

284 **26. SEVERABILITY:** In the case that any one or more of the provisions contained in this Agreement, or any application thereof, shall be invalid,
285 illegal or unenforceable in any respect, the validity, legality or enforceability of the remaining provisions shall not in any way be affected or impaired
286 thereby.

287

288 **27. ATTORNEY'S FEES:** If either party initiates or defends any arbitration or legal action or proceedings which are in any way connected with this
289 Agreement, the prevailing party shall be entitled to recover from the non-prevailing party reasonable costs and attorney's fees, including such costs and
290 fees on appeal.

291

292 **28. DEFAULT:** **If BUYER defaults** in the performance of this Agreement, SELLER has the option of: (1) accepting the Earnest Money as liquidated
293 damages or (2) pursuing any other lawful right and/or remedy to which SELLER may be entitled. If SELLER elects to proceed under (1), SELLER shall
294 make demand upon the holder of the Earnest Money, upon which demand said holder shall pay from the Earnest Money the costs incurred by
295 SELLER'S Broker on behalf of SELLER and BUYER related to the transaction, including, without limitation, the costs of title insurance, escrow fees,
296 appraisal, credit report fees, inspection fees and attorney's fees; and said holder shall pay any balance of the Earnest Money, one-half to SELLER and
297 one-half to SELLER'S Broker, provided that the amount to be paid to SELLER'S Broker shall not exceed the Broker's agreed to commission. SELLER
298 and BUYER specifically acknowledge and agree that if SELLER elects to accept the Earnest Money as liquidated damages, such shall be SELLER'S
299 sole and exclusive remedy, and such shall not be considered a penalty or forfeiture. If SELLER elects to proceed under (2), the holder of the Earnest
300 Money shall be entitled to pay the costs incurred by SELLER'S Broker on behalf of SELLER and BUYER related to the transaction, including, without
301 limitation, the costs of brokerage fee, title insurance, escrow fees, appraisal, credit report fees, inspection fees and attorney's fees, with any balance of
302 the Earnest Money to be held pending resolution of the matter.
303 **If SELLER defaults**, having approved said sale and fails to consummate the same as herein agreed, BUYER'S Earnest Money deposit shall
304 be returned to him/her and SELLER shall pay for the costs of title insurance, escrow fees, appraisals, credit report fees, inspection fees, brokerage fees
305 and attorney's fees, if any. This shall not be considered as a waiver by BUYER of any other lawful right or remedy to which BUYER may be entitled.

306

307 **29. EARNEST MONEY DISPUTE / INTERPLEADER** Notwithstanding any termination of this contract, BUYER and SELLER agree that in the event
308 of any controversy regarding the Earnest Money and things of value held by Broker or closing agency, unless mutual written instructions are received by
309 the holder of the Earnest Money and things of value, Broker or closing agency shall not be required to take any action but may await any proceeding, or
310 at Broker's or closing agency's option and sole discretion, may interplead all parties and deposit any monies or things of value into a court of competent
311 jurisdiction and shall recover court costs and reasonable attorney's fees.

312

313 **30. COUNTERPARTS**: This Agreement may be executed in counterparts. Executing an agreement in counterparts shall mean the signature of
314 two identical copies of the same agreement. Each identical copy of an agreement signed in counterparts is deemed to be an original, and all
315 identical copies shall together constitute one and the same instrument.
316

317

318 **31. REPRESENTATION CONFIRMATION:** Check one (1) box in Section 1 and one (1) box in section 2 below to confirm that in this transaction, the
319 brokerage(s) involved had the following relationship(s) with the BUYER(S) and SELLER(S).

320

321 Section 1:

322 ☐ **A. The brokerage working with the BUYER(S) is acting as an AGENT for the BUYER(S).**

323 ☐ **B. The brokerage working with the BUYER(S) is acting as a LIMITED DUAL AGENT for the BUYER(S), without an ASSIGNED AGENT.**

324 ☐ **C. The brokerage working with the BUYER(S) is acting as a LIMITED DUAL AGENT for the BUYER(S) and has an ASSIGNED AGENT**
325 **acting solely on behalf of the BUYER(S).**

326 ☐ **D. The brokerage working with the BUYER(S) is acting as a NONAGENT for the BUYER(S).**

327 Section 2:

328 ☐ **A. The brokerage working with the SELLER(S) is acting as an AGENT for the SELLER(S).**

329 ☐ **B. The brokerage working with the SELLER(S) is acting as a LIMITED DUAL AGENT for the SELLER(S), without an ASSIGNED AGENT.**

330 ☐ **C. The brokerage working with the SELLER(S) is acting as a LIMITED DUAL AGENT for the SELLER(S) and has an ASSIGNED AGENT**
331 **acting solely on behalf of the SELLER(S).**

332 ☐ **D. The brokerage working with the SELLER(S) is acting as a NONAGENT for the SELLER(S).**

333
334 Each party signing this document confirms that he has received, read and understood the Agency Disclosure Brochure adopted or approved by the Idaho real estate commission and
335 has consented to the relationship confirmed above. In addition, each party confirms that the brokerage's agency office policy was made available for inspection and review. EACH
336 PARTY UNDERSTANDS THAT HE IS A "CUSTOMER" AND IS NOT REPRESENTED BY A BROKERAGE UNLESS THERE IS A SIGNED WRITTEN AGREEMENT FOR AGENCY
337 REPRESENTATION.

338

339 **BUYER'S** Initials (_____)(_____) Date _____   **SELLER'S** Initials (_____)(_____) Date _____

340

343 RE-21 RESIDENTIAL PURCHASE AND SALE AGREEMENT PAGE 5 of 6 JULY, 2006 EDITION

F I G U R E 7.1

Real Estate Purchase and Sale Agreement and Receipt for Earnest Money (continued)

RE-21 RESIDENTIAL PURCHASE AND SALE AGREEMENT PAGE 6 of 6 <u>JULY, 2006 EDITION</u>

PROPERTY ADDRESS:_____ **ID#:**_____

32. ENTIRE AGREEMENT: This Agreement contains the entire Agreement of the parties respecting the matters herein set forth and supersedes all prior Agreements between the parties respecting such matters. No warranties, including, without limitation, any warranty of habitability, agreements or representations not expressly set forth herein shall be binding upon either party.

33. TIME IS OF THE ESSENCE IN THIS AGREEMENT.

34. AUTHORITY OF SIGNATORY: If BUYER or SELLER is a corporation, partnership, trust, estate, or other entity, the person executing this agreement on its behalf warrants his or her authority to do so and to bind BUYER or SELLER.

35. ACCEPTANCE: BUYER'S offer is made subject to the acceptance of SELLER on or before (Date)_____ at (Local Time in which property is located)_____ ☐ A.M. ☐ P.M. If SELLER does not accept this Agreement within the time specified, the entire Earnest Money shall be refunded to BUYER on demand.

36. BUYER'S SIGNATURES:

☐ **SEE ATTACHED BUYER'S ADDENDUM(S):** _____   (Specify number of BUYER addendum(s) attached.)

BUYER Signature_____   **BUYER (Print Name)**_____

Date _____ Time _____ ☐ A.M. ☐ P.M.   Phone # _____ Cell #_____

Address_____   City_____ State _____ Zip _____

E-Mail Address_____   Fax #_____

BUYER Signature_____   **BUYER (Print Name)**_____

Date _____ Time _____ ☐ A.M. ☐ P.M.   Phone # _____ Cell #_____

Address_____   City_____ State _____ Zip _____

E-Mail Address_____   Fax #_____

37. SELLER'S SIGNATURES:
On this date, I/We hereby approve and accept the transaction set forth in the above Agreement and agree to carry out all the terms thereof on the part of the SELLER.

☐**SIGNATURE(S) SUBJECT TO ATTACHED COUNTER OFFER**

☐ **SIGNATURE(S) SUBJECT TO ATTACHED ADDENDUM(S) #** _____

SELLER Signature_____   **SELLER (Print Name)**_____

Date _____ Time _____ ☐ A.M. ☐ P.M.   Phone # _____ Cell #_____

Address_____   City_____ State _____ Zip _____

E-Mail Address_____   Fax #_____

SELLER Signature_____   **SELLER (Print Name)**_____

Date _____ Time _____ ☐ A.M. ☐ P.M.   Phone # _____ Cell #_____

Address_____   City_____ State _____ Zip _____

E-Mail Address_____   Fax #_____

CONTRACTOR REGISTRATION # (if applicable)_____

RE-21 RESIDENTIAL PURCHASE AND SALE AGREEMENT PAGE 6 of 6 <u>JULY, 2006 EDITION</u>

Receipt of earnest money.   The amount of earnest money accepted by the broker should be sufficient to compensate the seller if the contract is not consummated and the sale is not completed. This amount should be written out in words as well as figures. It is also important to indicate whether the earnest money will be deposited immediately into a trust account or if the money will be held pending acceptance of all parties.

The receipt or earnest money provision also must indicate whether the deposit was cash, a personal check, a promissory note, or some other form of payment in lieu of cash. If the manner of payment is not indicated, the seller can assume that the deposit was made in cash; should the buyer forfeit the deposit, the seller then may demand the money in cash (unless the contract provides otherwise). If the buyer plans to deposit additional earnest money in the future, the contract should provide a definite date for such payment.

In addition, the agreement must provide for a division of the earnest money (including any portion paid to the broker) in the event that the transaction is not completed and the earnest money is forfeited.

The agreement must state which of the brokers will hold the earnest money for the benefit of the parties and which broker shall hold the completely executed copy of the agreement and be responsible for the closing.

Adequate legal description.   The definite description given must be sufficient for the property to be located from the description alone.

Excepted property.   Most purchase and sale agreement forms include a paragraph listing fixtures, which are articles that are part of the property and are to be included in the sale. If the seller plans on removing any of these fixtures, this intention should be written into the agreement to avoid misunderstandings between the parties.

Most contract forms also include a paragraph in which any items of personal property included in the sales price may be listed and described. If this provision is acceptable to the buyer, a separate bill of sale from the seller to the buyer for the personal property should be made out and transferred when the transaction is closed.

Sales price and terms.   The agreement should set forth the full sales price and describe the manner in which it will be paid. The contract will not be binding unless the terms of payment are specifically stated. If the buyer plans to obtain financing, a brief description of the type of loan, its amount, and the amortization period should be included so that the seller will know what kind of financing the buyer is planning to obtain. If the buyer will assume an existing loan, the terms of that loan—approximate balance, interest rate, due date, monthly payments, and who will pay any costs to assume the loan—should be clearly specified. If the buyer is asking the seller to carry a contract (installment contract or contract for deed) as part of the purchase price, the following items must be specified:

- Amount owing on the contract
- Interest rate
- Date interest is to begin
- Amount of monthly payments and dates due
- Date the first payment is due
- Who is to pay the escrow filing fee, escrow collection fee, and escrow closing fee
- Who, or what entity, will be the responsible custodian of the escrowed documents
- Any prepayment penalties or restrictions (if applicable)
- Whether the property can be transferred subject to the indebtedness, or whether there is a due-on-sale clause

It is dangerous to assume that the parties will understand the contract unless *all* conditions are set forth in clear and concise language. If additional space is necessary, the broker may use a separate sheet of paper, known as an "addendum." Any added pages or writings must be signed by all parties to the agreement.

Anything beyond filling in the blanks on preprinted forms, altering information in such blanks, or what is customarily allowed for brokers in the area should be dealt with by an attorney. Be careful to watch for anything unusual or technical in the transactions with which you are dealing. If such unusual or technical circumstances arise in any transaction, you should suggest that the client or customer see an attorney.

Other conditions.   Any additional conditions or concessions requested by the buyer, such as repairs to the property, should be clearly set forth in the agreement to ensure that the seller understands them.

Encumbrance clause.   This section of the contract includes what is sometimes known as the "subject to" clause; each contract form has its own wording. Basically, the seller agrees to furnish title evidence that his or her property is free and clear of all liens and encumbrances except any named that will remain outstanding against the property, such as mortgages, trust deeds, leases, easements, or restrictions. These must be stipulated in the agreement.

Conveyance and prorations.   The contract should state the type of conveyance or deed the seller will deliver to the purchaser. Real property usually is conveyed by warranty deed unless otherwise stipulated. Real property is never conveyed by an abstract of title or title insurance policy.

All taxes, assessments, rents, insurance, mortgage interest, or contract indebtedness should be prorated to the date of possession or any other date that is agreeable to the seller and buyer. If a definite date can be established, it should be made part of the contract.

Performance.   The performance clause usually stipulates that the seller must accept the offer and sign the agreement within a specified period of time and that the seller's title to the property must be merchantable and insurable. If the conditions are met and the purchaser then neglects or refuses to complete the sale, the contract provides that the earnest money is forfeited to the seller as *liquidated damages* or the seller may take legal steps to enforce his or her rights under the contract.

Damage to property.   Most contract forms provide that if the property is destroyed or materially damaged before the sale is consummated, the agreement, at the purchaser's option, becomes null and void and the earnest money is to be returned to the purchaser. This clause reminds the seller to keep the property in good condition and repair until the transaction is closed and the buyer has taken possession. It also provides for the possibility of damage to or destruction of the property by forces such as wind, fire, or flood.

Possession.   The agreement always should state a definite date of possession. In determining a possession date, the broker and the parties to the agreement must take many factors into consideration. How much time does the purchaser need to arrange for financing? When must the purchaser vacate his or her premises? When can the seller move into new premises? To avoid any misunderstandings, the buyer and seller should agree on the best possible possession date and include that date as a provision of the agreement.

Independent investigation.   The agent is responsible for making certain that all details of the sale are written into the agreement and are completely understood by both parties. Any verbal agreements pertaining to the sale that are made at any time during the negotiations or before the sale is closed can only cause problems. The agreement should clearly state that the purchaser enters into the contract upon his or her independent investigation and judgment and that no additional agreements, verbal or otherwise, affect the written contract.

Time is of the essence.   This clause prevents either party from unjustly delaying the closing of the transaction. The phrase "time is of the essence" means that one party must perform his or her obligations within the time specified in the contract in order to be able to require performance from the other party.

Purchaser's signature.   In the final clause, the purchaser agrees to pay a stipulated price for the property under the terms and conditions set forth in the contract and then signs the offer.

Seller's acceptance.   The seller agrees to sell and convey the property under the terms and conditions of the contract and to pay the agent's stipulated commission. Because Idaho is a community property state, whenever the sellers in a transaction are husband and wife, both must sign the agreement. When the seller(s) signs the agreement and accepts the offer, it becomes binding on both parties upon acknowledgment by the buyer.

Unless specified otherwise, the earnest money is held in trust by the broker until the closing, at which time it becomes the property of the seller.

Agency Confirmation [IC 54-2085]

Whether representation is involved or not, agency representation confirmation will be included in the purchase and sale agreement.

This confirmation does *not* create an agency relationship. A *separate*, signed, written agreement is required for that purpose.

Offers to Purchase [IC 54-2051]

A broker or sales associate shall, as promptly as practicable, tender to the seller *every* written offer to purchase obtained on the real estate involved, up *until time of closing.*

Broker's responsibility.   It is part of the licensee's legal duty to make certain that the seller understands all the terms and conditions of the contract; the agent's responsibility also includes explaining the contract's provisions to the buyer. When both parties understand the implications of the agreement, the likelihood of misunderstandings, dissatisfaction, or withdrawal by either party diminishes.

The unauthorized practice of law is covered by Idaho Code [IC 3-420]. This is often a confusing area for real estate brokers and salespersons because they come in contact with the law in every transaction and necessarily must know a good deal of the law to function in the real estate industry. Further adding to the confusion is that there is often a fine line between what is considered brokerage allowed under the law and what is considered the unauthorized practice of law.

Under a decision in the Idaho courts, a real estate licensee may fill in blanks in preprinted forms that are approved by an attorney but may not draft, draw, or formulate instruments that in effect include legal advice and counsel. Some of the problem areas where a real estate broker and sales associate could step over into the unauthorized practice of law are leases, options, quitclaim deeds, well agreements, exchange agreements, powers of attorney, and road maintenance agreements.

The broker must always be in a position to encourage the client to see an attorney and to seek legal advice and counsel. The broker or sales associate should never discourage a client or customer from seeing an attorney.

The consequences of practicing law without a license can include criminal charges, loss of commission, and suit for damages.

Idaho law makes the licensee responsible for the content of the contract as well. The broker or salesperson should make certain that all the terms and conditions of the sale are included in the contract. The law also provides that, upon accepting an earnest money deposit and a signed offer to purchase from a prospective purchaser, the agent must give that purchaser a copy of the agreement as a receipt.

Furthermore, the agent shall as promptly as practicable convey to the seller every written offer to purchase and, upon the seller's acceptance, deliver to each party a true copy of the contract signed by both buyer and seller.

In practice, the person making an offer to purchase should sign the original and at least four copies of the contract. One copy is retained by the purchaser as a receipt; the original and the other three copies are presented to the seller. Upon accepting the offer, the seller signs the original and the three copies. The seller keeps one copy; one copy is given to the purchaser; the other copy and the original are retained by the broker.

Purchase and Sale Agreement

Complete the Purchase and Sale Agreement form found in Figures 7.1, 7.2, 7.3, and 7.4 using the facts given in the following description of a real estate transaction.

On September 1, 2005, Mark and Sara Swenson make an offer on a home located at 1313 Honey Locust Drive in Boise, Idaho 83720. The legal description is lot 13, block 3 Randolf Addition to Boise, Ada County, Idaho.

The agent representing the Swensons is Frank Livermore, who is affiliated with Gold Carpet Realty. His phone number is 311-0011 and his e-mail is *liver@netcom.com*.

The purchase price is $165,000 subject to the Swensons securing a new mortgage in the amount of $148,500 with conventional financing at an interest rate of 6.5 percent fixed for 30 years.

The earnest money contract is accompanied by a personal check for $2,500 to be deposited in the Gold Carpet Realty real estate trust account. The responsible broker will be Gold Carpet Realty.

The buyer is asking the seller to pay 1 discount point toward securing the financing at 6.5 percent.

Personal property, which includes a Maytag washer and dryer, serial #09283475, and a Sears Craftsman 6.5 hp lawnmower, serial #74765584, is to be purchased from the seller for a total of $625. This purchase of personal property is separate from the real estate transaction but is included in the closing statement and is to be accompanied with a bill of sale from the seller.

The seller will keep the satellite dish and receiving equipment and is not included in the sale.

The buyer desires to have a home inspection at buyer's expense within five days of seller's acceptance.

Once a title commitment is provided to the buyer, the buyer shall have one day to object and the seller shall have one day to correct.

Because the property was built prior to 1978, the buyer waives the right for any testing.

Appraisal, appraisal reinspection, lender document preparation, tax service fee, and lender required inspections will be paid by the buyer.

The subdivision homeowner's association fees are $22 per month, and transferring from one owner to another is a one-time fee of $15.

Scheduled closing is for October 15, 2005, with possession on October 16, 2005.

The seller will have until September 2, 2005, to accept the offer.

The sellers, Jeff and Ronna Graham, are represented by Joe Wilson, who is affiliated with the Wilson, Wagner & Bills real estate firm. Joe's phone number is 333-0000. His e-mail is *joew@aol.com*.

On September 2, 2005, Jeff and Ronna Graham accepted the offer to purchase their home from Mark and Sara Swenson at 8:15 A.M.

A six percent commission is to be paid to the real estate brokerage firm of Wilson, Wagner & Bills by the seller.

The title insurance company will be Frontier Title Insurance Company, located at 2005 Sunnyside Drive, Boise.

The title insurance company's escrow closing fees will be shared equally between buyer and seller.

The Grahams are also responsible for providing a lender's (mortgagee) title insurance policy.

The seller is to provide Flood Certification.

Check your solution with the one given in the Answer Key.

Alterations in the Contract

The negotiating process in a real estate transaction may involve supplemental addendums and/or counteroffers. An addendum allows additional space, if needed but not available, within the offer to purchase or counteroffer form (see Figure 7.2).

If the seller wishes to make any changes in the contract, the best practice is to prepare a counteroffer form according to the seller's proposed terms and have both parties sign this agreement (see Figure 7.3).

Any material change or alteration by the seller of the buyer's written offer to purchase is equivalent to rejection of the buyer's offer, thereby canceling it. If the seller initials the changes, he or she is consenting to the change, which is a counteroffer (that is, an offer) by the seller to the buyer. The seller and buyer have reversed roles as offeror and offeree. The seller's offer (counteroffer) can be rejected, accepted, or ignored within the time limit stipulated in the document.

FIGURE 7.2

Addendum/Amendment

RE-11 ADDENDUM # _____ (1,2,3, etc.)

Date:_____

THIS IS A LEGALLY BINDING CONTRACT. READ THE ENTIRE DOCUMENT INCLUDING ANY ATTACHMENTS. IF YOU HAVE ANY QUESTIONS, **CONSULT YOUR ATTORNEY AND/OR ACCOUNTANT** BEFORE SIGNING.

1 This is an **ADDENDUM** to the Purchase and Sale Agreement.
2 ("Addendum" means that the information below is added material for the agreement {such as lists or descriptions} and/or means the form is being used
3 to change, correct or revise the agreement {such as modification, addition or deletion of a term}).
4
5 **PURCHASE AND SALE AGREEMENT DATED:**_____ **ID #**_____
6 **ADDRESS:**_____
7 **BUYER(S):** _____
8 **SELLER(S):** _____
9 The undersigned parties hereby agree as follows:
10 _____
11 _____
12 _____
13 _____
14 _____
15 _____
16 _____
17 _____
18 _____
19 _____
20 _____
21 _____
22 _____
23 _____
24 _____
25 _____
26 _____
27 _____
28 _____
29 _____
30 _____
31 _____
32 To the extent the terms of this ADDENDUM modify or conflict with any provisions of the Purchase and Sale Agreement including all prior
33 Addendums or Counter Offers, these terms shall control. **All other terms of the Purchase and Sale Agreement including all prior**
34 **Addendums or Counter Offers not modified by this ADDENDUM shall remain the same.** Upon its execution by both parties, this
35 agreement is made an integral part of the aforementioned Agreement.
36
37 **BUYER:** _____   Date: _____
38 **BUYER:** _____   Date: _____
39 **SELLER:** _____   Date: _____
40 **SELLER:** _____   Date: _____

F I G U R E   7.3

Counteroffer

RE- 13 COUNTER OFFER # _____ **(1, 2, 3, etc.)**

REALTOR®

EQUAL HOUSING
OPPORTUNITY

THIS COUNTER OFFER SUPERSEDES ALL PRIOR COUNTER OFFERS

THIS IS A LEGALLY BINDING CONTRACT. READ THE ENTIRE DOCUMENT INCLUDING ANY ATTACHMENTS. IF YOU HAVE ANY QUESTIONS, **CONSULT YOUR ATTORNEY AND/OR ACCOUNTANT** BEFORE SIGNING.

1   This is a COUNTER OFFER to the Purchase and Sale Agreement Dated:_____

2   ADDRESS:_____ ID# _____

3   BUYER: _____

4   SELLER: _____

5   The parties accept all of the terms and conditions in the above-designated Purchase and Sale Agreement with the following changes:

6   ☐ **This is a SELLER counter offer.** The SELLER reserves the right to withdraw this offer or accept any other offers prior to the receipt of a
7   true copy of signed acceptance of this Counter Offer within the time frame specified herein.

8   ☐ **This is a BUYER counter offer.** The undersigned BUYER reserves the right to withdraw this offer at any time prior to the receipt of a true
9   copy of signed acceptance of this Counter Offer within the time frame specified herein.

10 _____
11 _____
12 _____
13 _____
14 _____
15 _____
16 _____
17 _____
18 _____
19 _____
20 _____
21 _____
22 _____
23 _____
24 _____
25 _____
26 _____

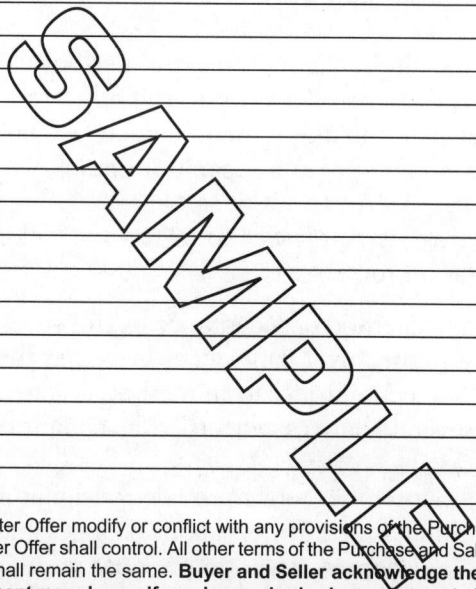

27 To the extent the terms of this Counter Offer modify or conflict with any provisions of the Purchase and Sale Agreement including all prior
28 Addendums, the terms in this Counter Offer shall control. All other terms of the Purchase and Sale Agreement including all prior Addendums
29 not modified by this Counter Offer shall remain the same. **Buyer and Seller acknowledge the down payment and/or loan amount on**
30 **Page 1 of Purchase & Sale Agreement may change if purchase price is changed as part of this Counter Offer.** Upon its execution by
31 both parties, this agreement is made an integral part of the aforementioned Agreement.
32
33 If a signed acceptance is not delivered on or before (date:) _____ at _____ ☐A.M. ☐P.M. this Counter
34 Offer shall be deemed to have expired.
35
36 DELIVERY: Delivery shall be to the agent/broker working with the maker of the Counter Offer in person, by mail, facsimile or electronic
37 transmission of any signed original document, and retransmission of any signed original document. Retransmission of any signed facsimile
38 or electronic transmission shall be deemed to be the same as delivery of an original.
39
40 **SELLER**_____ Date _____ Time_____ ☐A.M. ☐P.M.

41 **SELLER**_____ Date _____ Time_____ ☐A.M. ☐P.M.

42 **BUYER**_____ Date _____ Time_____ ☐A.M. ☐P.M.

43 **BUYER**_____ Date _____ Time_____ ☐A.M. ☐P.M.

If the changes required by the seller are minor, the seller may choose to make the changes on the original document, then initial and date these changes. To complete the contract, the buyer also initials the changes, noting the date of the initialing.

Because there are problems with this alteration route, its use is *not recommended*.

First, usually there is no time limit set for acceptance by the buyer. Second, there is no specified method of acceptance by the buyer. Unless the listing agent has great faith in the knowledge and integrity of the selling agent and the buyer is readily available to initial the document, the alteration route can be a dangerous method for the seller.

What appears to be a simple counteroffer situation develops into a complex situation. For example, if the price is changed, this can affect the down payment amount, loan amount, and monthly payments. Problems may be compounded if the contract is handwritten, making alterations difficult to distinguish from the original.

Technically speaking, only the person who originates the offer can change any part of the offer prior to the other party accepting. Changes made by the other party on the same document would constitute forgery. Thus, changes made should be on a separate form known as a counteroffer.

A written counteroffer form has the following distinct advantages over the alteration route:

- The method of acceptance by the buyer is specified on the form. The only way the buyer can accept is to sign the counteroffer form.
- The counteroffer form method is generally clearer and neater than when several changes, with their attendant dates and initials, are made on the original contract.
- Counteroffer forms provide for signatures, dates, and the times signed to eliminate confusion about changes and when such changes occurred.
- The counteroffer form provides more space and better ability for making corrections and additions that may be needed to make a good contract.

There has been considerable confusion and misunderstanding in the real estate industry as to how to deal with the counteroffer form in relation to the original purchase and sale agreement. First, the counteroffer form should be stapled—not paperclipped—to the top of the buyer's original offer before the form is signed by the seller. This is important because the combination of the two papers forms a contractual relationship between the buyer and the seller. Either one alone is incomplete and ineffectual. When both forms are attached, there can be no doubt in the minds of the buyer and seller that this combined document constitutes their agreement.

Counteroffer forms may be used to make any changes to the original offer. If the counteroffer form contains specific language incorporating it by reference into the original offer to purchase, it is not mandatory that the seller sign both documents. The seller may sign the counteroffer only. However, if the counteroffer form does not contain such incorporating language, the seller *must* sign both documents and reference the attached counteroffer on the original purchase and sales agreement. It is also permissible for the seller to sign the original purchase and sale agreement and include a reference to the counteroffer at the signature line, such as "signed subject to the counteroffer of (date)." To have a seller sign an original purchase and sales agreement that does not reference a counteroffer, and thereby does not reflect the actual agreement between the parties, would be improper. *Any and all questions regarding the effectiveness of the offer and acceptance should be referred to the attorneys for the buyer and seller.*

Once a Purchase and Sale Agreement, including any addendums or counteroffers, has been signed by both parties and acknowledged, the parties are in a contractual agreement. Should there be a need to modify or change the terms of the already agreed-upon agreement, an addendum form should be used to verify such changes.

■ NOTICE TO TERMINATE CONTRACT

In the event an accepted contract is terminated, the buyer and seller should agree in writing that the transaction will not be completed. In addition, disbursement or release of any earnest money deposits should be agreed upon, in writing, by both buyer and seller (see Figure 7.4).

The proper signature from an out-of-town seller is essential. While the broker is waiting for the purchase and sale agreement to make its rounds through the mail, an additional precaution can be taken. After an offer is made to purchase the property of an out-of-town seller, a facsimile (fax) of the original offer or a telegram describing the exact terms of the offer immediately should be sent to the seller with a request for a return accepted or rejected fax or a telegram of acceptance or rejection.

The broker should retain for the record a copy of the fax or telegram containing the offer and a copy of the reply. If the offer is rejected and no further action is taken by either party, the fax or telegram should be attached to the original purchase and sale agreement, dated, marked "rejected," and placed in the broker's rejection file. If the offer is accepted, the fax or both telegrams (one from the seller and one from the broker) should be attached to the original purchase agreement. As of this writing, facsimiles of legally binding agreements or instruments are lawful substitutions for originals. However, the parties may confirm facsimile transmitted signatures by signing an original document.

■ DOUBLE CONTRACTS [IC 54-2004, 54-2054, 54-2060]

Real estate brokers and salespeople are prohibited from using double contracts. *Double contract* refers to two separate contracts (for loan applications) concerning the same parcel of real estate, where one states the true purchase price and the other states a larger amount as the purchase price. Such contracts are used

F I G U R E 7.4

Notice to Terminate Contract

RE- 20 NOTICE TO TERMINATE CONTRACT AND RELEASE OF EARNEST MONEY

REALTOR

THIS IS A LEGALLY BINDING CONTRACT. READ THE ENTIRE DOCUMENT INCLUDING ANY ATTACHMENTS. IF YOU HAVE ANY QUESTIONS, **CONSULT YOUR ATTORNEY AND/OR ACCOUNTANT** BEFORE SIGNING.

EQUAL HOUSING OPPORTUNITY

1 **RE: Purchase and Sale Agreement Dated:** _____ **ID#** _____
2 Hereinafter referred as "Contract" covering the following described property:
3
4 **Property Address:**_____
5
6 **Legal Description:** _____
7
8 **BUYER:** _____
9
10 **SELLER:** _____
11
12 The undersigned BUYER and SELLER agree that the above real estate Contract WILL NOT be completed and
13 hereby mutually release each other from all further obligations to buy, sell or exchange under the Contract and
14 all related documents, and from all claims, actions, and demands which each may have against the other by
15 reason of said Contract. It is the intent of this agreement that all rights and obligations arising out of said
16 Contract are null and void. BUYER and SELLER further agree to release brokers and their associates from any
17 claims, actions and demands by reason of releasing and disbursing of said earnest money deposit.
18
19 **Earnest Money Holder:** _____
20
21 **Amount of Earnest Money:** _____ $_____
22
23 Earnest money holder, is hereby instructed to release and disburse said earnest money deposit in the following
24 manner:
25
26 $ _____   TO: _____
27
28 $ _____   TO: _____
29
30 $ _____   TO: _____
31
32
33 **BUYER:**_____   **Date:** _____
34 **BUYER:**_____   **Date:** _____
35
36 **SELLER:**_____   **Date:** _____
37 **SELLER:**_____   **Date:** _____
38

to induce a lender to make a mortgage loan commitment for a larger amount based on the false, inflated purchase price quoted on the second contract.

This fraudulent activity represents a "flagrant course of misconduct. . . constituting dishonorable or dishonest dealing" and could result in the suspension or revocation of an agent's license.

■ HANDLING EARNEST MONEY DEPOSITS (TRUST ACCOUNTING)

The Rules addressed in Chapter 10 of this book state specific requirements for handling earnest money deposits and other funds entrusted to a real estate broker.

Failure to account for trust funds properly, no matter what the reason, is grounds for suspension or revocation of the broker's license. In the interest of the broker's fiduciary obligations, he or she must deposit all funds received from and belonging to others on or before the next *banking* day unless directed in writing by the parties to do otherwise. The deposit must go to a neutral escrow depository or in a special trust checking account that is maintained in an Idaho bank, licensed title insurance company, or other approved depository. When a salesperson receives these funds, they must be turned in to the broker at once for deposit. There are provisions currently on the form purchase and sale agreements that direct the earnest money to be deposited upon the contract's acceptance by all the parties.

The trust account must be identified with the broker's business name, the broker's address, and the phrase "Real Estate Trust Account" to distinguish it from any other accounts the broker may have. A broker may have more than one trust account; however, it is best if each account is maintained in a different banking institution. In no case shall entrusted funds be commingled with funds of a real estate broker or salesperson.

Brokers are required to keep all documents and records pertaining to a real estate transaction on file for at least three calendar years after the year in which the transaction was closed. In addition, certain records must be kept concerning a broker's trust account (see Chapter 10).

The Idaho Real Estate Commission does not intend to dictate a specific record-keeping system. Any system that properly accounts for trust funds and is approved by the Commission may be used. In addition, the Commission staff is available to help a broker set up an adequate record-keeping system.

The Commission or its representative may make periodic inspections (audits) of a broker's trust account to ensure that the broker is complying with all rules and keeping accurate and adequate records.

■ OPTIONS

Usually an option to purchase or lease real estate gives the optionee (buyer) an exclusive right to purchase or lease the property in question. Some options, however, grant the optionee the right of first refusal (the first chance) to purchase or lease the property when it becomes available for sale or lease.

An option will often be given in connection with a lease; the optionee leases the property with the option to purchase it at a specified price. Such an option clause usually terminates when the lease expires; if the lease is renewed, the option may be renewed as well. It is recommended that leases with option clauses be drafted and reviewed by an attorney.

QUESTIONS

1. Sergei verbally leases an apartment from Hans for two years for $500 per month. The agreement between Sergei and Hans was
   a. valid.
   b. void.
   c. unenforceable.
   d. voidable.

2. When a contract appears to be good and binding, but in fact one of the parties may legally reject it, the contract is said to be
   a. unenforceable.
   b. valid.
   c. void.
   d. voidable.

3. Broker Gordon contracted with Dale to sell a parcel of land that Dale owned. Gordon was to be paid a specified commission and the parties signed a written agreement. Gordon found a buyer who made an offer that Dale accepted and the sale was completed, but Gordon never received a commission. If Gordon wishes to institute legal proceedings to force Dale to pay the commission as provided in the contract, Gordon must do so within how many years after payment is due?
   a. Seven   c. Five
   b. Six   d. Four

4. According to Idaho law, which of the following persons has the legal capacity to enter into a valid real estate contract?
   a. An exceptional psychiatric patient, legally declared to be of unsound mind, who obtains written authorization from the attending physician
   b. An 18-year-old student
   c. A criminal currently imprisoned for automobile theft who receives special permission from the warden
   d. A 21-year-old felon

5. Homeowner Paul puts a For Sale sign in front of his house. Diane, after inspecting the property, offers to purchase it for $115,000. Paul accepts; however, the agreement is never expressed in a written contract. Should Diane fail to perform the agreement and purchase the property, Paul
   a. cannot take legal action to force Diane to purchase the house as promised.
   b. may sue Diane for damages.
   c. may sue Diane for specific performance.
   d. may sue Diane for partial performance.

6. Which of the following items need NOT be included in a purchase and sale agreement?
   a. A list of fixtures attached to the property that specifies which of them will be included in the sale
   b. A physical description of the land and improvements, including the type of construction, the number and dimensions of the rooms, and the type of heating equipment
   c. A legal description of the location and boundaries of the property given in enough detail so that the exact property can be identified from the description
   d. A list of any personal property that will be included in the sale

7. Which of the following statements is TRUE regarding an earnest money provision?
   a. The contract must provide for a disposition of the earnest money if the buyer does not complete the sale.
   b. The contract should state only the sales price, leaving the details of how the buyer will pay for the property to be settled at the closing.
   c. The seller promises to furnish the buyer with evidence that he or she owns the property. Any liens or encumbrances that will remain outstanding against the property will be detailed in the title evidence and need not be listed in the earnest money agreement.
   d. After the buyer has signed the agreement and thus made an offer, the seller has an unlimited amount of time in which to reject it or accept and sign it.

8. Which of the following is NOT included in a broker's responsibilities regarding a purchase and sale agreement he or she has negotiated?

a. Giving a copy of the agreement to the buyer after he or she signs it as a receipt for the earnest money accepted by the broker.

b. Conveying the written offer promptly to the seller and then, after the seller accepts, giving a true copy of the executed agreement to both buyer and seller.

c. Obtaining both parties' written approval for any changes or alterations in the contract.

d. Suggesting that neither buyer nor seller needs to engage an attorney because the broker can adequately explain the terms and conditions of the contract.

9. Clark has signed a purchase and sale agreement to purchase a parcel of real estate for $50,000; however, Clark must borrow $45,000 (or 90 percent of the purchase price) in order to complete the sale. The lender to whom Clark will apply for financing has a policy of never lending a real estate purchaser a sum that is greater than 80 percent of the purchase price. Clark asks the broker to draw up a second purchase and sale agreement stating that Clark will purchase the property for $60,000. Clark plans to present this second contract to the lender when applying to borrow $45,000. This kind of practice is

a. known as novation.

b. standard procedure in many Idaho localities.

c. prohibited by the Idaho Real Estate Commission rules.

d. permitted, if the broker obtains the seller's written consent before completing the second contract form.

10. An earnest money deposit received by a broker immediately must be

a. placed in the broker's office safe, where it must remain until the transaction is closed.

b. deposited in a special trust account maintained by the broker for this purpose or with a neutral escrow depository.

c. delivered to the seller to whom it belongs.

d. attached to the broker's copy of the earnest money agreement and retained in the broker's files until the transaction is closed.

CHAPTER EIGHT

TRANSFER OF TITLE

■ DESCENT AND DISTRIBUTION

Idaho has adopted a modified version of the Uniform Probate Code that provides for the ownership succession of real property owned by a person who died intestate (without leaving a valid will). The deceased's surviving spouse and issue are always heirs. Other heirs are detailed in the following sections of the law. This pattern of succession does not apply to real estate that the decedent owned as a joint tenant or a tenant by the entirety.

One-half of the community property is owned by the surviving spouse, who receives, in addition, property and estate enumerated in Idaho Code [IC 15-2-102]:

15-2-102. *Share of the spouse*—The intestate (without a will) share of the surviving spouse is as follows:

  (a) *As to separate property:*
    (1) if there is no surviving issue or parent of the decedent, the entire intestate estate;
    (2) if there is no surviving issue but the decedent is survived by a parent or parents, one-half (½) of the intestate estate;
    (3) if there are surviving issue all of who are issue of the surviving spouse, one-half (½) of the intestate estate.
  (b) *As to community property:*
    (1) the one-half (½) of community property that belongs to the decedent passes to the surviving spouse.

The share of the estate taken by heirs other than the surviving spouse is described in Idaho Code Section 15-2-103:

15-2-103. *Share of heirs other than surviving spouse*—The part of the intestate estate not passing to the surviving spouse under Section 15-2-102 of this part, or the entire intestate estate if there is no surviving spouse, passes as follows:

(a) to the issue of the decedent; if they are all of the same degree of kinship to the decedent they take equally, but if of unequal degree, then those of more remote degree take by representation;

(b) if there is no surviving issue, to his or her parent or parents equally;

(c) if there is no surviving issue or parent, to the issue of the parents or either parent by representation;

(d) if there is no surviving issue, parent, or issue of a parent, but the decedent is survived by one or more grandparents or issue of grandparents, half of the estate passes to the paternal grandparents if both survive, or to the surviving paternal grandparent, or to the issue of the paternal grandparents if both are deceased, the issue taking equally if they are all of the same degree of kinship to the decedent, but if of unequal degree those of more remote degree take by representation; and the other half passes to the maternal relatives in the same manner; but if there be no surviving grandparent or issue of grandparents on either the paternal or the maternal side, the entire estate passes to the relatives on the other side in the same manner as the half.

15-1-201. *Issue* of a person means all his or her lineal descendants of all generations, with the relationship of parent and child at each generation being determined by the definitions of child and parent contained in this code.

15-3-914. If no heirs are found, the entire intestate estate passes to the state of Idaho, subject to administration by the public administrator. The estate is then disposed of under the Unclaimed Property Act, and if not claimed within 1,827 days (five years) from the date the property is paid to the State Tax Commission, it will escheat to the state and is apportioned to the public school fund.

■ TRANSFER OF TITLE BY WILL

A will must be prepared and executed by the property owner during his or her lifetime but cannot take effect until after the property owner's death. In Idaho any emancipated minor or any person 18 or more years of age who is of sound mind may make a will.

Every will (with certain limited exceptions) must be in writing and signed by the testator or in the testator's name by some other person in the testator's presence and by his or her direction. It also must be signed by at least two persons, each of whom witnessed either the signing of the will or the testator's acknowledgment of the signature or of the will. A *holographic* will is one in which the material provisions of the will and the signature are in the handwriting of the testator. There need be no witnesses to a holographic will. A *nuncupative* will is a verbal will made under special circumstances in immediate anticipation of the maker's death; however, the Idaho Uniform Probate Code has no provision for the use or enforceability of this type of will.

■ TRANSFER OF TITLE BY INVOLUNTARY ACTION OF LAW

Involuntary transfer comes in many forms. *Accession* is a growth or an increase of real property, frequently involving riparian or littoral (shoreline) property. Such land may be increased by *accretion,* which means through natural forces. Accretion may be accomplished by the process of *alluvion,* in which soil is washed up on the banks and deposited gradually, or by *reliction,* in which the water recedes permanently and lowers the waterline. Accession also may include improvements made by others to an owner's land or buildings that cannot be removed and so become *fixtures.*

A person who claims to acquire title to a parcel of real estate by *adverse possession* in Idaho must have been adversely in possession for *five years.* Such a person also *must have paid all taxes legally assessed against the property during this period.* A person who claims title through adverse possession may transfer the interest as with any other form of title. The similar acquisition of an easement by prescription is discussed in Chapter 3 of this book.

Bankruptcy is a legal proceeding created to protect the rights of debtors and their creditors when an insolvent person is unable to repay debts. Bankruptcy may be either voluntary or involuntary and takes the form, for most individuals and businesses, of a Chapter 7, a Chapter 11, or a Chapter 13. However, big changes in the law in the fall of 2005 make it much harder to qualify for bankruptcy. Fewer people will be eligible for filing Chapter 7. Fewer people will be able to stick to Chapter 13 repayment plans. Creditors' collections efforts will offer less protection. Fewer debts will be allowed to be wiped out. Increased costs and delays in filing will result in most people being required to get credit counseling.

A *Chapter 7* bankruptcy is total insolvency. The court appoints a *trustee,* who takes control of the bankrupt's nonexempt assets and liquidates them to repay the creditors.

A *Chapter 11* bankruptcy is available to individuals in business or businesses and is a form of reorganization that usually allows the bankrupt to dispose of assets in such a manner as to suffer the least amount of asset devaluation due to a forced sale. Also there must be, in the opinion of the court, enough assets available to satisfy the creditors. The court appoints a trustee, who may be the bankrupt. (Such a debtor is called a *debtor in possession.*) The trustee then takes control and title of the bankrupt person's nonexempt assets; those assets are sold with court approval, and the funds are applied toward the bankrupt's debts and other provable claims.

A *Chapter 13* bankruptcy is often called a *wage-earner plan.* It allows the bankrupt to file a plan that is approved by the court for repayment of debts to all the creditors.

The two other methods of involuntary transfer by operation of law are eminent domain and escheat.

Confiscation

Confiscation is the taking of property by a government in time of emergency or war without paying compensation. Generally only property of enemies of the government is confiscated. Private property can also be confiscated when someone profits from an illegal act.

▧ GIFTS

Title to real property may be transferred voluntarily by gift or sale. Gifts of real estate may involve transfers to private persons or to municipal governments by *dedication*. Land for streets, alleys, parks, and other public uses may be dedicated for public use by one of two methods.

Statutory dedication involves a recorded subdivision plat that indicates that specific streets or areas are set aside for public use. Such a plat must include a certificate executed by all parties who have a recorded interest in the property and are offering the specified areas for dedication as well as a certificate of acceptance executed by the proper municipal officials.

Common law dedication includes all other less formal dedications, for example, when a property owner clearly indicates in some way that a certain portion of his or her land is intended for public use. Acceptance of such a common law dedication may be by actual public use of the property or by a resolution of the city council. A common law dedication is considered to convey an *easement* to the public, with the landowner retaining the fee title to the property.

▧ DEEDS

The execution and delivery of a deed is the method provided by law for landowners to convey, transfer, or release their interests in real estate while they are living. After a deed has been executed and delivered, the grantor's interest in the property is transferred subject to the legal rights and covenants that the law attaches to the kind and form of deed used.

A deed may be delivered only once. In addition to the general requirements for a valid deed of conveyance, the following additional information is important to an understanding of the deeds used in Idaho.

Forms of Deeds

The most common form of deed used in Idaho is the *warranty deed*, which incorporates the grant deed. A *grant deed* is a statutory form of deed in which the word "grant" implies that the grantor and his or her heirs are bound by the following covenants and no others:

- The grantor previously has not conveyed the same estate or any part of it to any person other than the grantee.
- The estate conveyed is free from encumbrances done, made, or suffered by the grantor or any person claiming under the grantor.

In warranty deeds and bargain and sale deeds that customarily use the words "grant" or "grant, bargain, and sell" as words of conveyance, the covenants by which the grantor is bound are written out. Such covenants may grant full warranty or they may grant special warranty, which covers only the grantor's acts during the ownership period.

Grant deeds, warranty deeds, and bargain and sale deeds are generally interpreted by Idaho law as passing *after-acquired title*. For example, a grantor actually had less of an interest in the property at the time of conveyance than supposed, or a defective interest. If the grantor acquired title or perfected the title after the conveyance, such after-acquired title would automatically pass to the grantee.

By using a quitclaim deed, the grantor releases whatever interest in the property he or she may have, if any, to the grantee. No warranties or covenants are implied or written in this type of deed. It transfers only such title, right, or interest in the property that the grantor has at the time the quitclaim is delivered. After-acquired title does not pass under a quitclaim deed unless specifically provided for on the face of the deed.

A deed conveying real estate as a gift may state that "love and affection" is the consideration given for the property; this is known as a *gift deed*.

A special type of deed called a *reconveyance deed* (sometimes referred to as a *release deed*) conveys or releases the title or interest of a trust deed under a deed of trust loan after the debt has been paid in full by the landowner borrower.

Acknowledgment

Acknowledgment enables deeds and other instruments to be recorded. In Idaho acknowledgments may be taken by a notary public, county recorders, clerks, judges of courts of record, and certain other public officials. Any acknowledgment is void if a notary or another authorized person who is also a party to the transaction takes it. Idaho statutes provide for the specific wording of the acknowledgment depending on the capacity of the signatory (e.g., attorney-in-fact, corporate officer, etc.).

Revenue Stamps

Idaho has no documentary stamp tax, transfer fee, or other tax on real estate conveyances.

QUESTIONS

1. Peter is survived by his wife, Ruth, and their two daughters. Peter and Ruth's community property is worth $50,000, but Peter also has left a separate estate worth $150,000. Because Peter died suddenly without leaving a will, Ruth

   a. acquires sole ownership of the community property and her daughters each receive $75,000 from Peter's separate property.
   b. acquires sole ownership of all of the property.
   c. receives $50,000 (all of the community property) and $75,000 (half of the separate property), and her daughters each receive $37,500.
   d. receives one-half of the entire estate, or $25,000 from the community property and $75,000 from Peter's separate property, while her daughters each receive one-half of the balance of the entire estate, or $50,000.

2. Estelle died intestate leaving an estate worth $30,000. Because Estelle had no family, after five years her property passed into the state public school fund through the principle of

   a. accession.
   b. escheat.
   c. eminent domain.
   d. dedication.

3. Shortly before his death, Herb wrote out his will, signed it, and placed it on his desk for his family to find. This is known as what type of will?

   a. Holographic
   b. Nuncupative
   c. Probate
   d. Formal

4. Karl's property lies on the bank of a river. Over the years, the river has deposited soil along the bank. This gradual increase of Karl's land is

   a. littoral distribution.
   b. dereliction.
   c. escheat.
   d. alluvion.

5. Which of the following is NOT an example of transfer of title by involuntary action of law?

   a. Accretion
   b. Confiscation
   c. Bankruptcy
   d. Eminent domain

6. Zachary inherited Stately Manor from his aunt but was too busy to inspect the property immediately. Hank found the empty farmhouse and moved in. Six months later there still was no sign of the absent owner, and Hank began to make repairs on the property. In order to claim title to this property by adverse possession, Hank must

   a. immediately pay all real estate taxes and assessments for the current year.
   b. locate Zachary and pay him a token consideration for title to the property after using Stately Manor continuously for five years.
   c. occupy and use Stately Manor continuously for five years, paying all real estate taxes and assessments for the property during that time.
   d. file a declaration of homestead in the county record and occupy and use the property for five years.

7. Donald sold his home and delivered a warranty deed to the new owners. One month later Donald was informed that a third party, Walt, had a claim to the property arising from an improperly executed deed to a former owner. To correct this situation, Walt executed a quitclaim deed to Donald conveying his interest in the property. This perfected interest, which passed to the new owner, is known as

   a. after-acquired title.
   b. quitclaim title.
   c. accession.
   d. involuntary alienation.

8. Which of the following statements describes a grant deed?

   a. It warrants that the grantor has not conveyed the same estate to any other person other than the grantee.
   b. It conveys any interest the grantor may have in the real estate.
   c. It usually lists love and affection as the consideration given in exchange for the real estate.
   d. It is subject to the Idaho realty transfer tax.

9

TITLE RECORDS

■ RECORDING DOCUMENTS

Any conveyance, instrument, or judgment affecting title to or possession of real estate may be recorded. The grantor's signature of an instrument must be acknowledged (notarized), or proven and certified, in order to be eligible for recording. Then it is deposited and recorded in the recorder's office of the county in which the property is located and the proper fee is paid. (*Note:* Deeds must contain the grantee's correct mailing address.)

The courts charge the prospective buyer of real estate with constructive notice, making him or her responsible for knowing what documents are in the public record concerning the property. Documents are filed and indexed in the public record according to the grantor's and grantee's names and according to the legal description of the property involved. Recorded documents give constructive notice from the time they are filed with the county recorder.

Recording also establishes the priority of rights. A deed or another interest in real property that is recorded outside the chain of title may not be easily located at the recorder's office. The recorder, using a grantor/grantee index, lists any and all documents recorded in either name. If these names are not known, the recorded document cannot be easily found.

Unrecorded documents, including deeds, are valid between the parties to the transaction. However, unrecorded documents do not protect the rights of such parties against subsequent purchasers. Also, lenders could be at risk if they cannot find evidence of unrecorded documents by inspecting the public record. Thus, most lenders require lender's (mortgagee) title insurance for protection against unrecorded instruments.

Foreign Language Documents

Idaho law makes no special provision for documents written in a foreign language. The recorder will accept for recording any document that is properly acknowledged and notarized.

■ UNRECORDED INTERESTS

Constructive notice charges the buyer of real estate with the responsibility of inspecting the property as well as searching the public record. A person claiming an interest in a parcel of real estate can give notice of his or her right by being in possession of the property.

For example, a purchaser who has not recorded the deed may take possession and thus give notice of the interest. (This is not to suggest that a purchaser need not record the deed; all deeds should be recorded promptly.) An inspection of the property will reveal who is in possession and other possible unrecorded interests, such as an easement that is in actual use, a neighbor's fence or wall encroaching on the property, or evidence of recent construction work indicating the possibility of as yet unrecorded mechanics' liens against the property. This type of constructive notice is referred to as "inquiry notice."

■ TITLE EVIDENCE

In most Idaho real estate sales transactions, the seller furnishes evidence of his or her good and legal title to the property being sold.

In Idaho the title abstract is acceptable evidence of title. This history of recorded documents affecting the title to a parcel of real estate must be examined and evaluated by a real estate attorney, who then prepares an opinion of the title or ownership rights.

The protection afforded by a title company is that it cross-indexes all the documents recorded in a given county against a plat.

Asking for a preliminary title report or title information ensures that all transfers outside the chain of title have been picked up by someone who has been keeping records on a day-to-day basis on a plat index and not just by a grantor-grantee index.

The Idaho Real Estate Commission's Rules 302 and 303 expressly forbid real estate licensees to pass judgment or give opinions on the merchantability or condition of the title to a parcel of real property.

This is a task for an attorney and the licensee must not discourage either party to the transaction from consulting an attorney in such matters.

Title Insurance

In Idaho the title insurance industry is closely regulated by the Department of Insurance as to rates charged, rebates of fees, kinds of free services allowed, and gifts that may be offered to the title insurance clients.

If federally related financing is involved, the *buyer* has the right to choose the title insurance company. Real estate licensees could create liability for the seller if they advise the seller, as a condition of a sale, to use a particular title insurance company; especially if the buyer indicates a different title insurance company in their offer to purchase real estate.

Title 12 (Banks and Banking) of the United States Code, via Chapter 27 (Real Estate Procedures) section 2608 (Title companies; liability of seller) states the following:

(a) *No seller of property that will be purchased with the assistance of a federally related mortgage loan shall require directly or indirectly, as a condition to selling the property, that title insurance covering the property be purchased by the buyer from any particular title company.*

(b) *Any seller who violates the provisions of subsection (a) of this section shall be liable to the buyer in the amount equal to three times all charges made for such title insurance.*

Abstracts of title are seldom used in Idaho because of the preferable protection offered by title insurance policies. Title insurance protects against suits or claims based on items that are insured in the policy. The title company will defend any such suits at its own expense. It should be noted that there are various formats and coverage of title policies that can be issued and are standardized by the American Land Title Association (ALTA) and are known as ALTA forms.

Owner's Policy

The owner's policy insures the owner's title. The condition of the title is insured as of the date of the policy. As with most title policies, it insures against such problems as forged documents, improperly delivered deeds, and documents executed by incompetent parties. This policy is a standard policy and only insures against items that are recorded in the public record.

The owner's policy does not insure against those items that are listed as exceptions, including the following: defects in the title known to the owner; unrecorded easements; mechanics' liens and other liens, claims, or rights; rights of parties in possession not indicated in the public record; encroachments; factors that would be disclosed by an accurate survey and inspection of the property; and governmental regulations such as zoning requirements, building codes, or eminent domain.

Expanded coverage. Expanded coverage endorsement protects the buyer against mechanics' liens being placed against the property after the transaction has been closed. However, there may be limitations regarding exact coverage (usually coverage extends only to the drip line of the dwelling).

This endorsement attaches to and becomes a part of a standard owner's title policy. This endorsement shall be effective only if, at date of policy, there is located on the land described in the policy a one- to four-family residential structure in which the insured owner resides either at date of policy or any time prior to the time the insured owner acquires knowledge of a potential claim.

An example of what loss or damage a title insurance company would insure could include the following three situations:

1. Unrecorded mechanics' liens when the property is one to four units and is owner occupied
2. The forced removal of the residential structure or denial of the right to use thereof for ordinary residential purposes, as the result of a final court order of judgments, based upon the existence at the date of the policy of the following:

   ■ Encroachment of home onto easement or over property lines
   ■ Violation of covenants, conditions, or restrictions
   ■ Violation of zoning ordinances

3. Damage to the residential structure resulting from the exercise of any right to use the surface of said land for the extraction or development of the minerals from the description of said land or shown as a reservation in Schedule B.

Licensees should be aware there are limitations regarding exact coverage. The owner or buyer needs to talk to a title insurance company regarding the limitations and the exact coverage of the homeowner's expanded coverage endorsement.

Lender's Policy (Mortgagee Policy)

The mortgage or loan policy (lender's policy) provides coverage that is not usually included in the owner's policy. It insures the condition of the mortgage or deed of trust loan for the lender. All liens against a property must be determined to evaluate the priority of the mortgage lien.

This policy insures only the lender, not the owner. In a sale where the buyer is financing the purchase with a mortgage or deed of trust loan, however, both the owner's and lender's policies can be ordered together and prepared from the same title search.

Extended coverage.   The extended coverage policy considers matters of public record and additionally insures against certain matters not shown in the public record.

The extended coverage policy will be required by lenders and is also available to an owner and lessee. A title insurance company may insure against loss or damage resulting from the following:

1. Rights or claims of parties in possession not shown by the public records
2. Encroachments, overlaps, boundary line disputes
3. Easements, or claims of easements, not shown by the public record
4. Any lien, or right to lien, for services, labor, or material imposed by law and not shown by the public record

Before an extended coverage policy is issued, the premises must be inspected by the title insurance company agent and investigations must be made for possible off-record defects, liens, or encumbrances. The title company charges additional fees for the extended coverage and possibly for the inspection. In some cases, a survey may be required.

Torrens System   The Torrens system of registering title to real estate has not been adopted in Idaho.

■ BUSINESS OPPORTUNITY SALES [IC 54-2004]

Every business, no matter how small, must have a place of operation. Whether it is a small direct-mail sales enterprise operated from the owner's home or a large manufacturing concern with numerous factories and sales offices, the operation of a business involves the use of real estate. Consequently, when a business is sold, the title or lease to real estate used in the business is usually included in the sale.

Chapter 7 detailed what must be included in a valid real estate sales contract (earnest money agreement or receipt and agreement to purchase). When the sale includes chattel (i.e., trade fixtures) and other items of personal property as well as an interest in real estate, an additional agreement must be executed by the seller.

Items of personal property may be listed in the real estate sales contract. They should not, however, be included in a deed granting title to real property.

Upon the closing of a business sales transaction, a separate *bill of sale* should be executed by the seller for all chattel, stock, materials, and other items of personal property that are included in the sale.

QUESTIONS

1. An instrument affecting the title to a parcel of real estate gives constructive notice to the world when it is filed with the

   a. city clerk.
   b. county recorder.
   c. Idaho Real Estate Commission.
   d. title company.

2. To be eligible for recording in Idaho, a document *MUST* be

   a. in English.
   b. witnessed by two persons who are not affected by the document.
   c. acknowledged.
   d. drawn up by an attorney.

3. Vincent is interested in purchasing a certain large parcel of real estate from Derrick. Derrick does not live on the property. Which of the following facts about the property could Vincent discover by inspecting the title record?

   a. A family is, without Derrick's knowledge, living in an abandoned house on the property.
   b. The local bank holds a mortgage loan against the property.
   c. The local telephone company has an easement across the property where telephone poles and wires are installed.
   d. A fence, erected by the nearest neighbor to the east of the property, actually stands on Derrick's land, two feet west of the property line.

4. If a federally related loan is involved with a transaction, who has the right to choose a title insurance company?

   a. The lender
   b. The seller
   c. Either the buyer or the seller
   d. The buyer

5. Expanded title insurance coverage generally includes what coverage?

   a. Mechanics' liens, mortgage liens, street assessments
   b. Mechanics' liens to the property lines
   c. Mechanics' liens to fence line of property
   d. Mechanics' liens to drip line of house

6. An acronym used for standardized forms used by title insurance companies is

   a. EPA.   c. ALTA.
   b. UCC.   d. RESPA.

CHAPTER TEN

REAL ESTATE LICENSE LAW

Notice: It is important that you understand that the information in this section is a summary of the Idaho Real Estate License Law. You must check the current copy of the Idaho License Law and rules for the latest changes and updates that may have been adopted since this book was last printed and/or revised.

■ REAL ESTATE LICENSE LAW

The Idaho Real Estate Commission regulates real estate activity in the state. Although sketchy from various Idaho laws enacted in 1921, the Idaho Real Estate License Law, Chapter 20, Title 54 of the Idaho Code, was legislated in 1947 with the creation of the Real Estate Brokers Board to regulate the real estate profession in Idaho. The law was amended in 1951 to separate real estate licensure from the Bureau of Occupational Licensing with two types of licenses—broker and salesperson. Requirements of the 1951 legislation included successful completion of an exam, a satisfactory credit report, and a bond in the sum of $1,000 (credit report and bonding no longer required). The law has been amended numerous times since then.

You can obtain a current copy of the Idaho Real Estate License Law and Rules by writing to the Idaho Real Estate Commission, P.O. Box 83720, Boise, Idaho 83720-0077.

Online Information

You can also download the Idaho Real Estate License Law and Rules via the Idaho Real Estate Commission Web site at

WWWeb.Link

www.idahorealestatecommission.com
www.irec.idaho.gov

The license law is divided into two parts. In addition to the law itself, the Commission, as authorized by the law, has adopted a number of rules that elaborate on the basic law and provide additional requirements for Idaho real estate licensees. The summaries of the law and the rules of the Idaho Real Estate Commission in this chapter are intended to acquaint you with their general provisions. Idaho licensees are required to know the contents of the Idaho Real Estate License Law and Rules manual.

■ WHO MUST BE LICENSED [IC 54-2002]

No person shall engage in the real estate business or act as a real estate broker or salesperson in Idaho without first obtaining a license. The penalty for a person convicted of operating without a license is a fine of up to $5,000 and/or imprisonment for up to one year. The penalty for corporations or limited liability companies (LLCs) is a fine of up to $10,000 [IC 54-2065].

In addition, no person engaged in the real estate business or acting as a broker or salesperson may file a court suit to collect payment for such activities unless that person can prove that he or she was properly licensed at the time the activities or services in question were performed.

Definitions

Real estate broker [IC 54-2004].   A real estate broker means and includes any person who, while acting for another person for compensation or the promise of compensation—or any actively licensed broker under the provisions of this act while acting in his or her own behalf—performs any of the following activities with regard to real estate, business opportunities, or an interest in real estate or business opportunities:

- Sells or offers for sale
- Lists or offers to list
- Buys or offers to buy
- Negotiates or offers to negotiate
- Either directly or indirectly negotiates, purchases, sells, or exchanges real estate or any interest therein or business opportunity or interest therein for others
- Represents or advertises to the public in any way that he or she engages in any of these activities
- Takes part in any way in procuring prospects or in negotiating or closing any transaction that is intended to result in one of these activities
- Buys, sells, or offers to buy or sell options, or otherwise acts as a dealer in options

In addition, a real estate broker who sells, lists, buys, or offers to sell, list, or buy *personal property* in conjunction with or as a part of his or her real estate practice must comply with the law and the rules.

Associate real estate broker [IC 54-2004].   An *associate broker* is any person who qualifies as a real estate broker under the laws of Idaho, who is licensed under and associated with a designated broker, and who directly or indirectly represents that broker in the performance of any of the activities described under the definition of broker. The associate broker's license names the specific broker with whom he or she is associated.

Real estate salesperson [54-2004].   A real estate salesperson is any person who has qualified under the laws of Idaho, who is licensed under and associated with a designated broker, and who directly or indirectly represents that broker in the performance of any of the previously described activities.

Person [IC 54-2004].   The word *person* includes an individual, or any legal business entity such as a partnership, corporation, or limited liability company (LLC).

Business opportunity [IC 54-2004].   The term *business opportunity* is defined to include an established business, the goodwill of an established business, or any interest in a business for which a sale or transfer of an interest in land is involved in the transaction (this also includes an assignment of a lease).

Dealer in options [IC 54-2004].   An *option* is a contract conveying a right to buy or sell real estate at a specified price during a stipulated period. Any person, firm, partnership, association, or corporation that directly or indirectly takes, obtains, or uses options to purchase, exchange, rent, or lease real property for another person is a *dealer in options*. It makes no difference if the options are in the dealer's name or if title to the real estate in question is ever held briefly by the dealer in connection with the ultimate transaction.

**Exceptions
[IC 54-2003]**

The Idaho Real Estate License Law does not apply to the following persons, provided they are not active Idaho real estate licensees:

- Any person who purchases any real estate, option in real property, or business opportunity for his or her own account or use
- Any person who holds a property owner's power of attorney when that power of attorney was given for the purpose of completing a single transaction
- Any owner or any regular, salaried employee of the owner acting within the scope of his or her employment who sells, exchanges, purchases, or carries out any other disposition of property or business opportunity
- Any attorney at law acting in the performance of his or her regular duties
- Any receiver, trustee in bankruptcy, guardian, administrator, executor, or personal representative of an estate
- Any person acting under a court order or selling under a deed of trust
- Any property management, rental, or leasing agent

Any attempt to evade the exceptions to licensure shall be considered the unlawful and unlicensed practice of real estate.

■ THE IDAHO REAL ESTATE COMMISSION [IC 54-2005 THROUGH 54-2010]

**Organization and
Members**

The Idaho Real Estate Commission was created in 1947, as authorized by the license law. The Commission is composed of four members: one each from the northern, southeastern, southwestern, and south central sections of the state. Commission members are selected and appointed by the governor of Idaho. The law requires that Commission members be licensed real estate brokers with a minimum of five years experience in the real estate business in Idaho.

Each Commission member serves a four-year term and holds office until his or her successor is appointed and qualified. Upon the death, resignation, or removal of any member, the governor will appoint a qualified successor to serve out the unexpired term. The governor may also remove a member from office for neglect of duty, incompetency, or unprofessional or dishonorable behavior.

Duties and Powers

Each year the Commission selects one member to serve as chairperson. In administering and enforcing the license law, the Commission has the power to create and enforce any necessary rules.

Generally, these rules clarify the broader provisions of the law and describe more specific requirements for applicants and licensees. In addition, the Commission is specifically responsible for conducting examinations to determine the competency of real estate license applicants. A license may not be issued by the Commission unless a majority of the members agree on the applicant's qualifications.

Records and procedures.   The Commission is also responsible for maintaining records and for making these records open to public inspection. However, the Commission may refuse to disclose certain information without a court order. Refer to the open records law for more information on the specific types of information affected.

Executive Director

The executive director of the Commission is an administrator employed by the Commission to direct the operation of its activities. In general, the executive director operates the Commission's office, hires and supervises the staff, and maintains records of all Commission activities. The director's responsibilities also include preparing and conducting the examinations, issuing licenses, preparing a news bulletin that is sent to all licensees, investigating complaints of license law violations, taking any necessary action against a licensee, and correcting violations (subject to the Commission's approval). In addition, the executive director is responsible for promoting high standards of practice in Idaho's real estate industry by organizing and conducting educational programs.

■ LICENSING PROCEDURE

Applications and Requirements [IC 54-2012]

An application for a real estate license must be made on a form provided by the Idaho Real Estate Commission. Every applicant must

- be at least 18 years of age;
- furnish proof to the Commission that he or she is a high school graduate or holder of a certificate of general education development from any state;
- not have had a real estate license revoked or renewal refused in any state within five years before applying for a license in Idaho;
- not have been convicted of any felony in a state or federal court within five years from the date the person was convicted or completed any term of probation or confinement or period of parole;
- show proof of the successful completion of appropriate educational requirements;

- show proof of passing the license examination within 12 months prior to the license application date;
- sign and file with the Commission an irrevocable consent to service allowing the Commission's executive director to act as the licensee's agent upon whom all judicial and other process or legal notices to licensees may be served;
- be fingerprinted on a Commission approved form by a duly authorized law enforcement agency and have it on file with the Idaho Real Estate Commission; and
- certify to the Commission that he is in compliance with the errors and omissions insurance requirements.

Broker requirements [IC 54-2012].   In addition to these general requirements, an applicant for the real estate broker's (or associate broker's) license must have actively worked as a real estate salesperson for two years within the five years prior to the application date.

Active experience typically includes working a minimum of 30 hours per week, doing real estate business during at least 100 weeks of a 24-month period with approximately 15 to 20 sales and listings resulting in over $2 million in total sales volume. The Commission may, however, reduce or eliminate this requirement based on the applicant's educational background, experience as a real estate broker in another state, or experience in related business activities.

The broker's license applicant is also required to furnish a report, certified by his or her broker, of listings and sales accomplished by the applicant during two of the last five years of licensure.

Educational requirements [IC 54-2022].   Applicants for a salesperson's license must successfully complete a total of 90 classroom hours, or equivalent study approved by the Commission, in basic real estate principles and practices within five years prior to applying for a license.

Applicants for a broker's license must successfully complete, prior to licensing, a minimum of four courses totaling 90 additional classroom hours or equivalent correspondence study in real estate subjects as approved by the Commission. That is, a total of 180 hours is required to qualify for a broker's license. Courses may be taken at any university, college, junior college, or a privately owned real estate school approved by the Commission.

All courses must include a final examination and provide a certificate of successful completion that the applicant must furnish to the Commission. An applicant who has completed a course not previously approved by the Commission may submit a certificate of completion along with a course description; the Commission then will determine whether the course meets its requirements.

License Examinations [IC 54-2014]

Every applicant for a real estate broker's, associate broker's, or salesperson's license must take and successfully pass a state examination. Each applicant should understand the information in the *Candidate Handbook*, which is available from the Real Estate Commission, before applying to take the examination. This booklet explains the procedures necessary to take the state examination.

The Idaho broker's and salesperson's examination is offered four times a week in Boise (Tuesday through Saturday); the second and fourth Saturday in Coeur d'Alene; every Saturday in Pocatello; and Tuesday through Saturday in Spokane, Washington.

Candidates can register for the examination by calling Promissor at 1-887-540-5833 or by faxing the reservation form in the *Candidate Handbook* to 1-888-204-6291. Read the *Candidate Handbook* before making reservations so you have all the necessary information for processing.

Online Information

You may view Promissor examination dates, fees, and registration information and obtain a link to the Idaho *Candidate Handbook* at the Idaho Real Estate Commission Web site.

WWWeb.Link

www.idahorealestatecommission.com
www.irec.idaho.gov
www.promissor.com

Walk-in candidates still need to make phone reservations. Although every effort will be made by the testing service to accommodate all candidates, walk-in candidates cannot be guaranteed admission to the examination.

If a candidate with a disability needs special accommodations to be able to take the examination, he or she must notify the testing service by submitting a written request with his or her examination application. The request should indicate some explanation of the assistance needed.

All applicants are allowed four hours to complete the examination. A passing score on each part of the national and state portions is 70 on the salesperson's examination and 75 on the broker's examination.

The salesperson's examination consists of two parts. The first part is national in scope and contains 80 questions. Around ten percent of these questions involve mathematical computations. The second part consists of 40 questions (sales) and 50 questions (broker) specific to real estate laws and rules in Idaho.

Each portion of the exam contains five additional pretest questions that will not affect the final score in any way.

All persons taking the license examination must achieve a passing score on both the national and Idaho sections within a one-year period of passing the initial examination. What this means is that if an individual passes one portion of the examination but fails the other, the individual will then need to retake and pass the failed portion within one year of the date of the initial portion already passed. There is no limit to the number of times an applicant may retake an examination; however, passing scores on both the national and Idaho portions of the examination must be achieved within the one-year period described above.

Candidates will have their answer sheets scored immediately after finishing the examination. An applicant who fails the license examination may retake it on a regularly scheduled examination date. However, the applicant must wait a minimum of 24 hours before retaking. The applicant need only retake the portion he or she failed.

The candidate must then apply for a license within one year of the date he or she passed both portions of the examination or retake and successfully pass the whole examination.

■ FEES

As discussed previously, every preregistered applicant for a real estate broker's, associate broker's, or salesperson's license examination must pay a nonrefundable examination fee to the examination service. An original license fee is payable to the Idaho Real Estate Commission when the license is issued.

Fees for securing or retaining a real estate license include but are not limited to

- each preregistered or walk-in examination taken;
- each examination retake;
- fingerprinting;
- errors and omissions insurance;
- change of license information;
- each licensed branch office;
- issuance and renewal of an original license; and
- license and/or education history.

The actual amount of the fees charged by the Idaho Real Estate Commission or its duly authorized representatives can be determined by contacting the Commission.

Legal Business Entities [IC 54-2016]

A corporation, partnership, limited partnership, limited liability partnership (LLP), or limited liability company (LLC) may be granted a license provided that it complies with certain requirements. All five entities must appoint an officer, member, or general partner to be the *designated broker*. A sole proprietor does not have to make application as a legal business entity.

The designated broker must be an individual who qualifies as a broker and has passed the broker's examination.

To secure a broker's license, a licensee must provide proof of two years of active real estate experience within the last five years. To qualify as "active experience," factors considered include doing real estate business at least 30 hours a week during at least 100 weeks of a 24-month period with approximately 15 to 20 sales and listings resulting in over $2 million in total sales volume.

The designated broker's license application or notice of change is submitted at the same time as the entity's separate, properly completed application for a license, including proof of errors and omissions insurance. The entity's renewal date is the same as that of its designated broker. The Commission has the authority to investigate firms to determine their legal existence at the time a license or renewal application is submitted.

Corporations. The designated broker must be an officer of the corporation. In addition to the general application requirements, the corporation must submit a copy of its Idaho certificate of incorporation or an Idaho certificate of authority. The corporation must also submit a copy of the minutes or a resolution listing the names and addresses of its officers and directors and naming the person as a designated broker.

The license will be issued in the name of the corporation, listing the designated broker, and will use the designated broker's birth date for calculating the renewal date. If a licensee is the designated broker of more than one corporation, all such corporations must be located at the same business.

Partnerships. The designated broker of a general partnership, limited partnership, or limited liability partnership must be a general partner. A general partnership must also submit a list of its members' names and addresses and an agreement naming the designated broker. A limited partnership's application must include its certificate of limited partnership, a partnership agreement naming the designated broker, a list of all members' names and addresses, and an agreement naming the designated broker. A limited liability partnership must provide copies of its registration application and an agreement naming its designated broker.

Limited liability companies. In addition to the general application requirements, a limited liability company (LLC) must submit a copy of its filed and numbered articles of organization or registration application in the case of a foreign LLC. The LLC's operating agreement, in which the designated broker is named, and a list of the names and addresses of the LLC's members and manager must also be submitted to the Commission. The designated broker of an LLC may be either a member or a manager of the LLC.

Sole proprietorships. An individual not licensed by any other form of legal entity shall be licensed as a sole proprietor. Any such business under an assumed business name shall provide satisfactory proof of having filed a dba (doing business as) with the Idaho Secretary of State.

■ LICENSEES FROM ANOTHER STATE SEEKING AN IDAHO LICENSE [IC 54-2015]

An individual who holds an active license in good standing in another state or jurisdiction may, upon written request to the Commission, obtain a certificate of waiver of the national portion of the exam required for Idaho licensure.

An individual who is currently and actively licensed in another state or jurisdiction that administers a real estate exam may be issued a primary Idaho license without further exam or proof of educational prerequisites pursuant to written agreement between Idaho and the other state or jurisdiction, provided that such other state or jurisdiction allows the issuance of real estate licensees in substantially the same manner as set forth by Idaho license requirements.

Irrevocable consent to service [IC 54-2012]. All applicants for a real estate license shall sign and file with the Commission an Irrevocable Consent to Service, appointing the Commission's Executive Director to act as the licensee's agent upon whom all judicial and other process or legal notices directed to such licensee may be served.

All licensees shall provide the Commission a full and current mailing address and/or any changes within 10 business days of the change.

■ OUT-OF-STATE REAL ESTATE BROKERS/LICENSEES NOT LICENSED IN IDAHO

Out-of-state real estate brokers and sales associates who are *not licensed* as brokers or sales associates in Idaho should be aware that they

- may not enter Idaho to list, show, represent, or inspect Idaho property;
- may not advertise Idaho property in Idaho;
- may not have a sign placed on Idaho property;
- may not make initial contact by phone or mail to any potential clients in Idaho;
- probably could not sue for a commission if an owner of a property decided not to pay the brokers; and
- could be punished by a fine and/or one year in jail if acting as a broker or sales associate in Idaho without a license.

This does not prevent an out-of-state broker or sales associate from cooperating with an Idaho broker on the sale of Idaho property. An out-of-state broker or sales associate may accompany an Idaho licensee who is doing any of the above. In addition, a broker licensed in Idaho may share his or her commission with a broker licensed in another state as compensation for work done by the broker in the other state.

■ REAL ESTATE RECOVERY ACCOUNT [IC 54-2069 AND 2070]

Upon the original application or renewal of every license for a two-year period, the licensee shall pay a $20 fee, in addition to the original or renewal license fee. This fee is paid into the state treasury and is credited to the special real estate fund as provided in IC 54-2021. A balance of $20,000 is maintained in the account to satisfy claims against Idaho real estate licensees.

Recovery from the Fund [IC 54-2071]

The maximum claim that may be paid out of the account is $10,000 per licensee per calendar year. The claim must be based on some fraud, misrepresentation, or deceit practiced by the licensee in connection with a real estate transaction. An aggrieved party who wishes to collect a claim from the account has the following possible course of action.

The aggrieved party must start by filing a suit against the licensee. After obtaining a final judgment in any court of competent jurisdiction and after all proceedings, including appeals, are concluded, the aggrieved person then may petition the court to direct payment of the judgment out of the account. A copy of the petition must be served on the Commission and the court must hold a hearing and act on the petition within 30 days of that service.

At the hearing, the petitioner must show that he or she has obtained a proper judgment and complied with all requirements concerning the account. The petitioner also must show that all possible legal steps were taken to collect the judgment from the defendant licensee and that the licensee does not have enough funds or property to satisfy the judgment. In addition, the petitioner must prove that he or she is not the licensee's spouse or a representative of the licensee's spouse.

At any court action requesting money from the fund to satisfy a claim against a licensee, the Commission may take steps to defend the licensee and/or review the case. Based on the Commission's findings and subject to the court's approval, the Commission may be able to reach a compromise on a petitioner's claim.

Automatic suspension [IC 54-2074]. Whenever the Commission is directed by a court to pay out money from the account, the license of the broker, associate broker, or salesperson against whom the claim is made is automatically suspended.

This person's license will not be reinstated until he or she has repaid the account with the full amount plus interest at the highest rate allowed by law. The repayment of funds does not nullify or modify the effect of any other disciplinary action the Commission may take against the licensee.

Waiver of rights [IC 54-2077]. The failure of a person to comply with all of the provisions of the Recovery Fund shall constitute a waiver of any rights.

■ GENERAL OPERATION OF A REAL ESTATE BUSINESS

Place of Business [IC 54-2040]

Every Idaho real estate designated broker, except those brokers licensed by reciprocity, must maintain a physical office location as a principal place of business. The broker must conduct business only under the name and at the address indicated on his or her license. In that place of business, the broker's license must be prominently displayed along with those of all licensees who work there. It is unlawful for a salesperson to use the broker's license and operate a real estate business in the broker's name when the broker has only nominal control of the business affairs.

More than one broker, however, can maintain an office at the same address. Under these circumstances, each broker must keep separate records and trust accounts and operate under a separate and distinct business name that clearly identifies each individual broker.

Branch office [IC 54-2016]. When a broker establishes one or more licensed branch offices in which trust funds and original transaction files are maintained, a separate license must be obtained for each branch office. Each branch office must operate under the same name as the parent office. The designated broker is responsible for all business transacted in the branch office.

Every branch office licensed to do business in Idaho must be managed by a licensed broker or associate broker. The manager must be designated on the application for a branch office when it is filed with the Commission. The Commission must also be notified of any change in the designated manager of a branch office.

However, any salesperson acting as branch manager on July 1, 2005, shall have until July 1, 2006, to obtain an associate broker's license. Existing associate brokers managing a branch office will also need to complete a commission-approved business conduct and office operations course if they have not already done so within five years immediately prior to being named branch manager.

When a branch office is closed and real estate business is no longer transacted at that location, the broker must give the Commission written notice of the closing, along with the licenses of all people affiliated with that office. The Commission then will process the license transfer of each licensee individually.

Change of business name or location [IC 54-2040]. The Commission also must be notified of any change in a broker's business name, address, or licensed branch office. Inactive licensees have ten days following any change of address or personal telephone number to report the change to the Commission [IC 54-2018].

■ LICENSES

Every real estate license states the licensee's name and type of license and must be prominently displayed in the office designated by the Commission as the broker's main office location.

A salesperson's license is mailed to the designated broker at the office with which the salesperson will be affiliated. All new licenses issued by the Idaho Real Estate Commission must be signed by the licensee.

Personal information changes [IC 54-2018].   Any change of a personal name, change of personal residence, or personal telephone number must be provided to the Idaho Real Estate Commission in writing within ten days of the change. This requirement applies to active or inactive licensees.

If a personal name has been changed, legal proof together with a fee for printing a new license shall accompany notification to the Real Estate Commission.

License renewals [IC 54-2018].   The original license expires at 5 P.M. on the last day of the second consecutive birth month following the original license date. Subsequent license terms are based on a two-year period from birth month to birth month of each licensee. A renewal fee and an application must be submitted to renew either an active or inactive license. When renewing, an active licensee will certify successful completion of the continuing education requirement and compliance with the errors and omissions insurance requirement [IC 54-2013]. A portion of each license fee is deposited into the Real Estate Recovery Account [IC 54-2069].

Licensees who fail to renew their licenses on time may still renew within one year after the last renewal date, subject to the Commission's approval and a fine for late renewal and submission of the appropriate applications and fees. Such licenses are expired until they are renewed, and the licensees may not engage in real estate activities during that period.

The renewal fee is the same for a salesperson or broker as that charged for an original license.

When a broker, an associate broker, or a salesperson fails to renew a license promptly, the license expires, and the licensee must cease all real estate activities until the license is renewed.

A licensee can renew in person, by mail, or via the Internet (up to three months prior to license expiration). However, a word of caution is in order. When renewing over the Internet, a licensee is certifying that he or she has successfully completed all continuing education requirements and that errors and omissions insurance is in place as of the date the licensee files for renewal.

Continuing education [IC 54-2023].   Continuing education may be met by attending the entire "live" presentation of approved courses or by taking approved "distance learning" courses. A minimum of 16 hours of approved electives plus a "core course" is required to renew a license. By law, the core course shall not be more than four hours in length. The "commission core course," created annually by the Idaho Real Estate Commission, is effective July 1 of each year.

Errors and omissions insurance [IC 54-2013]. Full coverage by errors and omissions (E&O) insurance shall be certified by a licensee upon renewal as well. A licensee who elects not to participate in the insurance program administered by the Commission shall obtain a certificate of coverage, signed by an authorized agent or employee of the insurance carrier, reflecting proof of insurance. Upon request by the Idaho Real Estate Commission, the licensee shall produce the certificate for inspection.

Termination and transfer of a salesperson's license [IC 54-2056]. If a salesperson terminates with the broker, the broker shall remove from public view the former associate's license certificate. If the broker terminates the licensee, the broker shall notify the Commission in writing of the termination and the facts giving rise to such termination.

Termination of broker status. When an actively licensed broker changes his or her license status to one other than that of designated or individual broker, the broker must inform the Commission immediately of the location of all trust accounts and transaction file records for which he or she was responsible. These records must be available for inspection by the Commission for a period of three years following the year in which each transaction closed.

Surrender, suspension, or revocation of a license. When a real estate broker or sales associate surrenders his or her license or is notified that the license is suspended or revoked, he or she must immediately forward the license to the Commission.

Real Estate Contracts and Documents

The Idaho Real Estate License Law and Rules of the Idaho Real Estate Commission include specific provisions regarding the documents involved in a real estate sales transaction.

A buyer–broker or listing agreement may be established with the buyer or seller as either a customer or a client. If the buyer or seller is a client, then an agency relationship exists and must be explicitly stated in the agreement between the client and the broker.

Agreements for compensation. A licensee may assist, for compensation, either a buyer or a seller in a real estate transaction without establishing a formal agency representation relationship. In this case, the buyer or seller is a customer, and no agency relationship exists. In order to be enforceable in the event of default, this agreement for compensation should be in writing.

Listing agreements (seller representation). Any contract that promises payment of money or other valuable consideration as a commission for finding a purchaser for real estate must be in writing and signed by the owner of the property involved (or by a legal representative of the owner), as well as by the listing broker or the broker's agent. In addition, every listing must include a proper legal description of the property involved, the asking price and acceptable payment terms, the expiration date of the listing, and the commission to be paid to the broker. If the agreement is also creating an agency relationship, appropriate language must be included that identifies it as an agency representation contract. The licensee who obtains the listing must give a true copy of the agreement to the person or persons signing it.

Buyer broker agreements (buyer representation). Any agreement in which a broker is employed to represent a buyer to find a suitable property for purchase must be in writing and signed by the buyer. At the time the agreement is signed, a legible, signed, true, and correct copy must be given to the buyer. The agreement must state a definite expiration date and clarify specific points of agreement, including the level of buyer representation the broker will have with the buyer. If the buyer broker agreement also establishes an agency agreement, appropriate language must be included that identifies it as an agency representation agreement.

Purchase and sale agreements. After a listing agreement is signed, the licensee has certain obligations regarding any known offers to purchase that are executed by prospective purchasers or any offers that may be pending. A purchase and sale agreement, when signed by the prospective purchaser, is considered to be an offer to purchase with a receipt of earnest money, and the licensee must immediately give the prospective purchaser a copy of the agreement as a receipt for that earnest money. The licensee also must make sure that all terms and conditions of the proposed transaction are included in the purchase and sale agreement. In addition, the actual amount of earnest money received from the prospective purchaser and the form of payment must be specifically stated in the agreement.

The licensee is obligated to promptly deliver every written offer to purchase to the owner of the property involved. After the owner accepts an offer and signs the agreement, the licensee then delivers a true, executed copy to the purchaser and the seller. If the offer is rejected, however, the document must be clearly marked "rejected," dated, and retained in the broker's files.

Closing statement. At the closing of the transaction, the broker designated as the responsible broker is responsible for the accuracy of the closing statement and for delivery of a copy of the statement to the purchaser and the seller.

The responsible broker must show proof of proper delivery by obtaining the buyer's and seller's signatures on the file copies of the closing statements or by maintaining a copy of any closing statement transmittal letters kept in files. If the transaction was closed in escrow and the buyer's and seller's signatures are not obtained, the responsible broker must maintain in his or her files a written certification by the escrow officer attesting that the closing documents were properly delivered. A sales associate may handle the closing of a transaction only when authorized by his or her supervising broker.

If the transaction is a co-op sale between two or more brokers, the purchase and sales agreement must state which broker is responsible for closing the transaction. The broker must maintain copies of all documents pertaining to a transaction for three years after the year in which the transaction is closed.

In the broker's records, transactions must be numbered and filed in sequence by transaction number or filed alphabetically.

Double contracts [IC 54-2004, 54-2054, 54-2060]. A *double contract* refers to any separate undisclosed agreement between buyer and seller that contradicts any part of the primary agreement; or two separate purchase and sales agreements or loan applications concerning the same parcel of real estate, one stating the true purchase price and the other stating a larger purchase price.

Such contracts are used to induce a lender (or loan guarantor) to make a loan commitment for a larger amount based on the larger, inflated purchase price quoted on the second document or to include items of personal property that cannot be financed by the lender.

Any licensee found guilty of this act will be subject to disciplinary action by the Commission, including suspension or revocation of his or her license.

Care and Handling of Funds [IC 54-2041 and 54-2044]

All funds entrusted to a broker in connection with a real estate transaction must be immediately (or by the next banking day) placed in an approved escrow depository or in a special trust fund checking account that the broker maintains for this purpose. The separate real estate trust account may be maintained in a licensed title insurance company, a bank, or other approved depository.

A broker may establish more than one trust fund account. Each account should be identified as to the type of activity for which funds will be accounted. The broker may deposit funds in an interest-bearing trust account of an insured depository if directed in writing by the parties to the transaction and if the broker maintains control of the funds so that they are available on demand.

Approved depositories [IC 54-2042].   The broker is held personally responsible for these funds until they are disbursed and a full accounting is made to all parties to the transaction.

The money must be deposited on or before the next *banking* day after the broker receives it, except in situations where the purchase and sales agreement provides that a check given as earnest money is to be held for a specific length of time or to be deposited after the seller has accepted the buyer's offer, or where the agreement provides that the funds received by the broker are to be made payable to and held by a specified escrow closing agent. If any funds are to be deposited with some person, business, or agent other than the broker handling the transaction (such as an attorney or escrow closing company), the broker must keep written instructions signed by the parties as to how such funds are to be deposited and disbursed.

Trust account deposits [IC 54-2045].   All monies received by a broker must be deposited on or before the next *banking* day following receipt unless written instructions direct the broker to do otherwise. The broker must retain a dated receipt in his or her file. A salesperson receiving earnest money deposits or other funds belonging to others in connection with a real estate transaction must immediately turn them over to the broker.

Entrusted funds never may be commingled (mixed in) with a real estate licensee's personal funds.

A broker is prohibited from depositing any funds in the trust account that were not received in connection with a real estate transaction for which he or she is acting as agent, with the exception of a maximum deposit of $300 [IC 54-2042] as necessary to keep the trust account open.

Trust account disbursements [IC 54-2046].   Monies entrusted to a broker by a client may be disbursed only as provided by the terms of the purchase and sales agreement, on written authorization of both buyer and seller or by court order. A broker is not entitled to take any of the earnest money or other entrusted funds as part of his or her commission in advance of closing without written authorization by all parties involved. The purchase and sales agreement must provide for the disbursement of the earnest money if the transaction is not completed and such money is forfeited.

If the transaction is not completed and the consideration is returned before it is deposited in the broker's account, a dated notation to this effect must appear on the copy of the earnest money agreement to be retained in the broker's files.

Trust account record-keeping format [IC 54-2044].   The rules describe the specific records a broker is required to keep regarding deposits and disbursements of entrusted funds. First, the broker must have a set of checks and deposit slips for the special bank account that indicates the broker's business name and address and clearly identifies the account as a "real estate trust account." Checks drawn on this account must be identified as to the specific transactions and retained by the broker along with any voided checks in numerical sequence. The broker also must keep a duplicate bank deposit book that shows the source of each deposit and the date and place it was deposited.

In addition, the broker must keep a journal or record book of itemized deposits and disbursements of entrusted funds and an individual trust ledger sheet for each transaction that notes the details of the transaction and any entrusted funds taken in or paid out by the broker. A real estate trust fund account must be kept up to date. Ledger cards must be maintained in one location and not scattered throughout the broker's files.

The files must be maintained in sequence, either by transaction number or in alphabetical order. The individual transaction trust ledger sheets must be kept in the broker's records for at least three calendar years after the year in which the transaction was closed. Any record-keeping system approved by the Idaho Real Estate Commission or its appointed representatives may be used instead of this system.

Trust account audits [IC 54-2058].   The Idaho Real Estate Commission or its representatives may make periodic investigations of brokers' trust fund accounts. If any deficiency or irregularity is discovered during such an investigation, the Commission may order a complete audit of the account at the broker's expense.

Compensation, Commissions, Fees [IC 54-2054]

A person must obtain a real estate license before being entitled to collect a commission for engaging in real estate activities. IC 54-2002 of the Idaho Real Estate License Law makes it illegal for a licensee to pay part of a real estate commission to, or share a commission with, a person who does not have a real estate license. Splitting a fee with nonlicensed individuals is grounds for the revocation or suspension of a real estate license.

However, a licensee may pay any part of a commission, fee, or compensation received directly to either the buyer, seller, or both providing none of the fees received would directly or indirectly constitute a double contract.

Furthermore, a sales associate is prohibited from accepting any compensation for engaging in real estate activities from any person except the broker with whom he or she is associated. A broker may not accept compensation from more than one party to a transaction without first informing all parties to the transaction of all the facts, in writing.

The amount of commission earned by a broker in any real estate transaction is a matter to be decided between the broker and his or her principal. The Idaho Real Estate Commission does not set uniform rates of commission or recognize any agreement between brokers to standardize rates. The Commission will not interfere in any disputes between licensees concerning commissions.

Other Provisions and Ethical Considerations

Title opinion [Rule 302, 303].   An Idaho real estate licensee may not state a personal opinion on the condition of the title to real estate that is involved in a transaction. In addition, a licensee may not discourage any party to a transaction from consulting an attorney.

Licensee's personal interest [IC 54-2055].   Any licensee who directly, or indirectly through a third party, sells, purchases, acquires, or intends to acquire for personal use any interest in real property or an option to purchase real property must make written disclosure of this situation to the owner and state that he or she is a real estate licensee and the purpose for which the property will be used.

Furthermore, any actively licensed persons buying or selling property for their own account must conduct the transaction through the broker with whom licensed, *whether or not the property is listed.*

Kickbacks and rebates [IC 54-2054].   A licensee shall not receive a kickback or an unearned fee for directing any transaction to any lending institution or any escrow or title company as those practices are defined and prohibited by the Real Estate Settlement and Procedures Act of 1974 as amended [12

USC 2601 et. seq.]. Idaho code also forbids kickbacks or rebates for directing *any* transaction to *any* individual for financing.

Advertising [IC 54-2053]. Any advertisement of real property by an active licensee, whether for his or her own property or for property owned by others, must indicate that it is being made by a person engaged in the real estate business, not a private party. Every advertisement of property that is listed with a broker must be made under the broker's direct supervision, as provided in the listing agreement, and in the broker's business name; advertisements placed by a broker's branch offices also must clearly indicate the broker's business name. Advertising that identifies *only* a post office box number, a telephone number, or a street address is not permitted. These rules regarding advertising refer to all forms of advertising, including newspaper, magazine, and Internet advertisements.

■ SUSPENSION OR REVOCATION OF A LICENSE AND IMPOSITION OF CIVIL PENALTY [IC 54-2059]

The Idaho Real Estate Commission may investigate the actions of any licensee who is suspected of performing one or more prohibited acts while engaging in real estate activities. Such an investigation may be initiated solely by the Commission or it shall be prompted by the verified written complaint of anyone claiming to have been injured or defrauded by the actions of a licensee.

The real estate license of anyone who is found guilty of any number of acts may be suspended or revoked, and a maximum fine *not to exceed $5,000 [may be] imposed, plus costs and attorney fees against the person for the cost of any investigation and/or administrative or other proceedings*.

Any civil penalties collected by the Idaho Real Estate Commission shall be used exclusively for developing and delivering real estate education to the benefit of all Idaho real estate licensees.

Grounds for disciplinary action [IC 54-2060]. Forbidden acts of misconduct include

- making fraudulent misrepresentations;
- engaging in a continued or flagrant course of misrepresentation or making of false promises, whether done personally or through agents or salespersons;
- failure to account for or remit any property, real or personal, or moneys coming into the person's possession that belong to another;
- failure to keep adequate records of all property transactions in which the person acts in the capacity of real estate broker or salesperson;
- failure or refusal, upon lawful demand, to disclose any information within the person's knowledge or to produce any documents, books, or records in the person's possession for inspection by the Commission or its authorized representative;
- acting as a real estate broker or salesperson under an assumed name;

- employment of fraud, deception, misrepresentation, misstatement, or any unlawful means in applying for or securing a license to act as a real estate broker or salesperson in the state of Idaho;
- using, proposing to use, or agreeing to use a "double contract" as prohibited in IC 54-2054;
- seeking or receiving a "kickback" or rebate prohibited in IC 54-2054;
- violation of any provision of IC 54-2001 through 54-2097, or any administrative rule made or promulgated by the Commission, or any final order of the Commission;
- any other conduct whether of the same or a different character than hereinabove specified that constitutes dishonest or dishonorable dealings; and/or
- gross negligence or reckless conduct in a regulated real estate transaction. Conduct is grossly negligent or reckless if, when taken as a whole, it is conduct that substantially fails to meet the generally accepted standard of care in the practice of real estate in Idaho.

Under Idaho Code 54-2061, the Commission may temporarily suspend or permanently revoke a license by court action for some of the following three reasons:

1. The holder is convicted of any felony in a state or federal court or is convicted of a misdemeanor involving moral turpitude. The record of conviction, or a certified copy thereof, certified by the clerk of the court or the judge in whose court the judgment was had, shall be prima facie evidence of conviction in such cases.
2. The holder is declared insane by a court of competent jurisdiction, provided, however, that when a license shall have been revoked or suspended for this cause, such license may be reactivated by the commission upon a declaration of sanity being made.
3. The holder has a judgment entered against him or her in a civil action upon grounds of fraud, misrepresentation, or deceit with reference to any transaction for which a license is required.

If the Commission temporarily suspends or permanently revokes a license and/or imposes a civil penalty, the Commission may withhold execution of the suspension, revocation, and/or civil penalty on terms and for a time as it may prescribe.

A real estate license may be suspended for the licensee's failure to pay child support, as part of Idaho's welfare reform. A delinquency of more than 90 days or $2,000 triggers the commencement of the suspension through the Child Support Services of the Department of Health and Welfare.

If the license of the designated broker of a partnership or corporation is revoked or suspended, the license issued to the partnership or corporation also will be revoked or suspended by the Commission. However, the Commission may withhold execution of the revocation or suspension on terms and for a time as it may prescribe.

The Commission may also accept or reject, at its discretion, any offer to voluntarily terminate the license of a person whose activity is under investigation or against whom a formal complaint has been filed.

Review of agency action [IC 54-2063]. Any person whose real estate license has been suspended or revoked by the Commission has a right to request a review by the district court of the county in which he or she lives. The court will review the proceedings concerning the suspension or revocation.

Errors and Omissions Insurance [IC 54-2013]

Errors and omissions (E&O) insurance coverage insures licensees against lawsuits arising from their own errors or failures to act (omissions) in their capacity as real estate practitioners. A licensee seeking to obtain or renew an *active* license shall certify to the Commission that he or she is in compliance with E&O insurance requirements on the date the licensee makes application for renewal.

Under the Idaho Code, every actively licensed real estate agent and broker must, as a condition of licensing, carry E&O insurance to cover all licensed activities. The Idaho Real Estate Commission will make this insurance available to each licensee by contracting with an insurance provider for E&O insurance coverage.

The annual premium for the insurance provided by the Commission will be at a reasonable premium not to exceed $200 per year per licensee.

Any policy obtained by the Commission will be available to each licensee with no right on the part of the insurance provider to cancel coverage by the licensee.

The Commission will determine the terms and conditions of coverage required under the provisions of this law. The terms and conditions will include, but are not limited to, the minimum limits of coverage, the permissible deductible, and the permissible exemptions.

The licensees will also have the option of obtaining E&O insurance independently if the coverage contained in an independently obtained policy complies with the minimum requirements established by the Commission.

A certificate of coverage, showing compliance with the required terms and conditions of coverage, should be filed with the Commission by the license renewal date by each licensee who elects not to participate in the insurance program administered by the Commission.

The Real Estate Inspector

Periodically, a representative of the Idaho Real Estate Commission will visit a broker's office. The purpose of the inspector's visit is to find and correct problems before they become serious violations. He or she also answers licensees' questions and hears their recommendations regarding the real estate profession and the license law.

The real estate broker who conducts his or her business activities according to the provisions of the license law and principles of good business ethics will find these visits very beneficial.

The Inspector's Visit

Brokers are required to keep certain records of each transaction in their files for at least three calendar years after the year in which the transaction was closed. The inspector will examine all pending transactions, as well as some finalized transactions, comparing the provisions of the purchase and sales agreement of each with the manner in which the transaction was closed. Any deposits and disbursements will be scrutinized to make sure that the account was handled properly and that the broker was authorized to make the disbursements. Prorations, title costs, and other expense items will be checked for correctness.

In addition, the inspector will examine the licenses of all people who work out of the broker's office to make sure that they are current and properly displayed. Any violations will be noted and reported to the Commission. The broker will be advised by the Commission office of what action the Commission has decided to take regarding such violations.

In expectation of the inspector's visit, the broker's files must be kept in good order so that the inspector can easily relate them to the proper trust accounting records. Failure to keep records as required by law is a serious violation that will prompt a more complete investigation of the broker's activities by the Commission staff. Any attempt to hide or withhold information will not be tolerated; ignorance of the law is no excuse.

In general, the inspector's job is to help the broker and to advise the broker on any minor discrepancies. He or she is trained to do a thorough examination and will cooperate with the broker as much as possible under the law. The broker should be prepared to do the same.

When dealing with the inspector, however, the broker should remember that the inspector's authority and training are limited to the Idaho Real Estate License Law and the Commission's Rules. The inspector should not be expected to give advice or assistance on real estate problems that are outside this jurisdiction.

Citations

During the inspector's audit of an office, if certain numbers and types of license law or rule violations are noted within a category, the inspector will write the designated broker a citation for those violations which will carry a mandated civil fine. The amount of the civil fines range from $10 to $75 for each of ten categories.

These categories include: licensing; failure to account for funds; commingling; unauthorized conversion of trust funds; trust account deposits and checks; trust account check register and reconciliation; trust ledgers; transaction records; agency and agency disclosures; and broker supervision and office operations.

The broker must decide within ten days of issuance or receipt of the citation to

- admit to the violations and pay the civil fine;
- admit to only certain violations and pay the appropriate fine; or
- deny all violations and seek formal action by the commission.

The Commission still retains the right to prosecute separate and apart from this citation program those violations that are considered more serious and flagrant.

QUESTIONS

1. Which of the following persons *MUST* have a real estate broker's license in order to transact business?

   a. A person who owns a sixplex and personally manages the building, collects rents, and shows the apartments to prospective tenants
   b. A person who negotiates the sales of entire businesses, including their stock, equipment, and buildings, for a promised fee
   c. The superintendent of a large apartment building, who shows apartments to prospective tenants as part of his or her regular duties
   d. A person who has his or her parent's written authority to negotiate the sale of the parent's residence

2. The Idaho Real Estate Commission consists of how many members?

   a. Seven
   b. Five
   c. Four
   d. Three

3. An applicant for a real estate license in Idaho *MUST*

   a. have completed at least two years of college.
   b. be at least 21 years old.
   c. not have been convicted of a felony within five years before applying.
   d. show proof of passing the license examination any time up to six months prior to the application.

4. Which of the following statements regarding the Idaho Real Estate Commission is *NOT* true?

   a. Members of the Commission are selected by the Idaho Association of Realtors®.
   b. The Commission makes and enforces the rules by which all real estate licensees must abide.
   c. The examinations that must be taken by all applicants for real estate licensing are administered by an independent testing company.
   d. The operation of the Commission's activities is administered by an executive director specifically hired for that purpose.

5. Which of the following statements regarding the licensing of corporations, limited liability companies, and partnerships is *TRUE*?

   a. All the officers, managers, or partners must qualify as brokers and pass a written examination.
   b. The names and addresses of all officers, managers, directors, members, or partners must be submitted with the application.
   c. A separate fee must be paid for each individual broker's license, in addition to the fee for the commercial entity's license.
   d. All applicants must file an irrevocable consent agreement with the Commission.

6. If a person obtains an Idaho reciprocal real estate license, he or she

   a. must be licensed as a broker or salesperson in any state.
   b. must establish a principal place of business in Idaho or be licensed under a resident Idaho broker.
   c. must take all education course requirements in Idaho.
   d. must file an irrevocable consent agreement with the Commission.

7. Whenever the Commission is required to satisfy a claim against a licensee with money from the Real Estate Recovery Account

   a. the licensee may continue engaging in real estate activities under the Commission's direct supervision.
   b. the licensee must repay the full amount plus interest to the account if his or her license is to be reinstated.
   c. the aggrieved party may later collect additional damages by forcing the sale of any property newly acquired by the defendant licensee.
   d. the licensee must thereafter pay $25 per year into the account when applying to renew his or her license.

8. After Frank purchased a new home, Frank discovered that broker Walter had deceived Frank regarding the condition of the property. Frank sued Walter and obtained a judgment against Walter. In order to collect the judgment from the Real Estate Recovery Account, Frank *MUST*

   a. petition the Commission to hold a hearing on the matter.
   b. file a Request for Recovery with the executive director of the Commission.
   c. petition the court to direct payment from the account and then prove that the judgment cannot be collected from Walter in any other way.
   d. apply to the state treasurer for payment from the account.

9. Which of the following statements is *TRUE* of a real estate license?

   a. It is renewed every year.
   b. It must be prominently displayed in the real estate office out of which the licensee works.
   c. It must be carried by the licensee at all times.
   d. It indicates the licensee's home address.

10. Associate broker Jerry is not satisfied with ABC Real Estate and has decided to become associated with DEF Realty instead. Before Jerry can begin actively selling for DEF,

    a. the broker with ABC must transfer Jerry's license to DEF.
    b. Jerry's new broker, DEF, shall submit an approved written application to the Commission.
    c. Jerry must take his license to DEF and notify the Commission, within three days, of the transfer to a new location.
    d. Jerry's license must be returned to the Commission along with the proper fee and form signed by the broker with ABC.

11. A listing agreement entered into between a broker and a client is *NOT* required to

    a. be in writing.
    b. be notarized.
    c. state the amount of the broker's commission.
    d. state a definite termination date.

12. Broker Quincey has obtained an offer to purchase a residence that is listed with Quincey's firm. After the buyers sign a purchase and sale agreement and Quincey accepts their earnest money deposit, Quincey must

    a. deposit the earnest money in his personal checking account for safekeeping until closing.
    b. complete a second earnest money agreement form that states an exaggerated selling price and give the second form to the buyers to present to the lender so that they will be certain to obtain sufficient financing for their purchase.
    c. immediately give the buyers a copy of the agreement as a receipt for their deposit.
    d. file the agreement in his records and, when he has obtained two or three other offers for the property, present them all to the sellers, who then may choose the best offer.

13. In any real estate sales transaction that a broker negotiates, the broker is *NOT* required to

    a. inform the buyer of his or her personal opinion of the condition of the seller's title to the property.
    b. make sure that the written purchase and sales agreement includes all the terms of the parties' agreement.
    c. make sure that the closing statement is accurate and that a copy of it is delivered to both buyer and seller.
    d. keep copies of all documents involved in the transaction in his or her files for three years after the year in which the transaction was closed.

14. In Idaho, brokers are responsible for the accuracy of the closing of real estate sales transactions and the delivery of correct settlement statements to all parties. A salesperson may be delegated to supervise the closing of a transaction

    a. as part of his or her regular duties.
    b. only with the written consent of both buyer and seller.
    c. only when authorized by his or her supervising broker.
    d. only after obtaining written authorization from the Idaho Real Estate Commission.

15. Who is responsible to conduct a real estate related investigation or audit of a broker's records?

    a. The editor of a newspaper, published by the Idaho Real Estate Commission, in which brokers can advertise real property for sale

    b. A trained professional who can be engaged to inspect a parcel of real estate and furnish a written report of the physical condition of the property

    c. A representative of the Idaho Real Estate Commission who periodically visits a broker's office to make sure that the broker is operating according to the provisions of the Real Estate License Law and the Commission's Rules

    d. A county official who examines documents for their validity before they are recorded by the county recorder

16. Which of the following statements is *TRUE* of the commission earned by a broker in a real estate sales transaction?

    a. It is determined by agreement of the broker and his or her principal.

    b. It may be shared with an unlicensed person, provided that such person aided the broker in bringing the buyer and seller together.

    c. It must be deducted from the earnest money deposit and claimed by the broker as soon as the buyer and seller execute the purchase and sales agreement.

    d. It is based on a schedule of commission rates set by the Idaho Real Estate Commission.

17. Broker Annie took a listing for a small office building owned by Dominic. Because the property is in excellent condition and produces a good, steady income, Annie's salesperson has decided to purchase it as an investment. If Annie's salesperson wishes to buy this property, the salesperson *MUST*

    a. resign as Dominic's agent and make an offer after Dominic has retained another broker.

    b. have some third party purchase the property on the salesperson's behalf so that Dominic does not learn the true identity of the purchaser.

    c. obtain permission from the Idaho Real Estate Commission.

    d. inform Dominic in writing that the salesperson is a licensee before making an offer.

18. Broker Bart obtained an offer to purchase a residence and accepted an earnest money deposit from the buyers; the sellers accepted the offer. The parties agreed to deposit the earnest money and close the transaction in escrow, with GHI Title Insurance Company of Idaho acting as escrow agent. The earnest money was immediately deposited in a trust account maintained with GHI Title Insurance Company. Which of the following statements is *TRUE*?

    a. Bart's license will probably be suspended as a result of these actions.

    b. Bart acted improperly in depositing the earnest money with GHI, and so Bart's license will be revoked.

    c. Bart acted properly in this situation.

    d. Although Bart acted improperly in this situation, Bart's license will probably not be suspended or revoked.

19. A licensee purchased an unlisted property from a For Sale By Owner and correctly stated in the offer that the licensee was an active agent in the state of Idaho. What must the agent also do?

    a. Report the purchase to the Idaho Real Estate Commission

    b. Advise the closing agent (escrow) of the license status

    c. Make sure the transaction is processed through a title insurance company

    d. Conduct the transaction through the broker with whom licensed

CHAPTER ELEVEN

REAL ESTATE FINANCING

In Idaho, a *lien theory* state, a mortgage may not be considered a conveyance, regardless of its terms or wording. For this reason, the holder of a mortgage cannot recover possession of the real estate upon the borrower's default without a judicial foreclosure sale.

■ PROMISSORY NOTES

A promissory note is one of two instruments executed by a borrower in connection with a mortgage or deed of trust loan. The notes usually used in real estate financing are *negotiable instruments* that facilitate the holder's ability to transfer his or her right to payment to a third party.

The Uniform Commercial Code

The Uniform Commercial Code (UCC) governs negotiable instruments and defines a *negotiable instrument* as a written, unconditional promise or order to pay a certain sum of money, either on demand or on a certain date, payable to order or bearer, and signed by the maker.

The transfer may be accomplished by signing the negotiable note over to the third party or, in some cases, by merely delivering the instrument to another party. Endorsing the note over to a third party may be accomplished by a *blank endorsement*—the payee signing the back of the note.

Another method is by *special endorsement* where a specific person is named as the new payee on the back and then the original payee signs. When the payee does not want to be liable to the new owner of the note for future payments by the maker, he or she can state the endorsement is *without recourse*, and the issue of future payments will be between the maker and the new owner of the note.

If the new holder of the note has obtained the negotiable instrument in the ordinary course of business, before it is due, in good faith and for value, without knowledge that it has been previously dishonored, and without notice of any defect or setoff at the time it was negotiated, then that transferee meets all the requisites to qualify as a *holder in due course*.

Types of Notes

Two types of promissory notes are generally used with mortgages and trust deeds. A *straight note* calls for periodic payments of interest with the principal to be paid at the end of the loan term.

The second type, the *installment note*, may call for a set periodic payment of principal and additional amount for interest: the payments will not necessarily be the same for each period.

■ DEED OF TRUST

Idaho legislature authorizes the use of deeds of trust (trust deeds) in real estate loans in which the property securing the debt is *not more than 40 acres or is within an incorporated city*. A deed of trust is a three-party document involving the borrower, known in Idaho as the *grantor (trustor)*; the *lender* or *beneficiary*; and the *trustee*, the third party to whom legal title to the real estate is conveyed by the deed of trust.

Any one of the following may serve as a trustee in Idaho:

1. A member of the Idaho State Bar (attorney)
2. A bank or savings and loan association authorized to conduct business under Idaho or federal law
3. A corporation authorized to conduct a trust business under Idaho or federal law
4. A title insurance agent or company authorized to transact business under Idaho law

Because most deed of trust loans are long term, a trustee who will be able to serve for a long period of time should be chosen. Because the business affairs of a financial institution or title company do not terminate upon the death of one officer, the trusteeship of such an institution or company cannot be interrupted for this reason.

In the event of the death, incapacity, disability, or resignation of an individual trustee, the beneficiary may name another qualified trustee to acquire the same power and authority of the original trustee. In the event of a breach or default of the deed of trust, the trustee has the *power of sale* to foreclose and sell the property without court proceedings. Figure 11.1 is an example of a typical deed of trust form used in Idaho.

Repayment of Mortgage or Deed of Trust Loans

Deed of trust.   When a real estate loan secured by a deed of trust has been completely repaid, the beneficiary certifies this fact by completing the *request for reconveyance* form located on the reverse side of the deed of trust and delivering it to the trustee together with the paid promissory note. After receiving this written request from the beneficiary, the trustee executes and delivers a *deed of reconveyance* to the grantor conveying the property back to the grantor with the same rights and powers that the trustee was given under the deed of trust.

F I G U R E 11.1

Deed of Trust

A Pioneer Company

PIONEER TITLE COMPANY

OF ADA COUNTY

8151 W. Rifleman Ave. / Boise, Idaho 83704

(208) 377-2700

DEED OF TRUST

THIS **DEED OF TRUST**, Made this, BETWEEN _____, herein called GRANTOR, whose address is_____; PIONEER TITLE COMPANY OF ADA COUNTY, herein called TRUSTEE; and whose mailing address is,_____,, herein called BENEFICIARY;

WITNESSETH: That Grantor does hereby irrevocably GRANT, BARGAIN, SELL AND CONVEY TO TRUSTEE IN TRUST, WITH POWER OF SALE, that property in the County of Ada, State of Idaho, described as follows and containing not more than forty acres:

TOGETHER WITH the rents, issues and profits thereof, SUBJECT, HOWEVER, to the right, power and authority hereinafter given to and conferred upon Beneficiary to collect and apply such rents, issues and profits, for the purpose of securing payment of the indebtedness evidenced by a promissory note, of even date herewith, executed by Grantor in the sum of (), final payment due , and to secure payment of all such further sums as may hereafter be loaned or advanced by the Beneficiary herein to the Grantor herein, or any or either of them, while record owner of present interest, for any purpose, and of any notes, drafts or other instruments representing such further loans, advances or expenditures together with interest on all such sums at the rate therein provided. Provided, however, that the making of such further loans, advances or expenditures shall be optional with the Beneficiary, and provided, further, that it is the express intention of the parties to this Deed of Trust that it shall stand as continuing security until paid for all such advances together with interest thereon.

A.   **To protect the security of this Deed of Trust, Grantor agrees:**

(1)   To keep said property in good condition and repair; not to remove or demolish any building thereon; to complete or restore promptly and in good and workmanlike manner any building which may be constructed, damaged or destroyed thereon and to pay when due all claims for labor performed and materials furnished therefor; to comply with all laws affecting said property or requiring any alterations or improvements to be made thereon; not to commit or permit waste thereon; not to commit, suffer or permit any act upon said property in violation of law; to cultivate; irrigate, fertilize, fumigate, prune and do all other acts which from the character or use of said property may be reasonably necessary, the specific enumerations herein not excluding the general.

(2)   To provide, maintain and deliver to Beneficiary fire, vandalism and malicious mischief insurance satisfactory to and with loss payable to Beneficiary. The amount collected under any fire or other insurance policy may be applied by Beneficiary upon any indebtedness secured hereby and in such order as beneficiary may determine, or at option of Beneficiary the entire amount so collected or any part thereof may be released to Grantor. Such application or release shall not cure or waive any default or notice of default hereunder or invalidate any act done pursuant to such notice. The provisions hereof are subject to the mutual agreements of the parties as below set forth.

(3)   To appear in and defend any action or proceeding purporting to affect the security hereof or the rights or powers of Beneficiary or Trustee and to pay all costs and expenses, including cost of evidence of title and attorneys' fees in a reasonable sum, in any such action or proceeding in which Beneficiary or Trustee may appear, and in any suit brought by Beneficiary to foreclose this Deed of Trust.

(4)   To pay: (a) at least ten days before delinquency all taxes and assessments affecting said property, including assessments on appurtenant water stock; (b) when due, subject to the mutual agreements of the parties as below set forth, all encumbrances, charges and liens, with interest, on said property or any part thereof, which appear to be prior or superior hereto; (c) all allowable expenses of this Trust.

(5)   Should Grantor fail to make any payment or to do any act as herein provided, then Beneficiary or Trustee, but without obligation so to do and without notice to or demand upon Trustor and without releasing Grantor from any obligation hereof, may: make or do the same in such manner and to such extent as either may deem necessary to protect the security hereof, Beneficiary or Trustee being authorized to enter upon said property for such purposes; appear in and defend any action or proceeding purporting to affect the security hereof or the rights or powers of Beneficiary or Trustee; pay, purchase, contest or compromise any encumbrance, charge or lien which in the judgment of either appears to be prior or superior hereto; and, in exercising any such power, pay allowable expenses.

(6)   To pay immediately and without demand all sums so expended by Beneficiary or Trustee, with interest from date of expenditure at the amount allowed by law in effect at the date hereof.

F I G U R E   11.1

Deed of Trust (continued)

B.   It is mutually agreed that:

(1)   Any award of damages in connection with any condemnation for public use of or injury to said property or any part thereof is hereby assigned and shall be paid to Beneficiary who may apply or release such moneys received by him in the same manner and with the same effect as above provided for disposition of proceeds of fire or other insurance.

(2)   By accepting payment of any sum secured hereby after its due date, Beneficiary does not waive his right either to require prompt payment when due of all other sums so secured or to declare default for failure so to pay.

(3)   At any time or from time to time, without liability therefor and without notice, upon written request of Beneficiary and presentation of this Deed and said note for endorsement, and without affecting the personal liability of any person for payment of the indebtedness secured hereby, Trustee may: reconvey all or any part of said property; consent to the making of any map or plat thereof; join in granting any easement thereon; or join in any extension agreement or any agreement subordinating the lien or charge hereof.

(4)   Upon written request of Beneficiary stating that all sums secured hereby have been paid, and upon surrender of this Deed and said note to Trustee for cancellation and retention and upon payment of its fees, Trustee shall reconvey, without warranty, the property then held hereunder. The recitals in any reconveyance executed under this deed of trust of any matters or facts shall be conclusive proof of the truthfulness thereof. The grantee in such reconveyance may be described as "the person or persons legally entitled thereto."

(5)   As additional security, Grantor hereby gives to and confers upon Beneficiary the right, power and authority, during the continuance of these Trusts, to collect the rents, issues and profits of said property, reserving unto Grantor the right, prior to any default by Grantor in payment of any indebtedness secured hereby or in performance of any agreement hereunder, to collect and retain such rents, issues and profits as they become due and payable. Upon any such default, Beneficiary may at any time without notice, either in person, by agent, or by a receiver to be appointed by a court, and without regard to the adequacy of any security for the indebtedness hereby secured, enter upon and take possession of said property or any part thereof, in his own name sue for or otherwise collect such rents, issues and profits, including those past due and unpaid, and apply the same, less costs and expenses of operation and collection, including reasonable attorney's fees, upon any indebtedness secured hereby, and in such order as Beneficiary may determine. The entering upon and taking possession of said property, the collection of such rents, issues and profits and the application thereof as aforesaid, shall not cure or waive any default or notice of default hereunder or invalidate any act done pursuant to such notice.

(6)   Upon default by Grantor in payment of any indebtedness secured hereby or in performance of any agreement hereunder, all sums secured hereby shall immediately become due and payable at the option of the Beneficiary. In the event of default, Beneficiary shall execute or cause the Trustee to execute a written notice of such default and of his election to cause to be sold the herein described property to satisfy the obligations hereof, and shall cause such notice to be recorded in the office of the recorder of each county wherein said real property or some part thereof is situated.

Notice of sale having been given as then required by law, and not less than the time then required by law having elapsed, Trustee, without demand on Grantor, shall sell said property at the time and place fixed by it in said notice of sale, either as a whole or in separate parcels and in such order as it may determine, at public auction to the highest bidder for cash in lawful money of the United States, payable at time of sale. Trustee shall deliver to the purchaser its deed conveying the property so sold, but without any covenant or warranty express or implied. The recitals in such deed of any matters or facts shall be conclusive proof of the truthfulness thereof. Any person, including Grantor, Trustee, or Beneficiary, may purchase at such sale.

After deducting all costs, fees and expenses of Trustee and of this Trust, including cost of title evidence of title and reasonable counsel fees in connection with sale, Trustee shall apply the proceeds of sale to payment of: all sums expended under the terms hereof, not then repaid, with accrued interest at ten percent per annum; all other sums then secured hereby; and the remainder, if any, to the person or persons legally entitled thereto.

(7)   This Deed applies to, inures to the benefit of, and binds all parties hereto, their heirs, legatees, devisees, administrators, executors, successors and assigns. The term Beneficiary shall mean the holder and owner of the note secured hereby; or, if the note has been pledged, the pledgee thereof. In this Deed, whenever the context so requires, the masculine gender includes the feminine and/or neuter, and the singular number includes the plural.

(8)   Trustee is not obligated to notify any party hereto of pending sale under any other Deed of Trust or of any action or proceeding in which Grantor, Beneficiary or Trustee shall be a party unless brought by Trustee.

(9)   In the event of dissolution or resignation of the Trustee, the Beneficiary may substitute a trustee or trustees to execute the trust hereby created, and when any such substitution has been filed for record in the office of the Recorder of the county in which the property herein described is situated, it shall be conclusive evidence of the appointment of such trustee or trustees, and such new trustee or trustees shall succeed to all of the powers and duties of the trustees named herein.

Request is hereby made that a copy of any Notice of Default and a copy of any Notice of Sale hereunder be mailed to the Grantor at his address herein before set forth.

_____   _____

_____   _____

Read and Approved by Beneficiary:

Deed of Trust (continued)

_____

Notary Public of
Residing at
Commission expires:

REQUEST FOR FULL RECONVEYANCE
TO BE USED ONLY WHEN NOTE HAS BEEN PAID.

_____ Idaho, _____

TO: PIONEER TITLE COMPANY OF ADA COUNTY, Trustee:

The undersigned is the legal owner and holder of all indebtedness secured by the within Deed of Trust. All sums secured thereby have been fully paid. You are hereby requested and directed to cancel all evidence of indebtedness secured by said Deed of Trust and to reconvey, without warranty, the estate now held by you under the same.

Deliver to: _____

THE PROMISSORY NOTE OR NOTES, AND ANY EVIDENCES OF FURTHER AND/OR ADDITIONAL ADVANCES MUST BE PRESENTED WITH THIS REQUEST.

The deed of reconveyance, sometimes referred to as a release deed, should be acknowledged and recorded in the public record of the county in which the property is located.

Mortgage.   When a real estate loan secured by a mortgage has been completely repaid, the mortgage may be released in one of two ways.

First, it may be released by recording a separate satisfaction of mortgage, signed by the mortgagee, and stating that the mortgage loan has been paid, satisfied, or discharged.

Second, a notation acknowledging the release, or satisfaction, may be entered in the margin of the recorded mortgage document and signed by the mortgagee in the presence of the county recorder. A marginal release is the exception, not the rule, on property transactions in Idaho.

Release clause.   The *release clause* in a blanket mortgage document or deed of trust enables the lender to release portions of the property from the blanket encumbrance as those portions of the debt are repaid. In the case of a deed of trust, the lender instructs the trustee to execute and deliver a *partial reconveyance* to the grantor each time a portion of the debt is released.

Assumption of Mortgage and Deed of Trust Loans

Usually, when a purchaser of real estate assumes the seller's existing loan, the lender charges the purchaser a fee for transferring the loan. This is known as an *assumption fee* and is expressed in points or assumption points.

Frequently, when a real estate loan is made, the lender wishes to prevent some future purchaser of the property from being able to assume that loan, particularly at its old rate of interest.

For this reason some lenders include an *alienation (resale) clause* or a *due-on-sale clause*. An alienation clause provides that, upon the sale of the property by the borrower, the lender has the choice of either declaring the entire debt to be immediately due and owing or permitting the buyer to assume the loan. Sometimes an acceleration clause also is employed for this purpose.

By utilizing such clauses, the lender can choose to call the loan in the event of a sale and effectively reduce the number of notes with low interest rates that it holds and at the same time qualify new home purchasers on their income and paying ability before allowing them to assume an existing loan. It should be noted that the seller remains contingently liable for the loan.

Because virtually all loans contain due-on-sale clauses, it is imperative that the real estate agent check with the lender regarding a loan's assumability. If the loan can be assumed, the seller should be notified of his or her continuing liability as the original mortgagor. In order to be released from this continuing liability, the seller may require the buyer to create a novation or substitution of liability instead of an assumption.

Deed of Trust Foreclosure Procedure

If the grantor (or some person who owes an obligation, the performance of which is secured by a recorded deed of trust) defaults, the trustee may foreclose on the grantor by advertising and holding a sale of the property or by instituting legal proceedings to recover the debt through the mortgage (judicial) foreclosure procedure. The trustee may exercise his or her power of sale provided that no such action, suit, or proceeding has been instituted. If such a suit has been instituted, the trustee may advertise and sell the property only if that suit has been dismissed by the court.

Notice of default.   In order for the trustee to advertise and sell the property, the trustee (or the beneficiary) must file a *notice of default* with the county recorder identifying the specific trust deed involved and the nature of the breach and expressing the trustee's intention to sell the property to satisfy the obligation. This notice must be recorded in all counties in which the property or sections of the property are located. In addition, a copy of the notice must be sent to every person who has filed a request with the lender to receive one or has recorded a request for notice of default with the county recorder.

Notice of sale.   After recording the notice of default, the trustee must notify the following persons (or their legal representatives) of the sale by certified or registered mail at their last known addresses:

- The grantor
- Any person who has acquired the grantor's interest, provided that such successor's interest is indicated in the public record, the successor is in possession of the property, or the trustee has actual knowledge of the interest
- Any lessee or other person in possession of the property
- Any person holding a lien or an interest in the property that arose after the trustee's interest, provided that such lien or interest appears in the public record or the trustee has actual knowledge of it

The disability, incompetency, insanity, or death of any person who should receive a notice of the sale does not prevent the trustee from going ahead with the sale.

The following six items should be included in the notice of sale:

1. The names of the grantor, beneficiary, and trustee
2. A description of the property covered by the trust deed
3. The location of the recorded trust deed—the book and page number of the mortgage records or the recorded instrument number
4. A description of the default
5. The unpaid balance of the debt
6. The date, time, and place of the sale

At least three good-faith attempts must be made to personally serve a copy of the notice to any adult occupant of the property. The attempts must be made on different days over a seven-day period at least 30 days prior to the sale date. A copy of the notice must be conspicuously posted on the property each time an attempt at service is made, unless the posting from a previous attempt is still intact.

In addition, a copy of the notice of sale must be published in a newspaper of general circulation in each county in which a section of the property is located. This advertisement of the sale must be published once each week for four successive weeks, with the last publication at least 30 days before the sale.

IN PRACTICE   The trustee has 120 days in which to do the work described here. The notice of default and notice of sale are sent out within the first 60 days of the 120-day period.

The sale. The trustee's sale must be held at a designated time between 9:00 AM and 4:00 PM, standard time, and at a designated place in the county or one of the counties where the property is located.

Idaho's deed of trust statute allows for a postponement of a foreclosure sale past the date on which it was scheduled. Some lenders have seized upon foreclosure sale postponement as a technique for negotiating a repayment schedule with the borrower while keeping the borrower in what amounts to near perpetual default. By using this technique, lenders that have reached an agreement with a borrower for repayment avoid having to go through an additional 120-day period from notice to sale date. They are never more than 30 days away from a foreclosure sale. Despite the pressure of a possible foreclosure every 30 days, postponement provides a means by which borrowers who are unable to cure a default within the statutory period can still preserve their property.

The trustee's attorney may conduct the sale. The property is auctioned off to the highest bidder. It may be sold as one parcel or divided into sections and sold as two or more separate parcels.

Anyone, including the beneficiary under the trust deed, may bid on the property. After the sale and upon receiving the purchaser's payment for the property, the trustee executes and delivers a *trustee's deed* to the purchaser. A trustee's deed conveys to the purchaser all interest that the defaulted grantor had in the property. The purchaser is entitled to take possession of the property ten days after the sale.

Trustee sale proceeds. The trustee must apply the proceeds from the sale in four ways, as follows:

1. To pay the expenses of the sale, including reasonable fees for the trustee and the attorney
2. To pay off the debt secured by the trust deed
3. To pay off any liens recorded after the trust deed in the order of their priority
4. To pay any surplus funds from the sale to the defaulted grantor or his or her successor in interest

If, after the expenses are deducted, the proceeds of the trustee sale are not enough to cover the outstanding balance of the trust deed debt, the beneficiary is entitled to a *money judgment* or deficiency judgment as described in the text. Any such personal judgment must be sought within three months after the sale.

Foreclosure Procedure

Mortgage.   When mortgagors default, lenders must institute foreclosure proceedings under the *one-action rule*. This rule calls for a combined recovery of a debt and/or enforcement of a right secured by a mortgage in one action; no money judgment can be forced until the lender has foreclosed and the sale proceeds are insufficient to repay the lender. The mortgagee files a foreclosure suit that names all persons having a recorded interest in the property and requests a *sheriff's sale* of the property. At the court's direction, the sale is advertised. At the auction, the highest bidder for the property receives a *sheriff's deed*.

Right of redemption.   The equity of redemption enables a defaulted mortgagor (in the case of a mortgage) or grantor (in the case of a deed of trust) to redeem his or her property by paying all monies owed on the loan plus expenses at any time before the sheriff's sale (in the case of a mortgage) or trustee's sale (in the case of a deed of trust).

Idaho law also grants a defaulted mortgagor a time in which to redeem the property after a sale. The *statutory redemption period is one year after a sheriff's sale to foreclose a mortgage*, if the property sold consisted of *more than 20 acres*; it is *six months* if the property sold consisted of *20 acres or less*. During this period, the lender holds legal title to the property by holding a sheriff's Certificate of Sale.

At the foreclosure sale, if the lender (or some other party) acquires the property, it cannot market the property until the redemption period expires, or the debtor releases his or her right of redemption.

Deed of trust.   In a proceeding to foreclose on a deed of trust in Idaho, the trustor may stop the foreclosure proceedings by paying the delinquent amount of payments plus any costs incurred in the foreclosure process, which reinstates the loan. This action to reinstate the loan must be done within 115 days from the date the formal notice of default was recorded.

After the trustee's sale, the trustor has *no right* to redeem the property from the purchaser. The trustee's sale may not be held any earlier than 120 days after the date of the filing of the notice of default.

Although mortgages *must* be foreclosed judicially, deeds of trust *may* be foreclosed judicially; in either case, the one-action rule applies. If a deed of trust is foreclosed judicially, a payment of funds equal to the defaulted amount would not cure (i.e., reinstatement) the default. Standard note, mortgage, and deed of trust provisions require that upon default the entire indebtedness may become accelerated and due immediately at the lender's discretion.

Land sale contract foreclosure.   A *land sales contract*, also known as a *contract for deed*, is a form of security agreement between the buyer and seller. Once used extensively, it is not used as often as before because of court actions resulting from the foreclosure on the contract. If the contract for deed contains the necessary elements as required by Idaho Code 9-505, then it will also contain what constitutes default and the remedies that are available. The contract will usually state a time period during which the buyer may cure the default. Because this time period is not established by statute, it must be a matter of contractual agreement.

There are different alternatives when dealing with rescission and restitution on a land sales contract. Idaho Code 45-801 allows for judicial foreclosure, but this remedy for default is seldom used. Under this statute, the seller of the property has a lien on the property for as much as remains unpaid and the lien can be foreclosed.

Under what is defined as strict foreclosure, the seller indicates that he or she will perform as agreed and requests that the court determine a time limit for the buyer to (1) pay the total balance; (2) cure the default; or (3) quiet title to seller, free from all claims of the buyer. The contract is treated as being in full force until the court orders it canceled under strict foreclosure. There is no sale of the property or right of redemption after the time of performance set by the court has expired.

Another alternative for solving the default is forfeiture. The contract will contain a clause that stipulates that, in the event of a default, the seller can take possession of the property, keeping as liquidated damages any improvements and payments made by the buyer. This action by the seller can, in many cases, have a very disastrous financial impact on the buyer and give the seller a tremendous windfall in profit.

There have been a large number of court decisions where the courts have tried to stop the use of the forfeiture clause in the contract. Many of the court cases have come to conflicting positions by using some terms, such as "forfeiture" and "foreclosure," interchangeably.

Under court action, the enforcement of forfeiture provisions in the contract is enforced, but the court may require the seller to return money to the buyer. The amount is roughly equal to the difference between the rental value of the land during the term of the contract and the payments actually made by the buyer, plus the down payment and the value of any improvements made by the buyer during the contract period. This amount is referred to as a penalty and it must be paid in cash. If the seller cannot pay the amount in cash, the buyer is given a lien claim against the property. This equitable lien may then be foreclosed, forcing the property to be sold and the cash paid.

Judicial sale as a mortgage.   Because of the negative impact of court action on forfeiture, the remedy most often used by the seller in the market today is judicial sale as a mortgage.

Under this remedy, the seller can call the entire balance on the debt due and payable and foreclose on the contract as if it were a mortgage. When this remedy is used, the buyer would have the statutory right of redemption identical to the right granted to the mortgagor in a normal mortgage foreclosure.

When issues arise involving foreclosure on land sales contracts, licensees should direct the parties to an attorney.

■ DEED IN LIEU OF FORECLOSURE

The lender and the debtor may decide to satisfy the mortgage obligation by passing a *deed in lieu of foreclosure* to the lender; however, this action has the same result as an actual judicial foreclosure. Lenders generally use great caution before accepting a deed in lieu of foreclosure; the property may be subject to junior liens that could be discharged only by payment or by a notice and sale at some later date. In addition, the lender waives the right to any judgment if a deed in lieu is accepted.

■ USURY AND THE LEGAL RATE OF INTEREST

Idaho Code does not limit a maximum rate for usury when the rate of interest is expressly agreed to between parties in writing. With no expressed contract, a legal rate of 12 percent annual interest is allowed [IC 28-22-104].

Subdividers who sell real estate or licensees who finance their commission on installment contracts (carryback financing) must be constantly alert to whether their sales constitute *consumer credit sales*, which are regulated by the Idaho Department of Finance. The law provides for severe penalties for failure to comply with statutory notification, disclosure, and other requirements in connection with consumer credit sales.

Idaho Code [IC 28-41-301] defines *regulated credit sales* (item 35) as a sale of goods, services, or an interest in land in which (a) credit is granted either in conformance with a seller credit card or by a seller who regularly engages in credit transactions of the same kind and (b) the debt is payable in installments or a finance charge is made. Idaho Code describes notification and fees for regulated lenders, licensing, and related provisions [IC 28-46-201].

Points and late charges. Lenders charge the borrower a fee known as points at the loan's inception in addition to the stated interest rate on the face of the note. A point, which equals one percent of the loan amount borrowed, may be considered prepaid interest.

Points became a convenient method for many lenders to charge prepaid interest to compensate for low interest rates and provide a better return on their investments. If such points are, in fact, a bona fide service charge that can be justified or if they are actual brokerage or commitment fees, they are not considered prepaid interest to which the usury law applies.

Late charges are penalty fees charged by some institutional lenders to mortgagors that make their installment payments after the due date. Late charges are usually a specified percentage of the remaining unpaid principal or a percentage of the total payment, including tax and insurance impounds (PITI payment).

QUESTIONS

1. A promissory note is negotiable when
   a. it includes an alienation clause.
   b. it cannot be prepaid without penalty.
   c. the person who will collect payment on the note can transfer his or her right to collect to another party.
   d. the maker's debt may be assumed by another party.

2. Financier Krystal loaned $40,000 to Willie, who is opening a new restaurant. The promissory note executed by Willie states, "Pay to Bearer, the sum of forty thousand and no/100 dollars ($40,000.00)." Three months later, Krystal needed cash for some other project, so she sold Willie's note to Lance, an associate who was interested in a long-term investment. In order to transfer his rights under the note to Lance, Krystal had to
   a. give the note to Lance.
   b. have Willie execute a new note to Lance and destroy the original note.
   c. sign the note over to Lance.
   d. execute an endorsement agreement naming Lance as the official payee.

3. Roxanne borrowed some money from the local bank to finance some needed repairs to her farm. The note calls for Roxanne to make a monthly payment of $200 on the principal, plus interest at the rate of nine percent per year. This is what type of note?
   a. Amortized
   b. Straight
   c. Installment
   d. Balloon

4. In question 3, the outstanding balance of Roxanne's loan is $16,000. What is the total amount due for her next monthly payment?
   a. $320
   b. $300
   c. $220
   d. $200

5. A person who obtains a real estate loan secured by a trust deed is known as a
   a. holder in due course.
   b. trustee.
   c. beneficiary.
   d. grantor.

6. In Idaho, real estate loans secured by trust deeds may be made, provided that the property given as security is how many acres or less?
   a. 1
   b. 5
   c. 20
   d. 40

7. Which of the following persons or entities may NOT serve as the trustee of a trust deed loan in Idaho?
   a. A real estate broker
   b. A title insurance company
   c. An attorney
   d. A savings and loan association

8. Several years ago, Stan obtained a trust deed loan from the New Bank, which named an attorney, Barb, as trustee. Now Stan is six months behind in his payments, and New Bank has declared him in default and requested that Barb start the foreclosure process under her power of sale as trustee. The first step Barb must take is to
   a. schedule a time and place for the sale.
   b. record a notice of default in the county in which the property is located.
   c. notify Stan that his loan will be foreclosed unless he makes up the late payments.
   d. notify Stan's other creditors of the sale.

9. In question 8, the person who purchases Stan's property at the foreclosure sale will receive a
   a. reconveyance deed.
   b. release deed.
   c. sheriff's deed.
   d. trustee's deed.

10. A grantor's right to redeem a property that has been foreclosed upon through a trustee's sale must be exercised within
    a. 115 days.
    b. 120 days.
    c. 6 months.
    d. no time after sale.

11. The grantor may retain the property upon payment to the lender of all back payments and reasonable costs of foreclosure within
    a. 115 days.
    b. 120 days.
    c. 6 months.
    d. 1 year.

12

LEASES

Under Idaho law there are certain legal relationships between landlords and tenants. In addition to these legal relationships, the parties to the lease or rental agreement can establish other arrangements. In normal situations the terms of a lease agreement are binding on all parties to the agreement and are enforceable in a court of law.

Online Information

You can find and download the Idaho Landlord–Tenant Guidelines on the Attorney General Web page.

WWWeb.Link

www2.state.id.us/ag/consumer/forms/tips/landlordtenant.pdf

■ LEASE AGREEMENTS

A lease agreement can be either oral or written. It is strongly recommended that all lease agreements be in writing, no matter the length of period. Because the lease agreement is a contract, it must contain all of the essential elements of a contract. The courts use state statutes and certain implied covenants and terms when dealing with all leases, whether or not the lease is in writing.

Written Lease Agreements

Before either party signs a lease agreement, all questions and changes in the terms of the agreement should be resolved. An oral statement contrary to the terms of the written lease agreement cannot be relied on. *Idaho's Statute of Frauds requires that all leases of more than one year be in writing to be enforceable in a court of law* [IC 28-12-201].

The other requirements of a valid written lease include consideration, signatures, and legally competent parties. Consideration is normally the rent. The lease should spell out when the rent is to be paid, generally at the beginning of the period. If the lease agreement does not specify when rent is due, it will not be due until the end of the lease period. This could create added risk for the landlord, who would be unable to demand payment until the expiration of the lease period.

To be valid, the written lease agreement must be signed by the landlord (lessor). The tenant (lessee) need not sign the lease agreement, even though it is highly recommended. Acceptance by the tenant will be implied by his or her action, such as paying rent or taking possession of the property.

Oral Lease Agreements

If the terms of the lease have been agreed on, a legally binding oral lease agreement may exist. The greatest difficulty encountered with an oral lease is proving what specific terms were agreed to.

Most oral lease agreements result in periodic tenancy. That is, the parties agree that the tenant will pay rent on a periodic basis in return for the landlord giving possession of the property to the tenant. The period can be for any agreed-upon length and will be equal to the period for which the payment is made.

■ RIGHTS AND RESPONSIBILITIES OF LANDLORD AND TENANT

Idaho statutes provide for certain rights and require certain duties of both the landlord and the tenant in residential lease situations, regardless of whether a written lease agreement exists.

Possession

The tenant has the right to possession of the property during the term of the lease agreement; the landlord has the right to have possession of the property returned upon expiration of the term. However, if the tenant does not vacate the property at the end of the term, the landlord is prohibited from locking the tenant out without a court order. The landlord is required by Idaho law to give certain notice to the tenant and, if required, to institute formal legal proceedings to regain possession of the property.

Entry by the Landlord

Because Idaho laws do not speak specifically to the landlord's right to enter the premises, the lease agreement should spell out the rights of the landlord. The lease should, with the lessee's permission, allow the landlord to enter the property to make repairs, to inspect for damage, and to show the property to potential purchasers and prospective new tenants. If such entry is at a reasonable time and in a reasonable manner, there should be no problem, provided the lease agreement covers entry.

If the lease agreement does not address the landlord's right to enter, the landlord should notify the tenant as to the necessity for entry and request permission to enter at a reasonable time and in a reasonable manner.

The landlord probably has the right to enter for inspection of the property under the following two situations:

1. If the landlord has reasonable cause to believe that damage is occurring to the property, the landlord probably has the right to enter to inspect for such damage. Arrangements for entry should be made with the tenant, if at all possible.

2. If a tenant is in default in the rent and has been absent from the premises for a considerable period of time, the landlord probably has the right to enter and inspect. This situation should be provided for in the terms of the lease agreement to resolve any possible conflicts.

Security Deposits [IC 6-321]

Under Idaho law, a security deposit is for purposes other than the payment of rent. The lease agreement must specify the amount of the security deposit and what it can be used for.

The security deposit cannot be used for payment of rent unless the lease agreement or deposit receipt clearly indicates in writing that it will be used for payment of rent. The security deposit cannot be used to cover normal wear and tear. Normal wear and tear is defined as the deterioration that occurs based on the use for which the space is intended and without negligence, carelessness, accident, misuse, or abuse of the premises or contents by the tenants, their family, or their guests.

If the landlord finds it necessary to use the security deposit, Idaho law requires the landlord to provide the tenant with a signed statement as to the expenditures required, the amount to be retained, and the purpose for which the amount retained was used. This signed statement and the remaining amount of the security deposit, if any, or the full amount of the deposit, must be returned to the tenant within 21 days after the tenant surrenders the premises. In the original lease agreement, the landlord and tenant can agree to extend this period up to 30 days, but no longer.

The tenant is protected when the landlord refuses to comply with the requirements concerning security deposits. The tenant must first notify the landlord in writing of the violation and demand compliance. The landlord must be allowed three days to either refund the deposit or provide the necessary statement. After three days the tenant can institute a formal legal proceeding to require return of the security deposit. This lawsuit can be brought either in the district court with the aid of an attorney or in small claims court without the assistance of an attorney if the amount is not too large. If the tenant is successful, the court may award damages up to the amount of *three times* the security deposit.

Care of the Property

Safeguarding the property and ensuring that damage does not occur is one of a tenant's main responsibilities. A tenant will be held responsible and must pay for any damage that occurs due to tenant negligence or that of family members or guests.

The landlord is obligated to provide reasonable waterproofing and water protection and also to provide premises that are not hazardous to health and safety. A landlord who provides electrical, plumbing, heating, ventilating, cooling, or sanitary facilities must maintain them in good working order.

Tenant's Property

Upon termination of the lease agreement, the tenant has a right to remove personal property as long as such removal does not damage the premises. If the tenant's property has become part of the landlord's real property, it cannot be removed.

If a tenant leaves property of value behind after vacating the premises, the landlord has no legal right to *immediately* dispose of the property. In fact, the landlord has an obligation to reasonably safeguard the property until it can be disposed of properly. The tenant may reclaim the property or the landlord can dispose of it in accordance with the abandoned or unclaimed property laws of the state of Idaho.

Idaho law does *not* provide for a landlord's lien on property that belongs to a tenant. A lease agreement could contain a provision for the landlord to have a lien right on the tenant's property. The courts have upheld this type of lien right as long as the tenant knowingly and voluntarily enters into and understands the consequences of such an agreement.

Rent Increases

Proper notice is required before rent can be increased. A written notice must be given at least 15 days before the end of the term and prior to the date the rent increase is to become effective on all periodic tenancies. When the lease agreement, either written or oral, specifies the amount of the rent for a set time period, the rent cannot be increased during that period.

■ OTHER CHANGES IN LEASE AGREEMENT TERMS

None of the terms of a lease agreement for a specified time period can be changed unless both parties to the agreement consent to the proposed changes. Any changes made should be in writing as modifications to the lease agreement or be incorporated in an entirely new lease agreement.

The landlord may change the terms of the lease agreement in a periodic tenancy by giving the tenant written notice of changes at least 15 days before the end of the period and before the changes are to become effective. If the tenant continues to rent for the following period, the changes in the landlord's notice will automatically become effective for the new period.

Transfer of Property

During the term of the lease period, the owner has the right to sell the property. The lease cannot prevent the sale; however, the sale is made subject to the lease. This means that the buyer (new owner) must recognize the existence of the lease and honor the lease for the remainder of the term. The only exception is if the lease contains a sales clause term that allows the new landlord to terminate the lease agreement.

The tenant has certain additional rights unless a right is specifically prohibited by the provisions of the lease. These additional rights include the right to assign, sublease, or novate the lease interest. These three situations create different levels of liability for the first tenant. In the case of an assignment, the first tenant is not relieved of responsibility to pay rent and in fact is secondarily liable to pay. Under the sublease situation, the first tenant is primarily liable along with the new tenant. A novation allows the first tenant to terminate his or her liability under the old lease by replacing the old lease agreement with a new lease agreement with a new tenant.

■ TERMINATION DUE TO BREACH

Landlord's Remedies   Idaho law specifically speaks to the requirements that the landlord must follow when a tenant fails to pay rent or violates any terms of the lease agreement. The landlord must give the tenant *written notice* of the violation and provide three days in which the tenant can remedy the problem. If at all possible, the notice must be delivered personally. If personal delivery is not possible because the tenant is absent from his or her place of residence and usual place of business, then a copy of the notice may be left with a person of suitable age and discretion at either the tenant's residence or place of business. In that case, a copy of the notice must be mailed, addressed to the tenant at his or her place of residence. If these requirements cannot be fulfilled, the following steps must be taken:

- A copy of the notice must be posted in a conspicuous place on the property.
- If a person residing on the premises can be found, a copy must be left with that person.
- A copy must be mailed to the tenant at the address where the property is situated.

If the tenant does not remedy the violation, the landlord *cannot use force*. The next step would be to institute formal legal proceedings. The advice of an attorney should be sought.

When the landlord pursues formal legal eviction solely for the purpose of evicting a tenant due to nonpayment of rent, the legal proceedings are referred to as a *quick eviction*. The trial *must* be held within 12 days after the lawsuit is filed with the court unless the landlord requests a later date. The tenant must be given written notice of the action by being served with a copy of the summons and the complaint at least five days prior to the court hearing. The tenant can request a continuance, but only for two days unless the tenant deposits with the clerk of the court a security deposit such as a sum of money equal to the rent due and owing.

If the landlord is bringing an action for a breach of the lease other than nonpayment of rent, the quick eviction provision does not apply.

When the landlord is successful, the court judgment will be for restitution of the premises to the landlord and also may include the landlord's court costs and disbursements. If the property is less than five acres in size, the judgment may be enforced immediately. The sheriff is directed to remove the tenant and all of the tenant's possessions from the property and return the property to the landlord. If the property is larger than five acres in size, the judgment is delayed for five days. During this five-day period, if the tenant has not reinstated the lease, the judgment will be enforced and the tenant and his or her possessions can be removed.

In situations where the landlord not only brings action for possession but also brings action for other breaches, such as damages or rent, the judgment handed down by the court also may direct the sheriff to levy the tenant's property to satisfy the judgment. The amount of the judgment established by the court usually equals the amount of the unpaid rent or damage. However, the court may require the tenant to pay three times the amount of damages suffered along with court costs and the fees of the landlord's attorney.

Tenant's Remedies [IC 6-320]

The landlord is obligated to provide reasonable waterproofing and water protection; to provide premises that are free of hazard to the health and safety of the tenant; and to maintain in good working order electrical, plumbing, heating, ventilating, cooling, or sanitary facilities that are provided. If necessary, the tenant can resort to court action to get the landlord to provide these services. Idaho law has not been established as to whether the tenant has a legal right to withhold rent and/or to complete the repairs and then seek reimbursement from the landlord. Such rights apparently do not exist.

If the tenant's intent is to require the landlord to provide the necessary services, the tenant must give the landlord *written notice*, listing each violation and demanding that the violations be cured. This written notice should be delivered to the landlord or the landlord's agent personally, be mailed to the landlord or agent by certified mail with return receipt requested, or if the landlord or agent is absent from the place of business, be left with an employee at the usual place of business.

The landlord must be given three days in which to cure the violations. The tenant can institute formal legal proceedings to require the landlord to cure the violations if the landlord has not complied with the request. The court action has the same early trial provisions that the landlord has when suit is brought for possession.

The trial must be held within 12 days after the lawsuit is filed with the court unless the tenant requests a later date. The landlord must be given written notice of the action by being served with a copy of the summons and the complaint at least five days prior to the court hearing.

If the tenant prevails, the judge will order the landlord to fulfill the obligations and may order the landlord to pay the court costs and the fees of the tenant's attorney. The tenant also may bring formal legal proceedings to recover money damages, if the tenant has lost money or otherwise been injured as a result of the landlord's failure. If the tenant prevails in this situation, the court has the authority to require the landlord to pay three times the amount of the tenant's damages.

■ THE FLOATING HOMES RESIDENCY ACT [CH. 27, TITLE 55]

The Floating Homes Residency Act protects the rights and responsibilities of owners of floating homes located within a floating home moorage marina. A floating home moorage marina is a waterfront facility for the moorage of one or more floating homes and the land and water premises on which it is located.

Written Lease Agreement [IC 55-2706]

Any landlord offering a moorage site for rent must provide the prospective tenant with a written agreement. This agreement must include

- signatures of both landlord and tenant;
- a rental term of 12 months, or less or more than 12 months if mutually agreed upon by both landlord and tenant; and
- a clearly identified moorage site.

The lease agreement must not require or allow a tenant to waive any rights protected under the Act.

Marina Rules [IC 55-2707]

The marina landlord may establish reasonable rules and regulations governing the use and occupancy of a floating home marina with or without the tenant's consent, as long as the tenant is given at least six months' prior notice of the rule.

In addition, the landlord may enter a floating home in case of an apparent or actual emergency, when the tenant has abandoned the floating home, or has agreed to the landlord's right of entry in the rental agreement.

Rent Adjustments [IC 55-2708]

The lease agreement may provide for rent increases or decreases upon 90 days' notice. No fees may be charged except for rent, services, and utilities actually provided. Fees for services and utilities must be listed in the lease agreement, and any adjustments to these fees also are subject to 90 days' notice.

Renewal and Termination

A landlord cannot terminate or refuse to renew a tenancy, except for

- conduct by a tenant that is deemed a nuisance to others;
- substantial or repeated violation of the marina's rules;
- nonpayment of rent;
- material breach of a rental agreement; or
- condemnation of the marina.

The landlord must give notice to the tenant, allowing three days to comply by paying rent or remedying the violations. If the tenant does not comply within 15 days following the notice, the landlord may give 90 days' notice of eviction.

■ THE MOBILE HOME PARK LANDLORD–TENANT ACT [CH. 20, TITLE 55]

The Mobile (Manufactured) Home Park Landlord–Tenant Act of 1980 formally established a set of specific rights and responsibilities for both manufactured home park owners and manufactured home park tenants. Those situations not specifically covered under the 1980 Act are covered by the general provisions of the landlord–tenant laws.

Written Lease Agreement [IC 55-2005]

With limited exceptions, the manufactured home lot owner must provide a written lease agreement upon request. Either the landlord or the tenant may require the written agreement. This lease agreement must include

- payment terms, including the time and place of payment;
- a description of the utilities and services included in the monthly rent;

■ park rules;
■ the name and address of the manager of the manufactured home park;
■ the name and address of the owner of the manufactured home park or the name and address of an agent of the owner who resides within the state where the manufactured home park is located; and
■ the terms and conditions under which a security deposit may be withheld by the landlord upon termination of the lease agreement.

The lease agreement cannot provide for an entrance or exit fee, or restrict access for a tenant's guests; nor can it require or permit a tenant to waive any rights or remedies provided by the 1980 Act.

**Rent Increases
[IC 55-2006]**

The lease agreement may provide for rent increases (or decreases) upon 30 days' written notice. This 30-day provision applies only for the increases or decreases from ad valorem (property) taxes, utility assessments, or other service fees included in the monthly rent. All other rent increases require 90 days' written notice to the tenant.

**Park Rules
[IC 55-2008]**

The manufactured home park rules are enforceable only if they have been made part of the lease agreement signed by the tenant. Any changes become effective upon the consent of the tenant, upon 90 days' notice.

**Renewal and
Termination
[IC 55-2010]**

All lease agreements are automatically renewed unless the landlord gives the tenant at least 90 days' written notice of intent not to renew the lease agreement or the tenant gives 30 days' written notice of intent not to renew the lease agreement.

Also, a tenant may terminate upon 30 days' written notice if employment requires a change in residence and upon less than 30 days' notice if reassignment with the armed forces does not allow longer notice. The landlord may terminate the lease agreement during the term of the lease if the tenant

■ does not pay rent or other charges provided for in the lease agreement or
■ substantially or repeatedly violates the manufactured home park rules.

In either case, the landlord must give the tenant three days to comply by paying the rent or charges owed or by remedying the violations.

If the tenant does not comply at the end of three days, the tenant may be given 20 days in which to vacate the manufactured home park.

If the manufactured home space rental operation ceases to exist, the landlord may terminate the tenant's lease, provided at least 180 days' notice is given prior to cessation.

**Security Deposits
[IC 55-2013]**

Security deposits for manufactured homes are governed by the general landlord–tenant law, except that the manufactured home park landlord must maintain a separate record of deposits. A tenant's claim to a security deposit takes precedence over the claims of any other creditors of the landlord.

Notice to Lienholder
[IC 55-2009A]

Idaho law does not specifically provide for the creation of a lien on the manufactured home on behalf of a manufactured home park owner for unpaid rent and utilities. Any lienholder or legal owner of a manufactured home is required by Idaho law to notify the manufactured home park owner, in writing, of any secured or legal interest in the manufactured home.

If the tenant falls 60 days behind in rent or appears to have abandoned the manufactured home, the manufactured home park landlord must notify the lienholder or legal owner of responsibility for any costs accruing for the manufactured home space. The lienholder or legal owner shall be held responsible for utilities from the date of the notice. In addition, the lienholder or legal owner is responsible for the rent due, including the past rent up to a maximum of 60 days prior to the date of notice.

Before the manufactured home may be removed from the manufactured home space, a signed written agreement from the manufactured home park landlord, owner, or manager must be received giving clearance for removal. This clearance normally will not be obtained until all monies due have been paid in full or a written agreement has been reached between the legal owner and the landlord of the manufactured home park.

Sale of Manufactured Home

Any manufactured home owner has the right to sell his or her manufactured home. If the manufactured home lot owner helps the manufactured home-owner sell the manufactured home, a commission may be paid. For the commission to be paid, a written agreement voluntarily entered into by the manufactured home owner and lot owner must have been completed.

The manufactured home park owner may require 30 days' written notice prior to the sale if the purchaser of the manufactured home intends to leave the manufactured home in the park. A new lease agreement must be signed by the landlord and the prospective tenant prior to the sale of the manufactured home.

Retaliatory Conduct Prohibited
[IC 55-2015]

A manufactured home park owner may not take any action as retaliation because the tenant has exercised a legal right such as complaining about maintenance or the safety conditions of the park or becoming a member of a tenant's organization. The landlord cannot retaliate by terminating the lease, refusing to renew a lease, increasing rent, or decreasing services.

Under the general landlord–tenant laws the tenant is protected from a breach by the landlord. Under the manufactured home laws, the tenant is required to file an indemnity bond or monies to cover the landlord's legal expenses and court costs.

If the tenant is not awarded damages or specific performance, the landlord will be reimbursed for legal expenses and court costs from the bond or monies.

■ OIL AND GAS LEASES

When oil and gas exploration companies negotiate to lease land to explore for oil and gas, a special lease agreement must be negotiated. A cash payment is usually paid to the landlord when the lease agreement is executed. If no well is drilled within a year or the stated period in the lease, the lease expires.

When a producing well is found, the landlord usually receives one-eighth (12½ percent) of the production (or the value of that amount of production) as a royalty. The lease continues as long as oil or gas is obtained in significant quantities.

■ DISCRIMINATION

It is against both state and federal laws to have terms in a lease agreement that would violate fair housing laws. Care must also be taken in the way tenants are selected and treated to ensure that both federal and state laws are not violated. Fair housing issues are dealt with in more detail in Chapter 15.

QUESTIONS

1. Jim wanted to rent an apartment in Boise. Rick, the resident landlord of the four-story building Jim selected, gave Jim a blank, unsigned 18-month lease. Jim signed the lease, and the landlord filed it in a safe deposit box in a Montana bank without signing it. Jim's lease is
   a. valid, because only the tenant is required to sign a lease in the state of Idaho.
   b. valid, because the term of the lease is for more than one year.
   c. invalid, because the landlord (lessor) did not sign the lease.
   d. invalid, because Idaho law requires that a lease be stored in the state.

2. The Idaho Statute of Frauds requires a lease to be in writing if it is for a term of more than
   a. six months.
   b. one year.
   c. five years.
   d. any length of time.

3. Under the usual oil and gas lease, the property owner receives a
   a. set monthly rental, whether or not oil or gas is obtained from the land.
   b. separate fee for every well drilled.
   c. yearly fee for the use of the property plus an additional fee negotiated if and when oil or gas is obtained from the property.
   d. yearly fee for the use of the property plus a stated percentage of the production of the oil and gas as a royalty.

4. A landlord probably has the right to enter the property without permission to inspect it if
   a. the landlord has reasonable cause to believe that damage is occurring to the property.
   b. a tenant is in default in rent and has been absent from the premises for a considerable period of time.
   c. either of the above occurs.
   d. neither of the above occurs.

5. If the landlord plans a rent increase, a written notice MUST be given to the tenants at least how many days before the end of the term and prior to the date of the increase if the increase is to become effective on all periodic tenancies?
   a. 30
   b. 15
   c. No notice required
   d. 7

6. If a tenant leaves property of value behind after vacating the premises, how MUST a landlord legally dispose of the property?
   a. Dispose of it immediately
   b. Follow abandoned or unclaimed property laws
   c. Store it until tenant returns
   d. Safeguard it

7. The landlord is NOT obligated to provide
   a. reasonable waterproofing and water protection.
   b. premises that are not hazardous to the health and safety of the tenant.
   c. electrical, plumbing, heating, ventilating, cooling, and sanitary facilities in good working order.
   d. phone or TV service.

8. A security deposit can be used for all of the following EXCEPT
   a. rent.
   b. pets.
   c. negligent abuse of the premises.
   d. careless misuse of the landlord's property.

9. When a property is less than five acres in size and the landlord is successful in the court judgment for restitution of the premises, the maximum number of days the judgment may be enforced will be
   a. 5.
   b. 10.
   c. 20.
   d. immediately.

10. How much notice must be given to change rules of a marina to the tenant of a floating home rental agreement?
    a. 30 days
    b. 60 days
    c. 90 days
    d. 6 months

13

REAL ESTATE APPRAISAL

■ LICENSURE AND CERTIFICATION

Idaho, like all other states, has been mandated by federal law to license and certify real estate appraisers. The state of Idaho passed legislation that requires all appraisers be licensed or certified. There are three classes of appraisers in Idaho:

1. *Licensed Residential*: licensed to appraise one- to four-unit residential properties in noncomplex transactions valued under $1 million, or complex transactions valued under $250,000
2. *Certified Residential*: limited to appraising residential properties of four or fewer units, regardless of the complexity or value of the transaction
3. *Certified General*: certified to appraise all types of property

Each of these classes has its own set of educational, experience, and examination requirements. For complete information, write the Idaho Real Estate Appraiser Board at the Bureau of Occupational Licenses, 1109 Main Street, Suite 220, Boise, Idaho 83702-5642; or call 1-208-334-3233.

Online Information

The Idaho Real Estate Appraiser Board can be found on the Web at

WWWeb.Link

www.ibol.idaho.gov/rea.htm

Exceptions to Unlawful Practice of Appraisal [IC 54-4103 and 4105]

Under Idaho law, only a licensed or certified appraiser may perform an appraisal of property.

However, a licensed real estate broker, associate broker, or salesperson may in the ordinary course of his business give an opinion of the price of real estate *for the purpose of a prospective listing or sale*, provided that such person does not represent himself as being a state licensed or certified real estate appraiser.

In addition, an actively licensed broker or associate broker (a licensed sales-person is *not* included) *may charge a fee* providing the broker's price opinion complies with the following eight requirements in writing:

1. A statement of the intended purpose of the price opinion
2. A brief description of the subject property and property interested to be priced
3. The basis of reasoning used to reach the conclusion of the price, including the applicable market data and/or capitalization computation
4. Any assumptions or limiting conditions
5. A disclosure of any existing or contemplated interest of the broker(s) issuing the opinion
6. The name and signature of the broker(s) issuing the price opinion and the date of its issuance
7. A disclaimer that, unless the broker is licensed under the Idaho Real Estate Appraisers Act, Chapter 41, Title 54, Idaho Code, the report is not intended to meet the uniform standards of professional appraisal practice
8. A disclaimer that the broker's price opinion is not intended to be an appraisal of the market value of the property, and that if an appraisal is desired, the services of a licensed or certified appraiser should be obtained

The broker's price opinion permitted under this code chapter may not be used as an appraisal in a federally related transaction.

■ APPRAISAL AND MARKET VALUE

When professional real estate appraisers estimate the value of a property, they may use one or all of the three approaches to value, depending on the type of property being appraised and the applicability of each approach. The three approaches to estimating real estate values are the

1. *cost approach*, determined by computing the cost of reproducing or replacing the physical property, less depreciation, plus the estimated value of the land;
2. *income approach*, figured by analyzing the income (both net operating income and gross income) and choosing an applicable capitalization rate or gross multiplier from market information; and
3. *market approach*, estimating value based on comparison with other similar properties that have recently sold.

In contrast to these approaches, a real estate sales associate will do a *competitive market analysis*. How the real estate sales associate prepares and uses the competitive market analysis often will determine whether the property is listed at a reasonable probable market price.

The appraisal process of estimating value is not an exact science that can predict an exact sales price. Using the competitive market analysis, the real estate sales associate can suggest a reasonable range of listing prices. The limitation faced by a real estate appraiser actually turns out to be an advantage for the sales associate. By being presented with a range of possible prices, the seller will be prepared for a possible offer within that range.

■ COMPETITIVE MARKET ANALYSIS

To adequately prepare a competitive market analysis, the sales associate will need to gather as much information as possible, as discussed in the following sections.

Market Data

In gathering market information, a sales associate must attempt to find as many comparable sales as possible as well as currently listed properties. The sales should be recent actual sales of comparable properties in the area. The sales preferably should have closed no longer than three to six months earlier. Information also must be gathered about currently listed properties that the subject property will have as competition. The current competitive properties are important because they show the time the property has been on the market and still has not sold due to the pricing terms or the condition of the property.

Additional market information will be gathered about properties that were listed, did not sell, and are no longer on the market. These will help show the seller has consequences of not listing the property at a realistic price.

A broker's listings and/or multiple-listing service (MLS) files are a prime source for researching the data. *Note that the more similar the properties a sales associate selects for use in the analysis, the more accurate the market comparison will be.*

It is also important to make sure that all the facts are totally accurate. A real estate professional should physically visit each comparable to verify the information gathered.

Many standard competitive market analysis forms are available for use in presenting market data to a seller.

Other Listing Information

Location.   The location of the property will have a major impact on the listed price. A property located in a good neighborhood, close to schools and shopping, and with light traffic will usually sell at a higher price. The location, along with highly valued extras such as landscaping, view, covered patio, energy efficiency, and the like, will add to the buyer appeal. This buyer appeal usually equates to a higher selling price.

Energy-saving features.   The number and types of energy-saving features as well as the amount of money saved will have a significant impact on the buyer. If the savings are large enough, the buyer may be willing to pay more for the property.

Motivation.   The seller's reason for moving and his or her needs and emotional makeup will determine how the property is priced. The level of motivation will affect the seller's reaction to offers for sale and willingness to negotiate.

If the seller has bought a new home that will not be ready for five months and thinks the market value of properties is going up by $5,000 during that time, he or she may want the sales price much higher than the competition. Salespeople should be prepared to discuss the possible consequences of these actions.

People who change homes frequently to take new assignments often have a realistic view of pricing a house. Some sellers may choose to leave a house vacant for several months before becoming realistic. Others feel overextended and want to "get out from under" a major financial obligation. These are the kinds of motivators a salesperson must be aware of when listing the property.

Terms of financing.   What financing is available? Are conventional, FHA, IHFA, or VA loans available and what will be the cost to the seller? Can the buyer assume the seller's existing mortgage? Will the seller help finance by accepting a second mortgage, a contract for deed, or a low down payment? Answers to these questions will help determine the pricing strategy and the final listing price.

Drawbacks.   Needless to say, a property's drawbacks can reduce its market value dramatically. Certain construction flaws (e.g., a bad floor plan, small rooms, or low ceilings in the basement) cannot be corrected readily and may have to be left as is. Minor drawbacks (e.g., poor maintenance, leaky plumbing, or cracked plaster) can be repaired. By pointing out to the seller repairable drawbacks in the listing presentation and demonstrating the negative effects they can have on the property's market value, the sales associate may be able to persuade the seller to correct them in order to strengthen the seller's negotiating position.

■ THE FINAL LISTING PRICE

After all necessary information has been gathered and is ready to be presented to the seller, the sales associate should be able to advise the seller to list the property at a marketable price. The seller ultimately decides the listing price. However, a good presentation and comparative market analysis are influential in the decision.

Importance of an Appropriate Listing Price

Overpriced listings seldom sell. They create bad relations with the owner and harm the brokerage firm's reputation. Listings that expire unsold create an image of failure and eventually decrease your ability to obtain quality listings in your area. The larger the number of marginal listings you take, the lower your chances of success.

A licensee's confidence increases when his or her listings sell. The old adage, "A listing priced correctly is 'half sold,'" is still true today.

QUESTIONS

1. What method is generally used by a real estate sales associate or broker when preparing an analysis to assist the seller in determining a listing price?
   a. A formal appraisal
   b. County assessor's tax assessment
   c. Construction cost estimate
   d. Competitive market analysis

2. What type of appraisal accreditation would be required to perform all types of appraisals?
   a. Licensed general
   b. Licensed residential
   c. Certified residential
   d. Certified general

3. When a licensee offers an opinion of the price of real estate, the general purpose of performing a competitive market analysis is to secure a
   a. listing.
   b. sale.
   c. commission.
   d. listing or sale.

4. Who may offer a price opinion for a fee?
   a. An inactively licensed salesperson
   b. An active licensed salesperson
   c. An active broker
   d. An inactive broker

5. A broker's price opinion cannot be used for what purpose?
   a. Assisting a buyer with understanding the market before they make an offer
   b. Helping the seller with pricing their property for sale
   c. Appraising for a federally-related loan
   d. Verifying the marketplace with general values to structure an offer

6. What appraisal approach would most likely be used to verify value of a duplex?
   a. Income approach
   b. Cost approach
   c. Loan approach
   d. Market approach

CHAPTER FOURTEEN

ENVIRONMENTAL ISSUES AND CONTROL OF LAND USE

■ ENVIRONMENTAL ASSESSMENTS

As a result of the actions of our society and the enactment of federal and state law, environmental concerns have come to the forefront. This increased public awareness of pollution and its health and economic effects have made real estate transactions more complicated. Because of the possible costs that could be incurred by the cleanup and removal of pollution, buyers and lenders are requiring that environmental assessments be conducted for both commercial and residential property.

Idaho, like many other states, has passed legislation that is patterned after the federal National Environmental Protection Act (NEPA). The Idaho Environmental Protection and Health Act protects the environment and promotes the personal health, safety, and welfare of Idaho citizens by controlling air pollution, hazardous waste management, clean indoor air, and water quality. The enforcement will come from the State Department of Health and Welfare, Bureau of Environmental Health, or Department of Environmental Quality.

Online Information

The Idaho Department of Environmental Quality (DEQ) can be found on the Web at

WWWeb.Link

www2.state.id.us/deq

Lead-Based Paint

Before being banned in 1978, lead was used in alkyd oil-based paint as a pigment and a drying agent. An elevated level of lead in the body can cause serious damage to the brain, kidneys, nervous system, and red blood cells. The federal government has estimated that lead is present in approximately 75 percent of all private housing built before 1978. As a result, federal law has been created to mandate, under the Lead-Based Paint Hazard Reduction Act, the disclosure of any known lead-based paint hazards to *all potential buyers or renters.*

The Act does not require homeowners to test for lead; however, disclosure of any known lead-based paint hazards to prospective buyers or tenants is mandatory. A lead-based paint disclosure statement must be attached to all sales contracts and leases regarding residential properties built before 1978, and a lead hazard pamphlet must be distributed to all buyers and tenants.

More information about lead-based hazards and a copy of the required pamphlet is available from the National Lead Information Center (NLIC) at 1-800-424-LEAD (5323).

Online Information

The National Lead Information Center offers the above information on the Web at

WWWeb.Link

www.epa.gov/lead/regulation.htm

Radon Gas

One of the most common problems in Idaho is radon gas. The Bureau of Environmental Health will provide a list of testing and mitigating companies in the state of Idaho and surrounding areas that provide services to Idahoans, although it does not furnish testing devices or endorse any companies that sell testing equipment. This list is provided to the public for information purposes only, and the inclusion of a company on this list should not be interpreted as a certification or accreditation of that company by the state of Idaho. Most of the companies have successfully participated in one of the EPA's Radon Proficiency Programs, and all companies are encouraged to participate, although Idaho does not have any legislation that requires the certification of testers or contractors.

If you should need assistance, call the Idaho Department of Health and Welfare in Boise at 1-208-445-8647 or call the hotline at 1-800-44-LUNGS. District health departments are also available to provide information and conduct public meetings.

Online Information

Additional resources can be found on the Web at

WWWeb.Link

www.epa.gov/iaq/radon/pubs
www.healthandwelfare.idaho.gov

Waste Disposal

The Idaho Land Remediation Act allows for the voluntary remediation of abandoned or underutilized properties that are or are perceived to be contaminated with hazardous waste or petroleum.

Owners can work with the DEQ to remediate the property, protected by a "Covenant Not to Sue" from the state and a recordable "Certificate of

Completion." Property tax exemptions may also be available, based on the property's remediated value.

Underground Storage Tanks

In Idaho, federal laws governing underground storage tanks (USTs) apply. Buyers, sellers, and real estate practitioners alike may feel uneasy if a UST is or has been located on a particular piece of property.

A 12-page booklet specifically for real estate licensees is available at the DEQ Web site. The booklet, *Real Estate Professionals and Underground Storage Tanks*, addresses underground fuel oil tanks that could be leaking or abandoned together with suggested remedies. Any cleanup activity must comply with state law. The UST booklet is available from the DEQ or can be downloaded via the Internet by using the Web address shown above and then clicking on the booklet title.

Online Information

The Waste Program at Idaho's Department of Environmental Quality can be found on the Web at

WWWeb.Link

www.deq.state.id.us/waste/prog_issues/ust_lust/index.cfm

Underground storage tanks also include septic systems. Anyone who has a home with a well and septic system should be familiar with the operation and care of the system. A booklet, *A Homeowner's Guide to Septic Systems*, is also available from the DEQ and may be viewed on their Web site.

Online Information

The Water Quality Program at Idaho's Department of Environmental Quality can be found on the Web at

WWWeb.Link

www.deq.state.id.us/water/prog_issues/waste_water/onsite_septic_systems.cfm

For more information regarding the handling and cleanup of USTs, contact the Idaho Environmental Protection Agency or the Idaho Department of Environmental Quality at 1410 North Hilton, Boise, Idaho 83706. DEQ's telephone number is 1-208-373-0502.

Meth and Mold

Additional hazardous materials located on or around property include but are not limited to methamphetamine and mold. If the Idaho State Police Department seizes chemicals from a property, the property owner will be notified of such seizure. In addition, the Idaho State Police will notify various parties in the county in which the property is located including the County Commissioners and County Assessors in the county in which the property is located. In addition, letters will be sent to the Central Health District, Department of Health and Welfare, and the Bureau of Hazardous Materials. Cleanup should only be done by professionals trained in removing hazardous materials.

Online Information

Additional information about meth, including addresses of closed cases by the Idaho State Police, can be found at

WWWeb.Link

www.isp.state.id.us/citizen/drug_community.html

Mold is also causing concern in the real estate industry throughout the country, including Idaho. Causes of mold-related problems include but are not limited to: water in a crawlspace, leaking lines to ice makers of refrigerators, flooding dishwashers and/or clothes washing machines, and broken water lines. Sprinkler lines too close to foundations, improper grading and compaction of backfill away from foundations, and improper installation of insulation or venting in attic areas have also contributed to mold-related issues.

If mold is a concern, only properly trained professionals should evaluate the situation and suggest solutions. Again, removal of mold and water sources can be quite expensive, so caution should be exercised if a property has been exposed to water issues.

Remember, if meth, mold, or any other hazardous materials have been found on a property, a licensee must disclose to a buyer or seller, regardless of the agency relationship, "all adverse material facts actually known or reasonably should have been known by the licensee."

Manufacture of Controlled Substance [IC 6-303, 6-310, 6-311]

The Unlawful Detainer statute has been amended to allow landlords a more rapid method of evicting those who may be illegally using or producing controlled substances on the landlord's property.

The statute allows reasonable grounds, or the belief that a tenant is involved in illegal production, distribution, or use of controlled substances, as the basis for bringing an action for unlawful detainer before the court.

The landlord can use a 12-day window for action to initiate eviction. However, the landlord must have specific and articulate facts to believe that criminal activity is at hand to ensure frivolous actions are not brought before the court.

If wrong, the landlord could be held liable to pay all costs and fees associated with the tenant in their defense.

■ IDAHO LOCAL LAND USE PLANNING ACT [IC 67-6501 TO 67-6529]

The Local Land Use Planning Act repealed the former planning and zoning authority of cities and the former zoning authority of counties. With the enactment of the Local Land Use Planning Act, the Idaho legislature prescribed, in much greater detail, the terms and conditions for exercising regulatory authority over land use. A fundamental requirement is that the adoption of a comprehensive plan is a prerequisite to exercising zoning and subdivision control. Beyond this planning requirement, the Act established basic standards and procedures that local governments must follow in order to establish and administer a system of land-use controls.

Standards and procedures contained in the act fall into the following three categories:

1. Requirements for the organizational framework to enact and administer land-use regulations
2. Requirements for establishing and amending regulatory measures (the plan, the zoning ordinance, the subdivision ordinance)
3. Requirements for administration of permits under adopted regulatory measures (special uses, planned unit developments, subdivision approvals, and variances)

Organizational Framework

The Local Land Use Planning Act permits local governments to enjoy considerable leeway in establishing an organizational framework for regulating land use. The governing board (the city council or county commissioners) may exercise authority directly; delegate all or part of its authority (except for the authority to enact ordinances) to a planning commission and a zoning commission or a combined planning and zoning commission; or provide for initial decisions by a commission with appeal to the governing board. Governing boards in the affected jurisdictions also may establish joint planning, zoning, or planning and zoning commissions. Also, ordinances may provide for the appointment of hearing examiners to hear and make recommendations concerning particular permit applications.

Membership on commissions may range from 3 to 12 persons who have resided in the county at least five years. On county commissions, two-thirds of the membership must reside in unincorporated areas.

Membership may exceed 12 if necessary to achieve proportional representation on city commissions operating under impact area agreements or on joint planning commissions.

The commissions are required to adopt bylaws, hold regular meetings at least once a month for nine months of the year, and maintain records of meetings and other actions taken.

Members of governing boards and commissions are prohibited from acting in any case where the member—or a person with an employment, a business, or a family relationship with the member—has an economic interest. Members are required to reveal any conflict or potential conflict before the matter is considered.

■ THE COMPREHENSIVE PLAN

In contrast to the rather ambiguous role of planning in land-use regulation in the past, the Local Land Use Planning Act requires

■ preparation and adoption of a plan document;
■ zoning in accordance with the adopted plan; and
■ plan amendment before any rezone request is approved that is inconsistent with the plan.

The Local Land Use Planning Act requires local governments to adopt a plan covering historical and existing conditions, trends, and future goals and objectives for 11 specified elements unless an explanation is given as to why a particular element is unnecessary. The specificity required for each of these elements varies.

The apparent purpose in giving the plan greater than advisory effect is to require communities to articulate the policies they will pursue in exercising land-use controls so that interested persons are given notice of what to expect. The plan must be reviewed every five years.

Adoption, Amendment, or Repeal of Comprehensive Plan

The Local Land Use Planning Act requires the following for the adoption, amendment, or repeal of the comprehensive plan:

■ Two-stage notice and hearing process before the planning (or planning and zoning) commission and governing board
■ Republication of notice and additional hearing at the commission or governing board level "material changes" are made after a public hearing
■ Adoption by governing board via "resolution or ordinance"
■ Publication of plan (may be by reference)
■ Two special provisions applying to plan amendment:

  1. Standard: to correct "errors in the original plan or to recognize substantial changes in the actual condition of the area"
  2. Frequency of changes:
     a. Any person may petition for a plan change at any time.
     b. The commission may recommend amendments to the plan not more often than once every six months.

■ THE ZONING ORDINANCE

Historically, the use of private land in this country has been regulated by local units of government. Even today, with state and federal governments playing an increasing role in land-use regulation, local governments retain the principal mechanisms for regulating land use.

Of all the different powers local governments have to control the use and development of land, including regulatory authority (zoning, subdivision ordinances, and building codes), budgetary power (such as investments in water and sewer facilities and services and eminent domain), and taxing authority, *zoning* constitutes the most fundamental and far-reaching power.

Zoning authority consists of the power to regulate, for all legitimate police power purposes, the location and intensity of various uses of land as well as the power to regulate the physical design and arrangement of structures on land.

Thus zoning ordinances, which prescribe standards for development and building design, may overlap areas covered by building, subdivision, or other ordinances. However, the central and distinctive feature of zoning is the power to define different types and intensities of uses and to prescribe their location within a particular jurisdiction by means of mapped districts.

Regulatory Standards

The heart of a typical zoning ordinance is the sections setting forth different types and intensities of uses and the standards that apply to each. A typical zoning ordinance will recognize at least five major uses: residential, commercial, industrial, recreational, and agricultural. The agricultural category may represent an active use category, designed to conserve agricultural land and prevent conflict with agricultural operations, or it may represent a landholding category designed to be rezoned according to its highest and best use when the market creates a demand for its development.

Ordinarily, these major uses will be further subdivided into districts that represent different densities or types and intensities of these uses. Thus, residential use may be subdivided into high, medium, and low density and/or be categorized by different housing types (single family, multiple family, manufactured homes, and such).

In any event, uses predating new zoning restrictions must be allowed to continue as nonconforming uses, although they ordinarily will be restricted from expansion and may be subject to termination over a period of time.

Regulatory standards applying to the setup of manufactured homes have been established as well. All manufactured homes must be installed in accordance with the manufacturer's instructions. If the manufacturer's instructions are not available, the home must be installed in accordance with applicable setup codes.

Within the text of the ordinance setting forth the different use zones (or in a separate district designed to be superimposed over the use districts), standards for building design and arrangements of structures are specified. These regulations typically include height, yard, setback, and parking requirements and may include a variety of other design and performance standards.

Within any use district, allowable types of use are set forth. These uses fall into one of two categories:

1. "Permitted" uses (permitted as a matter of right, as long as the various design requirements are observed)
2. "Special" or "conditional" uses (can be permitted by the commission or governing board if such uses are determined to meet special design and performance standards and are compatible with neighboring uses)

IN PRACTICE

Any definition of "single family dwelling" must include group homes in which eight or fewer unrelated elderly or mentally or physically handicapped persons live under supervision by no more than two staff persons.

Administrative Procedures

Usually the latter portions of a zoning ordinance are devoted to administrative procedures. In these sections, the offices authorized to pass on disputed interpretations of ordinances and to act on variances, special-use, other permits, and requests for rezoning are designated.

Also, the procedures for dealing with each are set forth. Included in this portion of the ordinance are any general standards that apply to permits and rezoning requests. Steps must be taken to ensure that ordinance procedures follow minimum requirements established for various decisions by state statutes and that the prescribed procedures are adhered to in handling specific requests.

Standards and Procedures for Administration of Permits

The two general requirements for issuance of all permits under the Local Land Use Planning Act (special-use permits, planned unit development [PUD] permits, variance permits, and subdivision permits) are as follows:

1. Standards:
   a. Procedures for processing all permits for which a fee is charged must be set forth in the zoning, subdivision, or another ordinance.
   b. Rules must be adopted by the governing board establishing a time period for action by the commission and the board for all permits.
2. Procedures:
   a. All permits must be referred to the zoning (or planning and zoning) commission for recommendation and can be assigned to the commission for decision.
   b. The grant or denial of a permit must specify the following three items:
      i.   Ordinance or standards used
      ii. Reasons for the action
      iii. Actions, if any, the applicant could take to obtain a permit

Beyond the requirements of this section, the Act contains different minimum standards and procedures for the different types of permits.

■ SUBDIVISION CONTROLS

Subdivision regulations are intended to protect the local community from the creation and development of poorly designed and ill-equipped neighborhoods. The regulations require that

- new streets be properly constructed and logically related to the existing street system with which they connect;
- newly developed land be provided with basic services;
- other residents be protected from the financial impact of initial installation costs;
- the subdivision be consistent with zoning regulations; and
- the owners and developers of the subdivision occasionally bear the cost of providing open space necessary to serve the recreational and environmental needs of the future inhabitants of the subdivision.

The broad purpose of subdivision controls is to *guide* community development and to protect prospective residents and neighboring owners from the problems of poorly designed areas.

Regulation of the subdivision of land for the protection of the public health, safety, and welfare is within the police powers delegated to cities and counties. In Idaho, reasonable subdivision regulations have been upheld under the constitutional grant of police powers, even without enabling legislation. By statute, however, cities and counties now are required to provide standards for subdivision permits.

By statute, a *subdivision* is defined as a tract of land divided into five or more lots, parcels, or sites for the purpose of sale or building development, whether immediate or future, except for agricultural purposes.

Cities (but not counties) have the power to approve or disapprove subdivision plats within one mile outside of their corporate boundaries and, by agreement between an individual city and county, the city may be authorized to extend its subdivision regulations even further into the unincorporated areas of the county. Counties have no authority to exercise their subdivision controls within incorporated cities although, through use of a joint service agreement, a city presumably could contract with a county to have the county's officers enforce the city's subdivision ordinances within the city. Sewer and water facilities provided to a subdivision must be approved by the Idaho Department of Environmental Quality (if the subdivision exceeds 25 lots) or the local health district before the subdivision plat may be recorded.

Typically, the local subdivision ordinances contain standards for street width and construction; continuity with existing streets; installation of paving, curbs, gutters, and sidewalks; drainage facilities; provision of water and sewer facilities, including easements; and dedication of required rights-of-way.

Such ordinances usually provide that no subdivision plat may be recorded, nor may any sales of lots or blocks within a subdivision occur, until provision has been made for the installation, immediately or in the future, of the required dedication and improvements.

Because the county recorder cannot accept a plat for filing without proof of the required approvals, subdivision regulations must be met before a subdivider may record the plat and sell the lots and blocks within the subdivision.

Subdivision standards may be included as part of the subdivision ordinance itself or as part of a zoning or planned unit development ordinance, or they may be set forth by a separate ordinance. Procedural requirements for adoption of subdivision ordinances are the same as for the adoption of comprehensive plans and zoning ordinances.

Hearings before the planning, or planning and zoning, commission, and the governing body are required for adoption or amendment. Existing subdivision ordinances may be updated and amended in the same manner.

At the heart of modern subdivision ordinances is the requirement of *dedication* of property within the subdivision for public use, such as streets, alleys, drainage, sewers, water lines, and sometimes (especially under the more recent subdivision ordinances) parks and even schools or other public facilities. Dedication is a conveyance of an interest in land to the government for a public purpose. A dedication of land has an important effect on the subdivider, the public, and purchasers of land in the subdivision. In effect, the subdivider parts with ownership, even where the dedication is only an easement. The public obtains the dedicated land without cost. The purchaser will be ensured proper access and utilities but probably will pay more for the land than otherwise would be the case.

Under Idaho law, the owner of land included in a subdivision plat must make a dedication, on the plat, of all the streets and alleys shown on the plat. Local ordinances usually require additional dedication for utility easements. The effect of acknowledging and recording the plat is equivalent to a deed in fee simple for the portion of the premises set apart for streets or other public use. No street or alley dedicated by plat shall be deemed a public street or alley until the dedication is accepted and confirmed by the governing body of the city or county.

■ BUILDING, HOUSING, PLUMBING, FIRE, ELECTRICAL, AND GAS CODES

Police power enables cities and counties, in the interest of public safety, to enact codes governing building and housing construction, fire prevention, and the installation of plumbing, electrical, and gas distribution systems and fixtures. Early Idaho Supreme Court cases upheld the power of cities to enact and enforce fire and building codes. Idaho statutes also recognize local governmental authority in this area. The Idaho legislature has expressly declared building codes to be in the interest of public health, safety, and welfare.

One common method by which local governments regulate construction of buildings is by adoption of the 2000 International Building Code (Building Code) published by the International Conference of Building Officials. Idaho statutes specifically authorize cities and counties to adopt such codes by ordinance without publishing the entire code.

In addition, the Idaho legislature has adopted the Building Code and other nationally recognized codes and has made them applicable (with certain exceptions, including farms) throughout the state. Local governments are required to comply with each code and may provide inspection and enforcement, or may leave the inspection and enforcement duties to the State Department of Labor and Industrial Services.

The purpose of the Building Code is to provide minimum standards to safeguard life or limb, health, property, and public welfare by regulating and controlling the design, construction, quality of materials, use and occupancy, location, and maintenance of all buildings and structures and certain equipment in them. The Building Code and its related codes, such as the Housing Code, Mechanical Code, Uniform Code on Abatement of Dangerous Buildings, the Northwest Energy Code, and others, must be constructed in conjunction with local zoning ordinances.

However, there is an exception relating to low-cost housing and mobile home parks. Section 34-4103 of the Idaho Code provides an exemption to the Building Code allowing the board to grant a variance from the standards where a need for reduced costs for housing has been established and the use of another standard would result in reduced costs while maintaining a reasonable level of safety.

A related, nationally recognized code is the Uniform Fire Code, published jointly by the International Conference of Building Officials and the Western Fire Chiefs Association. The intent of the Uniform Fire Code is to prescribe regulations for safeguarding life and property from the hazards of fire and explosion arising from the storage, handling, and use of hazardous substances, materials, and devices and from conditions hazardous to life or property in the use or occupancy of buildings or premises. The code contains specific regulations on explosives, gases, lumberyards, building exits, and the like.

Additional fire and life safety regulations are contained in the Life Safety Code, published by the National Fire Protection Association. The provisions of this code overlap to some extent with the Uniform Fire Code. A local government that adopts both codes must specify in the adopting ordinance which code will prevail where overlap occurs.

Nationally recognized codes on plumbing, electrical, and gas installation are also adopted by local governments in Idaho. All of these codes are directed at promoting public safety and must be used for that purpose. The codes are not intended as devices to prevent growth but are important and necessary growth guidance tools in that they require a certain quality of growth by specifying minimum construction and safety standards.

■ ANNEXATION

Idaho law permits cities, in certain circumstances, to expand their boundaries by annexing adjacent property. This power is statutory, is not inherent in cities, and is not a part of a city's police power. Although county boundaries also may be altered, subject to certain constitutional provisions, and although some special districts also have annexation powers, the focus of this section is on the power of cities to annex adjacent unincorporated territory into the corporate limits, with or without the approval of the county or of the owners of the property.

Annexation is a *unilateral* power in that, as long as the requirements set forth by statute are met, Idaho cities may enlarge their boundaries merely by passing the proper ordinance, without the prior consent of anyone other than the city council.

Statutory Requirements [IC 50-222 through 50-233]

The first requirement is that the land to be annexed must be contiguous or adjacent to the city. The terms *contiguous* and *adjacent* have been defined in a number of Idaho Supreme Court decisions; the later cases have tended to strictly explain the requirement as meaning that the property to be annexed must be physically adjacent to or abutting the city and must be in the area of "city impact" as determined by the procedures in the Code.

After the requirement of contiguity is met, the area may be annexed if any one of the following conditions exists:

- The property has been, by the owner or by any person with the owner's authority or acquiescence, laid off into blocks containing not more than five acres of land each, whether platted or not.
- The owner or proprietor or any person by or with the owner's authority has sold or begun to sell off such lands in tracts not exceeding five acres.
- The owner or proprietor or any person by or with the owner's authority requests annexation in writing to the council.
- The tract is entirely surrounded by properties lying within the city boundaries.

The courts have construed the statute to mean that after a single sale has occurred from a tract of five acres or less, regardless of whether it is subdivided and platted, the entire tract may be annexed, even though the remainder is more than five acres. Even the acts of prior owners of the property may subject the land to annexation. The court has held that, if the tract is presently larger than five acres and the present owner has not subdivided or begun to sell in tracts of five acres or less, the burden of proof is on the city to show that some property in question was in his or her ownership.

There is an additional limitation on a city's power to annex. Idaho Code provides that a city may annex "only those areas which can be reasonably assumed to be used for orderly development of the city."

Assuming that the annexation ordinance has been enacted validly, certain additional procedural requirements must be observed. First, the city must comply with Idaho Code by filing certified copies of the annexation ordinance, legal description, and map with the appropriate county offices and with the State Tax Commission.

Second, following the procedures set forth in the Local Planning Act, the city must provide for the zoning designation of the annexed area. Zoning must take place simultaneously with the annexation because the Idaho Code provides: "Concurrently or immediately following the adoption of an ordinance of annexation, the city council must amend the comprehensive plan and zoning ordinance."

An important limitation on cities' annexation powers is the Idaho Code provision that permits agricultural lands, whether platted or unplatted, to be detached from a city through proceedings in district court.

The requirements for the detachment of agricultural lands are fairly simple, and if an owner can show that all requirements are met, the owner has a legal right to deannexation from the city, regardless of the effect on the city's comprehensive planning process.

For agricultural deannexation to occur, the property must

- contain not fewer than five acres;
- be within the corporate limits of a city;
- be used exclusively for agricultural purposes (the existence of a railroad or canal on the property does not amount to a nonagricultural purpose); and
- not receive sufficient special benefits to justify its retention in the city.

In addition, the symmetry of the city must not be materially marred by the detachment of the lands.

■ POTENTIAL TAKINGS OF PRIVATE PROPERTY [IC 67-80]

The Idaho legislature enacted legislation requiring the attorney general to develop an orderly, consistent process for state agencies to use in evaluating whether or not a proposed regulatory or administrative action would result in an unconstitutional "taking" of private property in violation of the fifth and fourteenth Amendments to the U.S. Constitution. In 1995, the statute was extended to local governments and political subdivisions. Under Article I, section 14 of the Idaho Constitution, *private property may be taken for public use, but not until a just compensation, to be ascertained in the manner prescribed by law, shall be paid therefore.* "Private property" for the purposes of this law means only real property.

The following are three situations in which a government action may require compensation to be paid to a property owner:

1. A government action caused *actual physical occupancy* of the property.
2. A government action causes a *physical invasion* of the property.
3. A government regulation *effectively eliminates all economic value* of the property.

The Attorney General of Idaho has established the following checklist of questions for agencies to ask in order to determine whether or not a proposed action should be reviewed for potential constitutional issues:

- Does the regulation or action result in a permanent or temporary physical occupation of private property?
- Does the regulation or action require a property owner to dedicate a portion of his or her property, or to grant an easement?
- Does the regulation deprive the owner of all economically viable uses of the property?
- Does the regulation have a significant impact on the landowner's economic interest?
- Does the regulation deny a fundamental attribute of ownership?
- Does the regulation serve the same purposes that would be served by directly prohibiting the use or action, and does the condition imposed substantially advance that purpose?

For example, the action of a city in demanding that the owner of private waterfront property provide a public easement as a condition for a building permit to construct a modest addition to an existing home would be an unconstitutional taking, as would an ordinance that required all privately held land within 500 feet of any public school to be left in its natural state forever.

Copies of the Attorney General's guidelines may be obtained by contacting the office of the Attorney General.

Online Information

The Office of the Attorney General for the State of Idaho can be found on the Web at

WWWeb.Link

www2.state.id.us/ag/

■ SPECIAL DISTRICTS

Numerous special districts may be created in Idaho to provide particular services to residents and owners of property. These include such special districts as auditorium, cemetery, drainage, fire protection, flood control, highway (including the old "good road" districts), hospital, irrigation, library, mosquito abatement, port, recreation, school, sewer, soil conservation, water, combined water and sewer, and watershed improvement districts, as well as city-created or county-created authorities, urban renewal agencies, housing authorities, and regional airport authorities.

Special districts differ from "general" governmental entities primarily in that special districts have no general governmental powers. They usually provide only a single, special governmental service. Special districts do not have the authority to pass general regulatory ordinances or to provide other governmental services beyond those specifically set forth in their enabling legislation.

QUESTIONS

1. The fundamental requirement of the Idaho Local Land Use Planning Act of 1975 is the adoption of
   a. a zoning ordinance.
   b. a comprehensive plan.
   c. a subdivision ordinance.
   d. all the above.

2. Any land use in existence prior to the adoption of a new zoning restriction must be allowed to continue as a
   a. conditional use.
   b. special use.
   c. nonconforming use.
   d. variance.

3. Any amendment or repeal of a zoning ordinance or change in a zoning boundary requires notice to be made to all landowners who are
   a. impacted.
   b. of legal voting age.
   c. both a and b.
   d. registered voters.

4. By statute, a subdivision is defined as a tract of land divided into _____ or _____ lots, parcels, or sites for the purpose of sale, building, or development, whether immediate or future, except for agricultural purposes.
   a. four/more
   b. five/fewer
   c. five/more
   d. six/more

5. Cities (but not counties) have the power to approve or disapprove subdivision plats within how many miles of their corporate boundaries?
   a. One-half
   b. One
   c. Two
   d. Three

6. Sewer and water facilities provided to a subdivision must be approved by the Idaho State Department of Health and Welfare if the number of subdivision lots exceeds
   a. 10.
   b. 50.
   c. 100.
   d. 25.

7. All but which of the following fall within a city's police powers?
   a. Zoning ordinances
   b. Annexation
   c. Building codes
   d. Fire codes

8. Lead-based paint hazards must be disclosed to prospective buyers and tenants of property built before
   a. 1968.
   b. 1978.
   c. 1987.
   d. 1979.

CHAPTER FIFTEEN

IDAHO FAIR HOUSING

◼ DISCRIMINATION IN HOUSING

The Idaho Fair Housing Law applies to apartments, condominiums, duplexes, and other attached housing; mobile homes and trailer courts; and vacant lands, commercial property, and private homes. Specifically, it prohibits discrimination in housing based on the following:

- Race
- Color
- Religion
- Sex
- National origin
- Familial status
- Handicap

In Idaho, discrimination based on any of these factors is prohibited in business transactions. The *prohibited acts* are set forth, along with illustrations, below.

◼ **Refusing to show, rent, lease, sell, or transfer housing.**

Jack, who uses a wheelchair, is told that the house he wants to rent is no longer available. The next day, however, the For Rent sign is still in the window.

◼ **Causing unequal terms, conditions, and privileges of housing.**

Samantha, a Roman Catholic, calls on a duplex and the landlord tells her the rent is $400 per month. When she talks to the other tenants, she learns that all the Lutherans in the complex pay only $325 per month.

◼ **Causing unequal terms, conditions, and privileges in obtaining and using financial assistance for the purchase, construction, or maintenance of housing.**

Anne, a single, divorced mother, is required to pay for a credit report and have her father cosign her mortgage loan. After talking to a male friend, she learns that he was given a loan without those requirements, despite his lower income.

■ **Segregating and/or separating housing.**

John wants to buy a house. He asks Berthold, a broker, to show him all the properties in his price range in the city. Berthold decides to show John only those houses located in a few areas "where people like John live."

■ **Including or honoring discriminatory restrictive covenants.**

A certain subdivision was established with a restrictive covenant limiting resale of homes to baptized Christians. A real estate agent informs a potential buyer that she cannot buy a home in the subdivision because she is Jewish.

■ **Advertising any discriminatory preference or limitation in housing, making any inquiry or reference that is discriminatory in nature.**

A real estate agent places the following advertisement in a newspaper: "Just Listed! Perfect home for white family, near an excellent parochial school!" A developer places this ad: "Sunset River Hollow—Dream Homes Just for You!" accompanied by a photo of several black families.

■ **Aiding and abetting unfair housing practices, preventing any person from complying with fair housing practices.**

David tells his real estate agent that he won't sell to "any of those darn Swedes." David's agent neglects to show the property to people she suspects are of Swedish descent. David's neighbor, Quigley, tells his agent that he will rent his house to anyone. However, Quigley's agent refuses to show the property to Native Americans.

■ **Retaliating against an employee or agent who complies with fair housing practices.**

The real estate agent who helped you find a home was given less than the normal commission split and told to move his license to another office that complies with "those stupid fair housing laws."

■ **Refusing to receive and transmit any bona fide offer to buy, rent, sell, or lease housing.**

A real estate agent receives three good offers on a property, but only tells the owner about the two that are made by people of the agent's ethnic group.

In Idaho, there is one exception to the general ban against discrimination in housing: A religious institution or organization is permitted to give preference in a real estate transaction to members of the same religion.

The discrimination laws also do not apply to an individual who offers a room or rooms for rent in a housing accommodation in which he or she, or a member of his or her family, lives. Similarly, the laws do not apply to multifamily dwellings (up to and including a fourplex) if the lessor or a member of the lessor's family lives in one of the units.

■ FAIR HOUSING PARTNERSHIP

A previous Voluntary Affirmative Marketing Agreement between the National Association of REALTORS® (NAR) and the U.S. Department of Housing and Urban Development (HUD) was replaced in 1996 with a Fair Housing Partnership agreement.

This partnership emphasizes a cooperative approach to addressing our nation's fair housing concerns. It focuses on the identification and eradication of housing discrimination in our communities. Because housing discrimination issues and priorities differ from community to community, the partnership is intentionally flexible. The partnership is based on the principle of providing support for and focusing attention on the implementation of local community incentives.

Residential Housing for Disabled [IC 67-6531]

Up to eight unrelated mentally and/or physically handicapped individuals may reside in a single family dwelling and still comply with the zoning law, ordinance, or code.

■ HOW TO FILE A CHARGE OF HOUSING DISCRIMINATION

A charge of discrimination may be filed with the Idaho Human Rights Commission, the U.S. Department of Housing and Urban Development (HUD), or the Boise HUD office within one year of the alleged discriminatory action. A suit may be filed in federal court within two years of the alleged discriminatory act.

The Idaho Commission on Human Rights is located at 1109 W. Main, Suite 400, Boise, Idaho 83720. The commission's telephone number is 1-208-334-2873.

Online Information

The Idaho Commission on Human Rights can be found on the Web at

WWWeb.Link

www2.state.id.us/ihrc/ihrchome.htm

The U.S. Department of Housing and Urban Development regional office is located at

U.S. Department of Housing and Urban Development
Regional Office of Fair Housing
Arcade Plaza Building
1321 Second Avenue
Seattle, WA 98101
Phone: 1-206-442-4307

The local office for Idaho is located in Boise at

HUD Department of Idaho State Office
Plaza IV, Suite 220
800 Park Boulevard
Boise, Idaho 83712-7743
Phone: 1-208-334-1990

Online Information

The Boise HUD Office can be found on the Web at

WWWeb.Link   *www.hud.gov/local/boi/index.html*

Additional information addressing various aspects of Fair Housing and Equal Opportunity can be found at

WWWeb.Link   *www.hud.gov/offices/fheo/index.cfm*

This Web site gives an overview of the act itself as well as addressing discrimination complaints, advertising guidelines, and HUD's advertising guidance.

■ WHAT HAPPENS WHEN A CHARGE IS FILED

The person charging discrimination signs a formal complaint form that allows the Idaho Human Rights Commission or HUD to investigate the case. Strict guidelines apply to the disclosure of information on a charge, and all information remains confidential unless a case is authorized for hearing or court action. Most cases are resolved prior to reaching that state, however.

A civil rights specialist will make every effort to settle the charge immediately, which often may result in a voluntary no-fault settlement. If a no-fault settlement does not occur, an investigation and interview will be conducted with all parties involved in the charge. If the facts do not support a finding of probable cause, the case will be dismissed. If the facts support the charge, a finding of probable cause, attempts will be made to conciliate the case. If the conciliation effort is not successful, the case may be taken to a hearing or court action, or it may be dismissed.

QUESTIONS

1. The Idaho fair housing laws apply to
   a. the rental of a room in a house by an individual who lives there.
   b. the rental of a duplex unit if a member of the lessor's family lives in the other unit.
   c. a church-owned retirement center that gives preference to church members.
   d. the sale or transfer of a mobile home.

2. A person who believes that he or she has been discriminated against may file a complaint with
   a. the Idaho Board of REALTORS®.
   b. the Idaho Attorney General.
   c. the Idaho Real Estate Commission.
   d. the Idaho Human Rights Commission or HUD.

3. A housing discrimination charge must be filed with the Idaho Human Rights Commission within
   a. 6 months.
   b. 1 year.
   c. 2 years.
   d. 30 days.

4. Which of the following is *NOT* a protected class under the Idaho Fair Housing Law?
   a. Race
   b. Handicap
   c. Sexual preference
   d. Ancestry

5. Which of the following acts is prohibited in a real estate transaction?
   a. A broker shows houses to a buyer only in certain neighborhoods in which the buyer has expressed an interest.
   b. A property manager refuses to rent to a blind person because he thinks the blind person will probably ask for special treatment.
   c. A loan officer requires that an unemployed male have his father cosign his mortgage loan but does not require a cosigner for an employed woman.
   d. An agent refuses to list a home in a subdivision if the seller insists on enforcing a restrictive covenant barring members of certain races and religions.

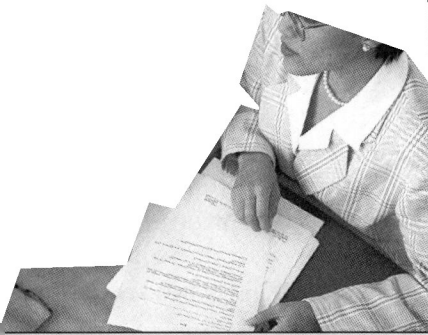

CHAPTER SIXTEEN

CLOSING THE REAL ESTATE TRANSACTION

■ THE CLOSING

In Idaho, the majority of real estate sales transactions are closed in the office of the escrow closing agent, the financial institution, or the broker. In a cooperative sale, either the listing broker or the selling broker can be the responsible broker.

The responsible broker is responsible for the accuracy of the closing and the delivery of the signed settlement statements; however, one or both parties may desire an attorney to represent them and/or direct the closing. An independent and impartial escrow (closing) agent may handle the closing for a fee. Transactions involving federally funded loans must be closed by either an attorney or a title company, as required by federal regulations.

However, a closing handled by an attorney or title company does *not* relieve the broker's responsibilities of accuracy and delivery of closing statements [IC 54-2048].

Broker's Responsibility

In supervising the closing of a transaction, a broker must make sure that all necessary information is obtained, documents prepared, and other details taken care of as provided by the terms of the purchase and sale agreement and/or earnest money agreement. Any deviation from these provisions should have the written consent of both buyer and seller.

The broker's responsibility in closing a transaction extends to every area that is listed on the closing statement or that otherwise affects ownership of the property being sold, including the following five:

1. *Financial arrangements of both parties.* Preparations for any new financing, loan assumptions, or loan payoffs must be coordinated by the broker so that any required mortgages, trust deeds, assignments, releases, contracts for deed, or other papers are provided for and ready to be executed at the closing.

2. *Title considerations.* Items such as the seller's deed, the required evidence of title, and any documents necessary to clear the seller's title must be obtained or prepared. In Idaho an abstract of title with an attorney's opinion or a title insurance policy is acceptable evidence of the seller's title; however, in recent years an owner's title insurance policy, furnished by the seller to the buyer, has been used almost exclusively.

   When the buyer is financing the purchase through a lending institution, the lender will require an additional title insurance policy called a *mortgagee extended coverage policy* (or *lender's policy*), which protects the lender's interest. The charge for this additional policy is customarily paid by the buyer/borrower.

3. *Taxes and other liens, including mechanics' and energy liens and assessments of the Local Improvement District (LID).* Some of these must be paid off at the closing; others will have been paid in advance or will be due in the future.

4. *Public utility charges.* Final readings must be taken so that current bills can be prorated. Some utilities are paid in advance for the upcoming service period; others are paid in arrears for the preceding service period.

5. *Insurance.* Buyers should be notified well in advance that they will have to obtain new homeowners' coverage to begin on the day of closing. While a lender will usually accept an insurance agent's binder as evidence of coverage, lenders are increasingly demanding the actual policy as part of the closing package.

Obtaining information and ordering documents.   Closing statement information must be carefully prepared and documented. In preparing to close a real estate transaction, the most reliable source must be used for information—for example, the county assessor or treasurer for information concerning real estate taxes and the lending institution involved in the transaction for information on the current balance of an existing loan.

The Idaho Code requires municipalities to record any LID lien with the county just like taxes and other liens. However, information regarding such assessments is apt to be more reliable when obtained from the clerk of the municipality where the payments are made instead of the county treasurer's office. Most public and private agencies will not accept liability for erroneous verbal information. The safest way is to get any loan payoffs, lien release amounts, irrigation company assessments, and LID assessments in writing, dated and signed by the person giving the information.

What about the existing loan? Discovering whether the loan payments are up to date is not sufficient; the date on which the interest is due must be known in order to prorate that interest correctly. Some lenders require at least 30 days' prior notice when a loan is to be paid off or they can charge interest for an additional 30 days.

If an existing loan is to be assumed by the buyer, the lenders often require both buyer and seller to execute several different documents. It is very important to order an *assumption package* from the lender well in advance of the designated closing date. Often the lender charges for this service, payable in advance. A closing statement based on incorrect information can create problems and unnecessary expense for all concerned parties.

The same kind of care should be taken when there is a need for the preparation of deeds, installment sales contracts, escrow instructions, property insurance policies, and title insurance policies. The accuracy of information supplied to the attorney, the title company, or another agency involved will determine the accuracy of the completed document.

Added care should be taken to ensure that all names are spelled correctly and that the exact legal description is given in any documents that will be recorded. Again, errors in such documents and papers will prove time consuming and costly to the parties involved in the transaction.

Making expenditures.   The experienced real estate broker will not disburse any of the funds held in trust for a client without considering important factors surrounding the circumstances of the transaction. All cash or like payments in lieu of cash received by a broker while acting as an agent are to be disbursed only in accordance with the terms of the purchase and sales agreement or another written authorization signed by the parties having an interest in such payments or by court order.

No disbursements from the real estate trust account shall be made in advance of the closing of a real estate transaction or before the happening of a condition set forth in the purchase and sales agreement to the seller, to the escrow agent, or to any other person for any reason without a written authorization signed by both the purchaser and seller. The trust accounting for a specific transaction must always balance; disbursements should not exceed the amount of money currently on deposit in that account.

Closing Statements

In every transaction, the designated closing broker is responsible for the correctness of the closing statements and for their delivery to the buyer and seller. The broker is not required to prepare the statements personally but is always held responsible for the accuracy of their content.

In the event of a cooperative sale, the earnest money agreement will state which broker is responsible for the closing of the transaction.

Customarily in Idaho, separate statements are prepared for the buyer and the seller. The statements, which may be delivered in person or by registered mail, should be signed and a signed copy returned to the broker. The buyer's and seller's signatures on their respective closing statements provide proof of statement delivery. If such statements are sent by certified mail with return receipt requested, a copy of the broker's letter, which accompanies the statement and acknowledges that the statement is enclosed, is sufficient proof of delivery, whether or not the recipient of the statement returns a signed copy to the broker.

In addition the broker must keep a true copy of each closing statement in his or her records for three years after the year in which the transaction was closed, along with copies of all other documents pertinent to the transaction, including the trust account records. This is required so that the Idaho Real Estate Commission inspector may examine the broker's records of completed transactions. In addition, the broker's copies of the closing statements may provide an invaluable service to a buyer or seller who has lost his or her copy and needs information to complete an income tax return.

In effect, the closing statement provides written evidence of the financial history of a transaction. A completed statement should include the following four parts:

1. A detailed account of the buyer's expenses and credits so that the buyer will know exactly what amounts have been expended on his or her behalf, what amounts have been credited, and how much money to bring to the closing
2. A complete accounting to the seller of expenses and credits and the amount of money to be realized from the sale
3. A detailed record of cash received by the broker and any disbursements made from that money (this reflects the accounting of the broker's trust fund for the transaction)
4. A disclosure of the amount of brokerage fee paid to the broker

Closing Action

Before the day of closing, the closing agent (escrow officer) or broker must advise both buyer and seller of the exact time and place of the closing. Usually the parties' spouses also must be present. A recent Idaho Supreme Court ruling requires that, whenever such a sales transaction involves the community property of a husband and wife, both spouses must execute (sign) any documents necessary for the transaction, such as the seller's deed to the buyer or the buyer's loan documents.

Many Idaho brokers prefer to close through a neutral escrow provider separately with the buyer and seller, holding that each party's financial considerations and arrangements are his or her private business.

Generally such brokers meet with the buyer first to accept payment of the sales price and take care of all details involving the buyer; then, after the buyer's check has cleared, they meet with the seller to complete the closing.

To close with the buyer first, however, the broker must have the deed and other papers prepared and signed by the seller before the closing. This way, the buyer can be given copies of the documents at closing. If a new or existing loan is involved, the buyer usually will close at the lending institution. In this case the seller's deed and assignment of the mortgage or trust deed (if there is an assumption) must be signed in advance and given by the broker to the lender before the buyer's closing.

Prior to the closing, the escrow provider or broker should inform the buyer of how much cash to bring to the closing. The buyer should bring a cashier's check or equivalency for the required sum, as required by most title companies. The broker also must make arrangements for the transfer of the keys to the property so that the buyer can gain access to the premises on the date of possession.

For money received in escrow, the real estate broker must comply with the Treasury Department Cash Reporting Regulations. In addition to reporting cash (coin and currency) deposits in excess of $10,000, the Department definition of cash requires reporting a deposit as a cash deposit if any combination of coin, currency, cashier's check(s), traveler's check(s), or money order(s) totals in excess of $10,000 *and* if any one of the deposits is less than $10,000.

■ **EXAMPLE**

— Deposit of $13,000 in currency—reportable
— Deposit of $13,000 in the form of a cashier's check—not reportable; single check in excess of $10,000
— Deposit of $6,500 in the form of two cashier's checks, one for $4,000 and one for $2,500—not reportable; individual amounts less than $10,000, but total deposit is also less than $10,000
— Deposit of $12,000 in the form of two cashier's checks, one for $8,000 and one for $4,000—reportable; individual amounts less than $10,000 for a total deposit in excess of $10,000
— Deposit of $25,000 in the form of two cashier's checks, one for $16,000 and one for $9,000—reportable; individual amount of less than $10,000 for a total deposit in excess of $10,000

The practice of a buyer exchanging currency for a series of cashier's checks or equivalents, each of which is less than $10,000, is called *structuring* by the IRS and is considered a possible effort to avoid the cash reporting requirement. IRS Form 8300 is used when reporting a transaction. A copy of the report must be provided to the depositor. The regulation provides for significant civil and criminal penalties for noncompliance; therefore, it would be prudent to err on the side of reporting too much rather than too little.

Buyer.   At the closing the broker or closing agent explains the closing statement to the buyer and the buyer executes the documents. All arrangements should be made in advance for the following papers so that they are completely prepared and awaiting the buyer's signature (unless they have been signed in advance):

■ Note and mortgage or trust deed, if a new loan is involved
■ Contract of sale and escrow instructions, if the sale is made on a land sale contract (contract for deed)
■ Closing statement
■ Any other documents in the transaction that require the buyer's signature

The broker collects from the buyer the amount indicated in the closing statement and delivers the following items to the buyer either at the closing or shortly afterward:

- Closing statement
- Copy of note and mortgage or trust deed (if possible), if a new loan is involved or if an existing loan is assumed
- Copy of contract, signed by the seller, and escrow instructions (if the sale is made on contract for deed)
- Deed (after it is recorded)
- Copy of insurance policy (usually supplied by the insurance company or agent)
- Copy of house plans (if available)
- Copy of survey (if available)
- Copy of title insurance policy

Seller. When closing with the seller, the broker also must make certain that the seller understands the closing statement, including the broker's accounting of cash received and disbursed in connection with the transaction. Any existing liens not being assumed by the buyer are paid off at this time. If the broker is paying off an existing mortgage or deed of trust loan for the seller and the lender is an individual rather than a lending institution, the broker should not disburse the check to the lender until a release of mortgage or deed of reconveyance and the canceled loan documents are received from that lender.

In addition, the seller executes the following documents, which may be signed in advance:

- Closing statement (should indicate the seller's new mailing address)
- Deed
- Contract of sale and escrow instructions (if the sale is made on contract for deed)
- Assignment of tax and insurance reserve account funds (if the existing loan is assumed by the buyer)
- Assignment of fire insurance policy required by lender (if the insurance company will permit such an assignment)
- Discount agreement (if any)
- IRS Form 2119 (to report the sale to the Internal Revenue Service)
- Any other documents in the transaction that require the seller's signature

The broker or closing agent pays the seller the amount indicated on the closing statement. If the seller is married, the check should be made payable to both spouses. In addition to the sale proceeds, the seller receives the following:

- Closing statement
- Old note and mortgage or trust deed (when received from lender), if existing loan is paid off
- Release of mortgage or deed of reconveyance (after it is recorded), if existing loan is paid off

- Copy of contract and long-term escrow instructions, if sale is being made on contract for deed
- Canceled insurance policy (if any)

Broker's accounts at title companies.   In the event the broker uses a title company instead of his own real estate trust account, the broker is still responsible for the trust funds held by the title company. The purchase and sales agreement must state which broker is responsible for deposit of the funds into the title company and that broker must have full control of the account and the trust funds. Also, the responsible broker must obtain a receipt of any deposit from the title company receiving such funds. In addition, the title company receiving funds from a brokerage must charge for this service and the broker must reconcile trust account funds at the title company monthly.

Recording.   Finally, the broker must make sure all documents in the transaction that should be recorded are filed with the county recorder. Such documents include the seller's deed to the buyer; the buyer's new mortgage or deed of trust; the seller's release of mortgage or deed of reconveyance if an old loan was paid off; and any documents necessary to clear the seller's title. These documents should be checked for correctness and completeness before they are recorded. Usually the recordings can be handled through the title insurance company if the broker gives the title company complete instructions on where to deliver the various documents after they have been recorded.

Escrow closings.   It is clear from the preceding discussion that many hours of work go into closing a real estate transaction. While using escrow closing departments of title companies, attorney offices, or other escrow closing agents does not relieve the broker of the responsibility for ensuring the accuracy of the settlement statements, a tremendous amount of time and work may be transferred to the closing agency. Typically, the buyer and seller split the cost of the closing escrow.

Where there is a contract for deed being closed, the closing agency will ensure that the collection of the debt is set up in a long-term collection or escrow account. The deed from the seller (the "vendor") to the buyer (the "vendee") is kept in this file until the terms of the contract have been satisfied, at which time the buyer receives the deed and can have it recorded to put title in his or her name. *No one except the seller's attorney should prepare this contract for deed.* The two parties usually split the attorney's fee, but the attorney works for and is the agent of the seller. The buyer typically will have his or her attorney review the contract.

Whenever a property is sold on contract, a separate escrow arrangement is usually set up for that contract and the contract remains in escrow until the buyer makes the final payment, at which time he or she obtains title to the property in the form of the deed from the seller.

■ CLOSING PROBLEM

Complete the closing statement form found in Figure 16.1 using the facts given in the following description of a real estate transaction.

On September 10, 2005, Jeff and Ronna Graham accept an offer to purchase their home from Mark and Sara Swenson.

The purchase price is $165,000.

The earnest money contract is accompanied by a personal check for $2,500.

The Swensons have at least $20,000 plus their share of the closing costs to put toward the purchase price.

The Swensons are securing a new mortgage in the amount of $148,500 at an interest rate of 6.5 percent for 30 years.

They are also responsible for the lender's (mortgagee) title insurance premium of $290 plus a credit report fee of $35, tax service fee of $72, and two months' tax and insurance reserves.

A 6 percent commission is to be paid to the real estate brokerage firm of Wilson, Wagner & Bills by the seller.

A first deed of trust currently recorded against the property has an unpaid principal balance of $94,120.59 as of October 1, 2005.

The principal and interest payment on this loan is $797.56 per month, including interest at 7.25 percent per annum, plus tax and insurance reserves of $162.03 per month.

The September payment has been made. There is a reserve account for taxes and insurance with a balance of $1,096.57.

The title insurance company's escrow closing fees are (A) $3 per thousand (or any portion thereof) of the purchase price, plus $45 or (B) $75, whichever is higher. Unless otherwise agreed, buyers and sellers equally split the cost of this service. (No agreements to the contrary have been made.)

The seller has agreed to pay 1 point for the benefit of the buyer.

The title insurance owner's policy to be charged is $880. A lender's policy is $240 plus endorsements totaling $50.

The recording fee for the new deed is $25 and $45 for a deed of reconveyance (paying off sellers' mortgage).

It is common for the buyer to be charged interest for the remaining days in the month the transaction is closed. The seller is also going to be charged interest from the last payment due date (October 1) to day of closing.

Real estate taxes for the previous year were $2,478.42. (*Note:* Current taxes are not available; use the previous year's taxes.)

Fire insurance will be provided by Greene Insurance Corporation for the buyers. Their first year's premium will be $315 and will be collected at closing.

Personal property, which includes a washer, dryer, and window air-conditioner, is to be purchased by the Swensons for a total of $625. This purchase is separate from the real estate transaction, but is included in the closing statement.

Note: Compute all prorations on the basis of a 360-day year/30-day month. Carry computations to four decimal places and round off when the computation is complete. Check your solution with the one given in the Answer Key.

F I G U R E 16.1

Closing Statement Form

CLOSING STATEMENT

Sale No. _____

Seller _____

Buyer _____

Property _____

Salesperson _____ Pro Rate Date _____

	BUYER		SELLER	
	DEBIT	CREDIT	DEBIT	CREDIT
Purchase Price				
Earnest Money				
Subsequent Payment				
Assumption				
First Mortgage Balance				
Interest				
Reserves				
Taxes				
Insurance				
FHA Insurance				
Assumption Fee				
Discount Points				
Contract Balance				
Interest				
New Mortgage Taken Out By Buyer				
Reserve for Taxes, Ins., Etc.				
Credit Report				
Loan Service Fee				
Appraisal Fee				
Interest Adj.				
MGIC Prem.				
Contract or Note Given Seller				
Taxes				
Special Assessments				
Fire Insurance				
Rent				
Title Insurance & Ats				
Recording & Release				
Attorney's Fees				
Escrow Fee				
Broker's Commission				
Cash From Buyer to Close				
Amount Paid To Seller				
BALANCE				

Prepared By _____

Date _____

APPROVED

BUYER _____

BUYER _____

SELLER _____

SELLER _____

STATE SOURCES OF INFORMATION

■ REAL ESTATE LICENSE LAWS/EDUCATION

Idaho Real Estate Commission
633 North Fourth Street
Boise, Idaho 83702
1-208-334-3285
Fax Number: 1-208-334-2050
Toll-free Number (within Idaho): 1-866-447-5411
www.idahorealestatecommission.com or *www.irec.idaho.gov*

The Idaho State Tax Commission
P.O. Box 36
Boise, Idaho 83722-0410
1-208-334-7500
Toll-free Number: 1-800-972-7660
http://tax.idaho.gov/

The Idaho Department of Water Resources (IDWR)
1301 North Orchard Street
Boise, Idaho 83706
1-208-327-7900
Fax Number: 1-208-327-7866
www.idwr.state.id.us

Idaho Real Estate License Law and Rules
via the Idaho Real Estate Commission Web page
www.idahorealestatecommission.com or *www.irec.idaho.gov*

State Real Estate Examination Dates, Fees, and Registration Information
Link to the *Idaho Candidate Handbook* via the Idaho Real Estate Commission
Web page
www.idahorealestatecommisson.com or *www.irec.idaho.gov*

Promissor—For State Exam
1-888-204-6231
Fax Number: 1-888-204-6291
www.promissor.com

■ LEASING

Idaho Landlord–Tenant Guidelines
via the Attorney General Web page
www2.state.id.us/ag/consumer/tipsandinfo.htm

■ APPRAISAL

Idaho Real Estate Appraiser Board at the Bureau of Occupational Licenses
1109 Main Street, Suite 220
Boise, Idaho 83702-5642
1-208-334-3233
www.ibol.idaho.gov/rea.htm

■ ENVIRONMENTAL AGENCIES AND ISSUES

Idaho Environmental Protection Agency
1435 North Orchard Street
Boise, Idaho 83706
1-208-378-5746
Fax Number: 1-208-378-5744
www.epa.gov/region10

Idaho Department of Environmental Quality
1410 North Hilton
Boise, Idaho 83706
1-208-373-0502
www.deq.state.id.us/

National Lead Information Center
www.epa.gov/lead/nlic.htm

The Idaho Department of Health and Welfare
450 West State Street, 4th Floor
Boise, Idaho 83702
1-208-334-5500
Fax Number: 1-208-334-6581
Hotline: 1-800-44-LUNGS
www.healthandwelfare.idaho.gov

The Waste Program at Idaho's Department of Environmental Quality
www.deq.state.id.us

The Water Quality Program at Idaho's Department of Environmental Quality
www.deq.state.id.us

The Office of the Attorney General for the State of Idaho
700 West Jefferson Street
P.O. Box 83720
Boise, Idaho 83720-0010
1-208-334-2400
Fax Number: 1-208-334-2530
www2.state.id.us/ag

■ FAIR HOUSING

The Idaho Commission On Human Rights
1109 Main Street, Suite 400
Boise, Idaho 83720
1-208-334-2873
www2.state.id.us/ihrc/ihrchome.htm

U.S. Department of Housing and Urban Development
Regional Office of Fair Housing
Arcade Plaza Building
1321 Second Avenue
Seattle, Washington 98101
1-206-442-4307
www.hud.gov/offices/fheo/index.cfm

Boise HUD Office
Plaza IV
800 Park Boulevard, Suite 200
Boise, Idaho 83712-7743
1-208-334-1990
www.hud.gov/local/boi/index.html

Please note: Internet addresses are subject to change.

ANSWER KEY

Following the answers in the Answer Key are explanations of the correct choices. These rationales are provided to help you make maximum use of the text. *Check your answers.* If you did not answer a question correctly, *restudy the course material until you understand the correct answer.*

CHAPTER 1
Real Estate Brokerage

1. c   Idaho code states: "A brokerage must disclose its relationship to both buyer and seller in any transaction no later than the preparation or presentation of a purchase and sale agreement" [IC 54-2085].

2. a   Addressing brokerage representation requires "all fees and commissions" to be addressed and included in the agreements [IC 54-2050].

3. d   When the broker actually knows but does not disclose, fraudulent misrepresentation occurs.

4. c   Disclosure of adverse material facts is required whether the consumer is a customer or client [IC 54-2086 and 54-2087].

5. c   Confidentiality applies to a client relationship, not a customer relationship.

6. b   Withholding is required only with an employee relationship, not with an independent contractor relationship.

CHAPTER 2
Buyer and Seller Representation Agreements

1. b   A property condition report does not require an "expert" but rather the seller. Also, there are exceptions in which the seller may not be required to supply a report.

2. a   Supply and demand plus appeal together with price and condition attract potential buyers.

3. c   The business name of the broker must be listed in any property advertising property for sale [IC 54-2053].

4. d   Whoever signs a "listing" agreement must receive a copy of such agreement upon signing [IC 54-2050].

5. b   Rob withdrew the listing without knowledge or approval of the broker; thus, a penalty could result.

6. b   Any "active" licensee must disclose he or she is licensed whether the property is listed or not [IC 54-2055].

7. d   A sex offender can be disclosed but such disclosure is NOT required [IC 55-2801].

8. d   A real estate licensee can sell a used unit on leased land but would be required to have additional licensing if selling a used unit off the lot of a manufactured home dealer.

9. c   Even though the agency relationship has ended, the licensee must maintain confidentiality beyond the termination of the listing [IC 54-2092].

10. c   If an active licensee owns any interest in real estate, he or she must disclose his or her license status as well as run the transaction through his or her broker [IC 54-2055].

CHAPTER 3

Interests in Real Estate

1. b   The condition was created when the transfer was made and subject to condition (determinable) and remains (executory) until such event is executed.

2. c   Because the mother is still alive, the property will not transfer (revert) back until her death.

3. c   Homestead exemption (protection against unsecured creditors) is $50,000.

4. a   The homeowner needs a waiver from the Idaho Department of Water Resources to abandon or have a licensed well driller verify abandonment.

5. b   To be eligible, the party claiming homestead must own and occupy for not less than six months a year to qualify.

6. b   The old saying "if you don't use it, you could lose it" applies to water rights if not used for five years.

7. d   Geothermal resources are classified as "sui generis," meaning neither water nor mineral.

8. a   When water right ownership transfers, don't assume it will happen automatically. The new owner should verify or report to the Idaho Department of Water Resources such transfer of water rights.

CHAPTER **4**
How Ownership Is Held

1. d   If two or more unmarried people acquire property, they will acquire as "tenants in common" unless otherwise stated.

2. c   In Idaho, community property includes wages earned by either spouse.

3. c   Both spouses must sign a sales contract and deed as verification to each other of the transfer.

4. d   If there is no will (intestate), the remaining half of the decedent's estate will pass to the remaining spouse.

CHAPTER **5**
Legal Descriptions

1. d   Government Rectangular Survey, metes-and-bounds, and recorded plats can be used individually or collectively in Idaho.

2. a   The township in question is north (township 10 north) and west (Range 2 west) of the initial point.

3. b   A street address, although a common method of identification, does not constitute a legal description.

4. d   The initial point is located in southwestern Idaho near the Kuna Caves.

5. a   The Canadian border is at township 65 north of the initial point.

6. d   The eastern border from the initial point is range 46 east.

CHAPTER **6**
Real Estate Taxes and Other Liens

1. a   The lien date for property taxes each year in Idaho is January 1.

2. b   Taxes must be paid by December 20 due to the fact there is only one payment.

3. d   The second installment of the current year is due no later than June 20 of the following year.

4. c   Tax delinquency takes place the next day after the appropriate tax is due.

5. a   A supplier of material to a job site must file a mechanic's lien no later than 90 days from when the material was delivered to the job site.

6. a   Fifty percent of the total combined value of the land and improvements, not to exceed $75,000, is multiplied by the tax levy to get the tax due.

7. c   The total tax due is divided in half to be paid in two equal installments.

8. d   After three years of unpaid property taxes, the delinquent property will be publicly sold at a tax sale.

9. a   A mechanic's lien for labor needs to be filed within 90 days after the work is completed.

10. d   In Idaho, a judgment lien is good for five years and can be renewed every five years until paid.

11. d   Judgment liens can be filed five years at a time, indefinitely.

12. b   A 26-year-old single parent is not eligible for a reduction in real property taxes.

13. c   A pre-existing home must be owned and occupied prior to April 15 of the existing tax year to be eligible for homeowner's exemption for the current year.

14. d   Laborers have priority over material providers if proceeds are insufficient to pay all claimants.

CHAPTER 7

Real Estate Contracts

(For answer to earnest money problem, see pages 203–208)

1. c   In Idaho, a rental agreement or lease for more than one year must be in writing to be enforceable.

2. d   A contract is voidable if one of the parties legally can reject what appears to be good and binding.

3. c   The statute of limitations in Idaho is five years for contracts in writing.

4. b   The legal age in Idaho to contract is 18.

5. a   In Idaho, a transfer of real property must be in writing to be enforceable to comply with the Statute of Frauds.

6. b   Although informational in scope, the physical description of land and improvements, room dimensions, and so on, need not be included in an offer to purchase real property.

7. a   "The purchase and sale agreement must include a provision for division of moneys taken as earnest money when the transaction is not closed and such moneys are retained by any person as forfeited payment" [IC 54-2046].

8. d   Real estate licensees should suggest legal counsel if the consumer does not understand the terms and conditions of a contract.

9. c   If a written contract would allow the buyer to qualify for a loan larger than the true sales price would allow, the agreement could be considered a "double contract," which is illegal [IC 54-2004].

10. b   All entrusted funds received by a broker shall be deposited into a real estate trust account maintained by the broker [IC 54-2045].

CHAPTER 8
Transfer of Title

1. c   Without a will, the survivor of community property will receive all of the community property. The separate property will be divided this way: one half to the surviving spouse and the remaining half divided equally between the daughters [IC 15-2-102].

2. b   Escheat occurs when there is no will or heirs; thus, property reverts to the state of Idaho [IC 15-3-914].

3. a   A holographic will occurs when the maker of a will signs but there are no witnesses.

4. d   The process in which soil is washed up onto banks is known as alluvian.

5. c   Bankruptcy is a voluntary action to transfer title.

6. c   Adverse possession in Idaho requires claim of right without owner's consent and occupying the property for a minimum of five years together with payment of taxes.

7. a   A quitclaim deed after the fact will be known as "after-acquired" title.

8. a   A grant deed grants that the same estate has not been conveyed to anyone else other than the grantee.

CHAPTER 9
Title Records

1. b   Constructive notice is filed with the county recorder.

2. c   "Acknowledgment" is usually accomplished with a notary public that verifies a voluntary act by the party making the original signature.

3. b   The bank will record a security instrument into the public records that will show up in a title search.

4. d   The purchaser has the right to choose the title insurance company for any federally related mortgage.

5. d   "Expanded" endorsement to a standard owner's title insurance policy usually extends only to the drip line of the dwelling.

6. c   Title policy forms used by title companies are standardized by the American Land Title Association (ALTA).

CHAPTER 10
Real Estate License Law

1. b   Anyone conducting a real estate activity for a fee must possess a real estate license defined as a "real estate broker" [IC 54-2004].

2. c   Four members make up the Commissioners, one from each district of Idaho [IC 54-2005].

3. c   Minimum requirements to secure a real estate license include not having been convicted of a felony within five years of license application [IC 54-2012].

4. a   Members of the Idaho Real Estate Commission are appointed by the Governor of Idaho.

5. b   All officers shall be included with application for licensure [IC 54-2016].

6. d   When Idaho issues a reciprocal license, an Irrevocable Consent to Service is required to be filed [IC 54-2017].

7. b   A licensee's license will not be reinstated until the amount paid out of the recovery fund has been repaid [IC 54-2074].

8. c   If a person obtains a final judgment, a copy of the petition shall be served upon the Commission and an affidavit of such service shall be filed with the court [IC 54-2071].

9. b   Real estate licenses shall be displayed for public inspection in the broker's main office location [IC 54-2040].

10. b   When changing brokerages, the new broker shall submit a written application for licensure to the Commission [IC 54-2056].

11. b   Although a listing agreement needs to be in writing and signed by the parties to the contract, it need not be notarized.

12. c   The broker or salesperson shall provide a copy of the offer to purchase signed by the buyer immediately as a receipt [IC 54-2051].

13. a   No broker or sales associate shall give an opinion regarding the title to property [Rule 302].

14. c   Although a salesperson may be delegated by the broker to supervise a closing, the responsible broker shall ensure the correctness of closings [IC 54-2048].

15. c   The Commission has the authority to conduct audits to verify a brokerage is in compliance with the Idaho Code and Rules of the Commission [IC 54-2058].

16. a   The fee or commission is between the principal and the broker based on the terms of a written agreement [IC 54-2050].

17. d   An active licensee shall disclose in writing that he or she is a licensee to a seller when buying real estate for his or her own account [IC 54-2055].

18. c   Entrusted money related to a regulated real estate transaction must be deposited into an approved depository including but not limited to a properly licensed title insurance company [IC 54-2042].

19. d   Licensees dealing with their own property must conduct the transaction through their broker [IC 54-2055].

CHAPTER 11
Real Estate Financing

1. c   A promissory note gives evidence of debt and is negotiable to the holder of the instrument.

2. a   Because the note stated "pay to the bearer," all Krystal has to do is give it to Lance.

3. c   An installment note includes payment of a specified principal amount in two or more installments.

4. a $16,000 divided by 12 (months) equals $120 (interest for one month on $16,000) which, added to the monthly principal payment of $200, equals $320.

5. d   The borrower is also known as the grantor; the person seeking the loan.

6. d   The maximum acreage that can be secured by a deed of trust in Idaho is 40.

7. a   A real estate broker is not allowed to serve as a trustee on a deed of trust in Idaho.

8. b   A foreclosure proceeding does not start in Idaho until the trustee has a notice of default recorded in the county in which the property is located.

9. d   A "deed of reconveyance" will be issued as a result of a foreclosure and sale of a deed of trust.

10. d   There is no "right of redemption" with a trustee's sale of a deed of trust in Idaho.

11. a   If the grantor brings the delinquency of a loan secured by a deed of trust current within 115 days the grantor will retain the property and stop the foreclosure.

CHAPTER 12
Leases

1. c   Even though the lease was in writing, it still has to be signed by the lessor to be valid.

2. b   If a valid lease is for more than one year, it must be in writing to comply with the Idaho Statute of Frauds.

3. d   A property owner will get an agreed-upon fee based on production of an oil or gas well.

4. c   If the property has been "abandoned" or if damage is occurring (such as a broken water pipe) a landlord would probably have the right to enter the rental unit.

5. b   In Idaho, a written notice of 15 days must be given before the end of the term of the existing lease.

6. b   A landlord must follow the laws of Idaho relating to abandoned property and its safekeeping.

7. d   A landlord needs to provide housing that offers safe, sound, and sanitary conditions.

8. a   The security deposit is to accommodate damage and not apply to rent unless landlord and tenant agree to allow the security deposit to apply toward rent.

9. d   If the property is less than five acres a judgment can be enforced immediately.

10. d   At least six months' notice must be given to the tenant to change the rules of a marina.

CHAPTER 13
Real Estate Appraisal

1. d   A competitive or comparative market analysis (CMA) is what real estate licensees use to assist the seller in pricing.

2. d   A certified general appraiser can perform residential and commercial appraisals regardless of complexity.

3. d   Providing the purpose is to secure a listing or sale, a licensee can offer a competitive market analysis to either buyer, seller, or both.

4. c   Only an active broker can offer a price opinion for a fee in Idaho [IC 54-4105].

5. c   Only a licensed appraiser can appraise a property for a federally related loan.

6. a   Because a duplex is income-producing, the most likely method of appraisal would be the income approach.

CHAPTER 14
Environmental Issues and Control of Land Use

1. b   The Comprehensive Plan, a plan to accommodate growth, was the focus of the Local Land Use Planning Act of 1975.

2. c   Because the use predated the adoption of a new zoning restriction, it will be allowed to continue. However, there may be restrictions of expansion and the use could be subject to a termination date.

3. a   A public notice will be sent to all property owners as well as a notice being published in a local newspaper [IC 50-222].

4. c   State statute identifies a platted subdivision as five or more, but local jurisdictions can be more restrictive.

5. b   Because of possible future annexation, cities have the power to approve or disapprove within one mile of their corporate boundaries.

6. d   Subdivisions exceeding 25 lots must have sewer and water facilities approved by the State Department of Health and Welfare.

7. b   Annexation by cities is regulated by state statute [IC 50-222].

8. b   Lead-based paint must be addressed and acknowledged between buyer and seller or landlord and tenant for residential homes built prior to 1978.

CHAPTER 15

Idaho Fair Housing

1. d   Even though a mobile home is personal property, it is still residential housing and is subject to fair housing laws.

2. d   The Idaho Human Rights Commission or HUD will answer complaints surrounding discrimination.

3. b   A complaint regarding discrimination must be filed within one year to be heard.

4. c   Fair housing laws categories include race, color, religion, sex, national origin, familial status, and handicap but not sexual preference.

5. b   Because a property manager is representing another, the property manager cannot discriminate against anyone, including a blind person who would be considered handicapped.

CHAPTER 16

Closing the Real Estate Transaction

Closing statement computations:

The problem states that the payments are current to September 1. Because interest is paid in arrears, we must charge the seller with interest to the date of closing.

- October 1 through October 15 = 15 days of interest owed
- $94,120.59 × 7.25% = $6,823.7428 per year
- $6,823.7428 ÷ 12 = $568.6452 per month
- $568.6452 ÷ 30 = $18.9548 per day
- $18.9548 × 15 days = $284.32

Even though the October payment was paid, the payment paid for principal and interest for September. Thus, interest must be paid from October 1 to October 15 (closing).

Because the real estate tax bills are not mailed out until the first week in November, we do not know the exact amount of taxes owed for the current year. We will prorate taxes based on the most recent information available; thus, we use the previous year's taxes as a figure. Idaho's tax year is from January 1 to December 31.

January 1 through October 15 = 9 months and 15 days
$2,478.42 ÷ 12 = $206.54
$206.54 × 9.5 months = $1,962.08

Because the taxes cannot be paid, the buyer is assuming the liability for the full payment when due. Therefore, we give the buyer credit for the seller's share of the taxes owed and charge the seller accordingly.

The escrow closing fee is to be shared equally by the buyer and seller. The fee is computed at $3 per thousand dollar value or portion thereof. Because $165,000 is more than $122,000, the fee is computed as though the price were $165,000.

$3 × 165 = $495 + $45 = $540

½ × $540 = $270

ANSWER KEY FIGURE 1

Completed Closing Statement

CLOSING STATEMENT

Sale No. _____ 2005–241 _____

Seller _____ Jeff and Ronna Graham _____

Buyer _____ Mark and Sara Swenson _____

Property _____ 1313 Honey Locust Dr., Boise, Idaho _____

Salesperson _____ Frank Livermore _____   Pro Rate Date _____ October 15, 2005 _____

	BUYER		SELLER	
	DEBIT	CREDIT	DEBIT	CREDIT
Purchase Price	165,000.00			165,000.00
Earnest Money		2,500.00		
Subsequent Payment				
Assumption				
First Mortgage Balance			94,120.59	
Interest 10/1/05 to 10/15/05			284.32	
Reserves				
Taxes				
Insurance				
FHA Insurance				
Assumption Fee				
Discount Points			1,485.00	
Title Insurance—Standard Owners			880.00	
Contract Balance				
Interest				
New Mortgage Taken Out By Buyer		148,500.00		
Reserve for Taxes, Ins., Etc. (2 months)	515.00			
Credit Report	35.00			
Tax Service Fee	72.00			
Appraisal Fee			450.00	
Interest Adj. 10/15/05 to 11/1/05	402.19			
MGIC Prem.				
Contract or Note Given Seller				
Taxes 1/1/05 to 10/15/05		1,962.08	1,962.08	
Special Assessments				
Fire Insurance (one-year premium)	315.00			
Rent				
Title Insurance lender (mortgagee)	290.00			
Recording & Release	25.00		45.00	
Attorney's Fees				
Escrow Fee	270.00		270.00	
Broker's Commission			9,900.00	
Cash From Buyer to Close		13,962.11		
Amount Paid To Seller			55,603.01	
BALANCE	166,924.19	166,924.19	165,000.00	165,000.00

Prepared By _____ Frontier Title Insurance Escrow _____

Date _____ October 15, 2005 _____

APPROVED

BUYER _____

BUYER _____

SELLER _____

SELLER _____

A N S W E R K E Y F I G U R E 2

Completed Real Estate Purchase and Sale Agreement and Receipt for Earnest Money

RE-21 REAL ESTATE PURCHASE AND SALE AGREEMENT

EQUAL HOUSING OPPORTUNITY

REALTOR® THIS IS A LEGALLY BINDING CONTRACT. READ THE ENTIRE DOCUMENT INCLUDING ANY ATTACHMENTS. IF YOU HAVE ANY QUESTIONS, **CONSULT YOUR ATTORNEY AND/OR ACCOUNTANT** BEFORE SIGNING.

1. ID# 41008326   DATE September 1, 2005
2.
3. **LISTING AGENCY** Wilson, Wagner & Bills   Office Phone # 333-0000   Fax # 333-0202
4. Listing Agent Joe Wilson   E-Mail joew@aol.com   Phone # 333-0000
5. **SELLING AGENCY** Gold Carpet Realty   Office Phone # 311-0011   Fax # 311-1117
6. Selling Agent Frank Livermore   E-Mail liver@netcom.com   Phone # 311-0011
7.
8. **1. BUYER:** Mark A. Swenson and Sara R. Swenson   (Hereinafter called
9. "BUYER") agrees to purchase, and the undersigned SELLER agrees to sell the following described real estate hereinafter referred to as "PREMISES"
10. **COMMONLY KNOWN AS** 1313 Honey Locust Drive   City Boise
11. Ada County, ID, Zip 83720   legally described as: Lot 13, Block 3, Randolf Addition
12. to Boise, Ada County, Idaho
13. **OR Legal Description Attached as addendum # —— (Addendum must accompany original offer.)**
14.
15. **2. $ 165,000 PURCHASE PRICE:** One Hundred and Sixty-Five Thousand **DOLLARS,**
16. payable upon the following **TERMS AND CONDITIONS** (not including closing costs) :
17.
18. **3. FINANCIAL TERMS: Note: A+C+D+E must add up to total purchase price.**
19.
20. $ 2,500 **(A). EARNEST MONEY:** BUYER hereby deposits Two Thousand Five Hundred DOLLARS as
21. Earnest Money evidenced by: ☐cash ☒personal check ☐cashier's check ☐note (due date):
22. ☐other and a receipt is hereby acknowledged. Earnest Money to be deposited
23. in trust account ☐upon receipt, or ☐ upon acceptance by all parties and shall be held by: ☐Listing Broker ☒Selling Broker
24. ☐other for the benefit of the parties hereto. The responsible Broker shall be Gold Carpet Realty .
25.
26. **(B). ALL CASH OFFER:** ☒NO ☐YES If this is an all cash offer do not complete lines 32 through 61, fill blanks with N/A
27. **(Not** Applicable). **IF CASH OFFER, BUYER'S OBLIGATION TO CLOSE SHALL NOT BE SUBJECT TO ANY FINANCIAL CONTINGENCY.**
28. BUYER agrees to provide SELLER within —— business days from the date of acceptance of this agreement by all parties, evidence of
29. sufficient funds and/or proceeds necessary to close transaction. Acceptable documentation includes, but is not limited to, a copy of a recent bank or
30. financial statement or contract(s) for the sale of BUYER'S current residence or other property to be sold.
31.
32. $ 148,500 **(C). NEW LOAN PROCEEDS:** This Agreement is contingent upon BUYER obtaining the following financing:
33. ☐ FIRST LOAN of $ 148,500 not including mortgage insurance, through ☐FHA, ☐VA, ☒CONVENTIONAL, ☐IHFA,
34. ☐RURAL DEVELOPMENT, ☐OTHER with interest not to exceed 6.5 % for a period of 30 year(s) at: ☒ Fixed Rate
35. ☐Other BUYER shall pay no more than —— point(s) plus origination fee if any. SELLER shall pay no more than 1 point(s).
36. Any reduction in points shall first accrue to the benefit of the ☐BUYER ☒SELLER ☐Divided Equally ☐N/A.
37.
38. ☐ **SECOND LOAN** of $ with interest not to exceed % for a period of 30 year(s) at: ☒Fixed Rate
39. ☐Other BUYER shall pay no more than —— point(s) plus origination fee if any. SELLER shall pay no more than 1 point(s). Any
40. reduction in points shall first accrue to the benefit of the ☐BUYER ☒SELLER ☐Divided Equally ☐N/A.
41.
42. **LOAN APPLICATION:** BUYER ☐has applied ☐ shall apply for such loan(s) within business day(s) of SELLER'S acceptance. Within
43. business days of final acceptance of all parties, BUYER agrees to furnish SELLER with a **written confirmation showing lender approval of**
44. **credit report, income verification, debt ratios in a manner acceptable to the SELLER(S) and subject only to satisfactory appraisal and final lender**
45. **underwriting.** If such written confirmation is not received by SELLER(S) within the strict time allotted, SELLER(S) may at their option cancel this
46. agreement by notifying BUYER(S) in writing of such cancellation within business day(s) after confirmation was required. If SELLER does
47. not cancel within the strict time period specified as set forth herein, SELLER shall be deemed to have accepted such written confirmation of lender approval
48. and shall be deemed to have elected to proceed with the transaction. SELLER'S approval shall not be unreasonably withheld. **If an appraisal is required**
49. **by lender, the property must appraise at not less than purchase price** or BUYER'S Earnest Money may be returned at BUYER'S request. BUYER
50. may also apply for a loan with different conditions and costs and close transaction provided all other terms and conditions of this Agreement are
51. fulfilled, and the new loan does not increase the costs or requirements to the SELLER.
52. **FHA / VA:** If applicable, it is expressly agreed that notwithstanding any other provisions of this contract, BUYER shall not be obligated to complete the
53. purchase of the property described herein or to incur any penalty or forfeiture of Earnest Money deposits or otherwise unless BUYER has been given in
54. accordance with HUD/FHA or VA requirements a written statement by the Federal Housing Commissioner, Veterans Administration or a Direct
55. Endorsement lender setting forth the appraised value of the property of not less than the sales price as stated in the contract. SELLER agrees to pay fees
56. required by FHA or VA.
57.
58. $ 0 **(D). ADDITIONAL FINANCIAL TERMS:**
59. ☐ Additional financial terms are specified under the heading "OTHER TERMS AND/OR CONDITIONS" (Section 4).
60. ☐ Additional financial terms are contained in a **FINANCING ADDENDUM** of same date, attached hereto, signed by both parties.
61.
62. $ 14,000 **(E). APPROXIMATE FUNDS DUE FROM BUYERS AT CLOSING** *(Not including closing costs)*: Cash at closing
63. to be paid by BUYER at closing in GOOD FUNDS, includes: **cash, electronic transfer funds, certified check or cashier's check. NOTE:** *If any*
64. *of above loans being Assumed or taken "subject to", any net differences between the approximate balances and the actual balance of said loan(s)*
65. *shall be adjusted at closing of escrow in:* ☐Cash ☐Other:
66.
67. **BUYER'S** Initials ( )( ) Date   **SELLER'S** Initials ( )( ) Date
68.

A N S W E R   K E Y   F I G U R E   2

Completed Real Estate Purchase and Sale Agreement and Receipt for Earnest Money (continued)

72 RE-21 RESIDENTIAL PURCHASE AND SALE AGREEMENT PAGE 2 of 6 JULY, 2006 EDITION
73
74 **PROPERTY ADDRESS:** 1313 Honey Locust Drive, Boise   **ID#:** 41008326
75
76 **4. OTHER TERMS AND/OR CONDITIONS:** This Agreement is made subject to the following special terms, considerations and/or contingencies
77 which must be satisfied prior to closing ____N/A_____
78
79
80
81
82
83
84
85
86
87
88 **5. ITEMS INCLUDED & EXCLUDED IN THIS SALE:** All existing fixtures and fittings that are attached to the property are **INCLUDED IN THE PURCHASE**
89 **PRICE** (unless excluded below), and shall be transferred free of liens. These include, but are not limited to, all attached floor coverings, attached television
90 antennae, satellite dish and receiving equipment, attached plumbing, bathroom and lighting fixtures, window screens, screen doors, storm windows, storm doors,
91 all window coverings, garage door opener(s) and transmitter(s), exterior trees, plants or shrubbery, water heating apparatus and fixtures, attached fireplace
92 equipment, awnings, ventilating, cooling and heating systems, all ranges, ovens, built-in dishwashers, fuel tanks and irrigation fixtures and equipment, all water
93 systems, wells, springs, water, water rights, ditches and ditch rights, if any, that are appurtenant thereto that are now on or used in connection with the premises
94 and shall be included in the sale unless otherwise provided herein. BUYER should satisfy himself/herself that the condition of the included items is acceptable. It
95 is agreed that any item included in this section is of nominal value less than $100.
96
97 **(A). ADDITIONAL ITEMS SPECIFICALLY INCLUDED IN THIS SALE:** Maytag stack washer and dryer serial # 09283475 and Sears
98 Craftsman 6.5hp lawnmower serial #74765584 to be purchased upon closing outside escrow for $625 with a bill of sale from seller
99
100
101 **(B). ITEMS SPECIFICALLY EXCLUDED IN THIS SALE:** satellite dish and receiving equipment as identified on 90 above shall remain
102 with the seller and is not included
103
104 **6. TITLE CONVEYANCE:** Title of SELLER is to be conveyed by warranty deed, unless otherwise provided, and is to be marketable and insurable except for
105 rights reserved in federal patents, state or railroad deeds, building or use restrictions, building and zoning regulations and ordinances of any governmental unit,
106 and rights of way and easements established or of record. Liens, encumbrances or defects to be discharged by SELLER may be paid out of purchase money at
107 date of closing. No liens, encumbrances or defects which are to be discharged or assumed by BUYER or to which title is taken subject to, exist unless otherwise
108 specified in this Agreement.
109
110 **7. TITLE INSURANCE: There may be types of title insurance coverages available other than those listed below and parties to this**
111 **agreement are advised to talk to a title company about any other coverages available that will give the BUYER additional coverage.**
112
113 **(A). PRELIMINARY TITLE COMMITMENT:** Prior to closing the transaction, ☐ SELLER or ☐ BUYER shall furnish to BUYER a preliminary commitment of a
114 title insurance policy showing the condition of the title to said premises. BUYER shall have ____ business day(s) from receipt of the preliminary commitment or
115 not fewer than twenty-four (24) hours prior to closing, within which to object in writing to the condition of the title as set forth in the preliminary commitment. If
116 BUYER does not so object, BUYER shall be deemed to have accepted the conditions of the title. It is agreed that if the title of said premises is not marketable,
117 or cannot be made so within ____ business day(s) after notice containing a written statement of defect is delivered to SELLER, BUYER'S Earnest Money
118 deposit will be returned to BUYER and SELLER shall pay for the cost of title insurance cancellation fee, escrow and legal fees, if any.
119
120 **(B). TITLE COMPANY: The parties agree that** ____Frontier_____ **Title Company**
121 located at ____2005 Sunnyside Drive_____ **shall provide the title policy and preliminary report of commitment.**
122
123 **(C). STANDARD COVERAGE OWNER'S POLICY:** SELLER shall within a reasonable time after closing furnish to BUYER a title insurance policy in the
124 amount of the purchase price of the premises showing marketable and insurable title subject to the liens, encumbrances and defects elsewhere set out in this
125 Agreement to be discharged or assumed by BUYER unless otherwise provided herein. **The risk assumed by the title company in the standard coverage**
126 **policy is limited to matters of public record.** BUYER shall receive a ILTA/ALTA Owner's Policy of Title Insurance. A title company, at BUYER's request, can
127 provide information about the availability, desirability, coverage and cost of various title insurance coverages and endorsements. If BUYER desires title
128 coverage other than that required by this paragraph, BUYER shall instruct Closing Agency in writing and pay any increase in cost unless otherwise provided
129 herein.
130
131 **(D). EXTENDED COVERAGE LENDER'S POLICY (Mortgagee policy):** The lender may require that BUYER (Borrower) furnish an Extended Coverage
132 Lender's Policy. This extended coverage lender's policy considers matters of public record and additionally insures against certain matters not shown in the
133 public record. **This extended coverage lender's policy is solely for the benefit of the lender and only protects the lender.**
134
135 **8. MECHANIC'S LIENS - GENERAL CONTRACTOR DISCLOSURE STATEMENT NOTICE:** BUYER and SELLER are hereby notified that,
136 subject to Idaho Code §45-525 *et seq.*, a "General Contractor" must provide a Disclosure Statement to a homeowner that describes certain rights afforded
137 to the homeowner (e.g. lien waivers, general liability insurance, extended policies of title insurance, surety bonds, and sub-contractor information). The
138 Disclosure Statement must be given to a homeowner prior to the General Contractor entering into any contract in an amount exceeding $2,000 with a
139 homeowner for construction, alteration, repair, or other improvements to real property, or with a residential real property purchaser for the purchase and
140 sale of newly constructed property. Such disclosure is the responsibility of the General Contractor and it is not the duty of your agent to obtain this
141 information on your behalf. You are advised to consult with any General Contractor subject to Idaho Code §45-525 *et seq.* regarding the General
142 Contractor Disclosure Statement.
143
144 **BUYER'S** Initials (_____)(_____) Date _____   **SELLER'S** Initials (_____)(_____) Date _____
145
149
150 RE-21 RESIDENTIAL PURCHASE AND SALE AGREEMENT PAGE 2 of 6 JULY, 2006 EDITION

A N S W E R   K E Y   F I G U R E   2

Completed Real Estate Purchase and Sale Agreement and Receipt for Earnest Money (continued)

152 RE-21 RESIDENTIAL PURCHASE AND SALE AGREEMENT PAGE 3 of 6 JULY, 2006 EDITION
153 **PROPERTY ADDRESS:** _____1313 Hone Locust Drive_____Boise_____ **ID#:** _41008326___

155 **9. INSPECTION:**
156 (A). **BUYER chooses** ☐to have inspection ☐not to have inspection. If BUYER chooses not to have inspection skip section 9C. BUYER shall
157 have the right to conduct inspections, investigations, tests, surveys and other studies at **BUYER'S expense**. BUYER shall, within _____ business
158 day(s) of acceptance, complete these inspections and give to SELLER written notice of disapproved of items. BUYER is strongly advised to exercise
159 these rights and to make BUYER'S own selection of professionals with appropriate qualifications to conduct inspections of the entire property.

161 (B). **FHA INSPECTION REQUIREMENT, If applicable: "For Your Protection: Get a Home Inspection", HUD 92564-CN must be signed on or**
162 **before execution of this agreement.**

164 (C). **SATISFACTION/REMOVAL OF INSPECTION CONTINGENCIES:**
165 1). If BUYER **does not** within the strict time period specified give to SELLER written notice of disapproved items, BUYER shall conclusively
166 be deemed to have: (a) completed all inspections, investigations, review of applicable documents and disclosures; (b) elected to proceed with the
167 transaction and (c) assumed all liability, responsibility and expense for repairs or corrections other than for items which SELLER has otherwise agreed in
168 writing to repair or correct.

170 2). If BUYER **does** within the strict time period specified give to SELLER written notice of disapproved items, **BUYER shall provide to**
171 **SELLER pertinent section(s) of written inspection reports**. SELLER shall have ___ONE___ business day(s) in which to **respond in writing.** The
172 SELLER, at their option, may correct the items as specified by the BUYERS in their letter or may elect not to do so. If the SELLER agrees to correct the
173 items asked for in the BUYERS letter, then both parties agree that they will continue with the transaction and proceed to closing. **This will remove the**
174 **BUYER'S inspection contingency.**

176 3).If the SELLER elects not to correct the disapproved items, or does not respond in writing within the strict time period specified, then the
177 BUYER(S) have the option of either continuing the transaction without the SELLER being responsible for correcting these deficiencies or giving the
178 SELLER written notice within ___ONE___ business days that they will not continue with the transaction and will receive their Earnest Money back.

180 4). If BUYER **does not** give such written notice of cancellation within the strict time periods specified, BUYER shall conclusively be deemed
181 to have elected to proceed with the transaction without repairs or corrections other than for items which SELLER has otherwise agreed in writing to
182 repair or correct. SELLER shall make the property available for all Inspections. BUYER shall keep the property free and clear of liens; indemnify and
183 hold SELLER harmless from all liability, claims, demands, damages and costs; and repair any damages arising from the inspections. No inspections
184 may be made by any governmental building or zoning inspector or government employee without the prior consent of SELLER unless required by local
185 law.

187 **10. LEAD PAINT DISCLOSURE:** The subject property ☒is/ ☐is not defined as "Target Housing" regarding lead-based paint or lead-based paint
188 hazards. If yes, BUYER hereby acknowledges the following: (a) BUYER has been provided an EPA approved lead-based paint hazard information
189 pamphlet, "Protect Your Family From Lead in Your Home", (b) receipt of SELLER'S Disclosure of Information and Acknowledgment Form and have
190 been provided with all records, test reports or other information, if any, related to the presence of lead-based paint hazards on said property, (c) that
191 this contract is contingent upon BUYERS right to have the property tested for lead-based paint hazards to be completed no later than
192 _____ or the contingency will terminate, (d) that BUYER hereby ☒waives ☐does not waive this right, (e) that if test results show
193 unacceptable amounts of lead-based paint on the premises, BUYER has the right to cancel the contract subject to the option of the SELLER (to be given
194 in writing) to elect to remove the lead-based paint and correct the problem which must be accomplished before closing, (f) that if the contract is
195 canceled under this clause, BUYER'S earnest money deposit will be returned to BUYER.

197 **11. SQUARE FOOTAGE VERIFICATION: BUYER IS AWARE THAT ANY REFERENCE TO THE SQUARE FOOTAGE OF THE REAL PROPERTY OR**
198 **IMPROVEMENTS IS APPROXIMATE. IF SQUARE FOOTAGE IS MATERIAL TO THE BUYER, IT MUST BE VERIFIED DURING THE INSPECTION PERIOD.**

200 **12. SELLER'S PROPERTY DISCLOSURE FORM:** If required by Title 55, Chapter 25 Idaho Code SELLER shall within ten (10) days after execution
201 of this Agreement provide to BUYER "SELLER'S Property Disclosure Form" or other acceptable form. BUYER has received the "SELLER'S Property
202 Disclosure Form" or other acceptable form prior to signing this Agreement: ☒Yes ☐No ☐N/A

204 **13. COVENANTS, CONDITIONS AND RESTRICTIONS (CC& R'S):** BUYER is responsible to obtain and review a copy of the CC& R's (if
205 applicable). BUYER has reviewed CC& R's. ☒Yes ☐No

207 **14. SUBDIVISION HOMEOWNER'S ASSOCIATION:** BUYER is aware that membership in a Home Owner's Association may be required and
208 BUYER agrees to abide by the Articles of Incorporation, By-Laws and rules and regulations of the Association. BUYER is further aware that the
209 Property may be subject to assessments levied by the Association described in full in the Declaration of Covenants, Conditions and Restrictions,
210 BUYER has reviewed Homeowner's Association Documents: ☒Yes ☐No ☐N/A Association fees/dues are $ __22.00_____
211 ___
212 per ___Month_____ ☒BUYER ☐SELLER ☐N/A to pay Homeowner's Association **SET UP FEE of** $_____0_____ **and/or property**
213 **TRANSFER FEES of** $___15.00___ at closing.

215 **15. "NOT APPLICABLE DEFINED:"** The letters "n/a," "N/A," "n.a.," and "N.A." as used herein are abbreviations of the term "not applicable." Where
216 this agreement uses the term "not applicable" or an abbreviation thereof, it shall be evidence that the parties have contemplated certain facts or
217 conditions and have determined that such facts or conditions do not apply to the agreement or transaction herein.

219 **BUYER'S** Initials (_____)(_____) Date _____   **SELLER'S** Initials (_____)(_____) Date _____
220
222 RE-21 RESIDENTIAL PURCHASE AND SALE AGREEMENT PAGE 3 of 6 JULY, 2006 EDITION

ANSWER KEY FIGURE 2

Completed Real Estate Purchase and Sale Agreement and Receipt for Earnest Money (continued)

223 RE-21 RESIDENTIAL PURCHASE AND SALE AGREEMENT PAGE 4 of 6 JULY, 2006 EDITION
224 PROPERTY ADDRESS: _____1313 Honey Locust Drive_____ Boise_____ ID#: _41008326_

225
226 **16. COSTS PAID BY:** Costs in addition to those listed below may be incurred by BUYER and SELLER unless otherwise agreed herein, or provided by
227 law or required by lender, or otherwise stated herein. The below costs will be paid as indicated. Some costs are subject to loan program requirements.
228 **SELLER agrees to pay up to $_____ of lender required repair costs only.**
229 BUYER or SELLER has the option to pay any lender required repair costs in excess of this amount.
230

	BUYER	SELLER	Shared Equally	N/A		BUYER	SELLER	Shared Equally	N/A
Appraisal Fee	X				Title Ins. Standard Coverage Owner's Policy		X		
Appraisal Re-Inspection Fee	X				Title Ins. Extended Coverage **Lender's** Policy – Mortgagee Policy	X			
Closing Escrow Fee			X		Additional Title Coverage				X
Lender Document Preparation Fee	X				Fuel in Tank – Amount to be Determined by Supplier				X
Tax Service Fee	X				Well Inspection				X
Flood Certification/Tracking Fee		X			Septic Inspections				X
Lender Required Inspections	X				Septic Pumping				X
Attorney Contract Preparation or Review Fee				X	Survey				X
Home Inspection	X								

231
232 **17. OCCUPANCY:** BUYER ☒ does ☐ does not intend to occupy property as BUYER'S primary residence.
233
234 **18. FINAL WALK THROUGH:** The SELLER grants BUYER and any representative of BUYER reasonable access to conduct a final walk
235 through inspection of the premises approximately __3__ calendar day(s) prior to close of escrow, NOT AS A CONTINGENCY OF THE SALE, but
236 for purposes of satisfying BUYER that any repairs agreed to in writing by BUYER and SELLER have been completed and premises are in
237 substantially the same condition as on acceptance date of this contract. SELLER shall make premises available for the final walk through and
238 agrees to accept the responsibility and expense for making sure all the utilities are turned on for the walk through except for phone and cable. If
239 BUYER does not conduct a final walk through, BUYER specifically releases the SELLER and Broker(s) of any liability.
240
241 **19. RISK OF LOSS: Prior to closing of this sale, all risk of loss shall remain with SELLER. In addition, should the premises be materially**
242 **damaged by fire or other destructive cause prior to closing, this agreement shall be void at the option of the BUYER.**
243
244 **20. CLOSING**: On or before the closing date, BUYER and SELLER shall deposit with the closing agency all funds and instruments necessary to
245 complete this transaction. **Closing means the date on which all documents are either recorded or accepted by an escrow agent and the sale**
246 **proceeds are available to SELLER.** The closing shall be no later than (Date)_____October 15, 2005_____.
247 The parties agree that the **CLOSING AGENCY** for this transaction shall be _____Frontier Title Insurance Company_____
248 located at_____2005 Sunnyside Drive, Boise, Idaho_____
249 If a long-term escrow / collection is involved, then the long-term escrow holder shall be _____N/A_____.
250
251 **21. POSSESSION:** BUYER shall be entitled to possession ☐upon closing or ☒date _____10/16/05_____ time ____9:00____ ☒A.M. ☐ P.M.
252 Property taxes and water assessments (using the last available assessment as a basis), rents, interest and reserves, liens, encumbrances or obligations
253 assumed and utilities shall be pro-rated as of _____10/15/05_____.
254
255 **22. SALES PRICE INFORMATION:** SELLER and BUYER hereby grant permission to the brokers and either party to this Agreement, to disclose
256 sale data from this transaction, including selling price and property address to the local Association / Board of REALTORS®, multiple listing service, its
257 members, its members' prospects, appraisers and other professional users of real estate sales data. The parties to this Agreement acknowledge that
258 sales price information compiled as a result of this Agreement may be provided to the County Assessor Office by either party or by either party's Broker.
259
260 **23. FACSIMILE TRANSMISSION:** Facsimile or electronic transmission of any signed original document, and retransmission of any signed facsimile
261 or electronic transmission shall be the same as delivery of an original. At the request of either party or the Closing Agency, the parties will confirm
262 facsimile and electronic transmitted signatures by signing an original document.
263
264 **BUYER'S** Initials (_____)(_____) Date _____ **SELLER'S** Initials (_____)(_____) Date _____
265

269

RE-21 RESIDENTIAL PURCHASE AND SALE AGREEMENT PAGE 4 of 6 JULY, 2006 EDITION

A N S W E R   K E Y   F I G U R E   2

Completed Real Estate Purchase and Sale Agreement and Receipt for Earnest Money (continued)

274 RE-21 RESIDENTIAL PURCHASE AND SALE AGREEMENT PAGE 5 of 6 JULY, 2006 EDITION

275 **PROPERTY ADDRESS:** _____ 1313 Honey Locust Drive _____ Boise _____ **ID#:** _41008326_

276 **24. SINGULAR AND PLURAL** terms each include the other, when appropriate.

278 **25. BUSINESS DAYS & HOURS** A business day is herein defined as Monday through Friday, 8:00 A.M. to 5:00 P.M. in the local time zone
279 where the subject real property is physically located.   A business day shall not include any Saturday or Sunday, nor shall a business day include
280 any legal holiday recognized by the state of Idaho as found in Idaho Code § 73-108. The time in which any act required under this agreement is to
281 be performed shall be computed by excluding the date of execution and including the last day. The first day shall be the day after the date of
282 execution. If the last day is a legal holiday, then the time for performance shall be the next subsequent business day.

284 **26. SEVERABILITY:** In the case that any one or more of the provisions contained in this Agreement, or any application thereof, shall be invalid,
285 illegal or unenforceable in any respect, the validity, legality or enforceability of the remaining provisions shall not in any way be affected or impaired
286 thereby.

288 **27. ATTORNEY'S FEES:** If either party initiates or defends any arbitration or legal action or proceedings which are in any way connected with this
289 Agreement, the prevailing party shall be entitled to recover from the non-prevailing party reasonable costs and attorney's fees, including such costs and
290 fees on appeal.

292 **28. DEFAULT: If BUYER defaults** in the performance of this Agreement, SELLER has the option of: (1) accepting the Earnest Money as liquidated
293 damages or (2) pursuing any other lawful right and/or remedy to which SELLER may be entitled. If SELLER elects to proceed under (1), SELLER shall
294 make demand upon the holder of the Earnest Money, upon which demand said holder shall pay from the Earnest Money the costs incurred by
295 SELLER'S Broker on behalf of SELLER and BUYER related to the transaction, including, without limitation, the costs of title insurance, escrow fees,
296 appraisal, credit report fees, inspection fees and attorney's fees; and said holder shall pay any balance of the Earnest Money, one-half to SELLER and
297 one-half to SELLER'S Broker, provided that the amount to be paid to SELLER'S Broker shall not exceed the Broker's agreed to commission. SELLER
298 and BUYER specifically acknowledge and agree that if SELLER elects to accept the Earnest Money as liquidated damages, such shall be SELLER'S
299 sole and exclusive remedy, and such shall not be considered a penalty or forfeiture. If SELLER elects to proceed under (2), the holder of the Earnest
300 Money shall be entitled to pay the costs incurred by SELLER'S Broker on behalf of SELLER and BUYER related to the transaction, including, without
301 limitation, the costs of brokerage fee, title insurance, escrow fees, appraisal, credit report fees, inspection fees and attorney's fees, with any balance of
302 the Earnest Money to be held pending resolution of the matter.
303   **If SELLER defaults**, having approved said sale and fails to consummate the same as herein agreed, BUYER'S Earnest Money deposit shall
304 be returned to him/her and SELLER shall pay for the costs of title insurance, escrow fees, appraisals, credit report fees, inspection fees, brokerage fees
305 and attorney's fees, if any. This shall not be considered as a waiver by BUYER of any other lawful right or remedy to which BUYER may be entitled.

307 **29. EARNEST MONEY DISPUTE / INTERPLEADER:** Notwithstanding any termination of this contract, BUYER and SELLER agree that in the event
308 of any controversy regarding the Earnest Money and things of value held by Broker or closing agency, unless mutual written instructions are received by
309 the holder of the Earnest Money and things of value, Broker or closing agency shall not be required to take any action but may await any proceeding, or
310 at Broker's or closing agency's option and sole discretion, may interplead all parties and deposit any monies or things of value into a court of competent
311 jurisdiction and shall recover court costs and reasonable attorney's fees.

313 **30. COUNTERPARTS**: This Agreement may be executed in counterparts. Executing an agreement in counterparts shall mean the signature of
314 two identical copies of the same agreement. Each identical copy of an agreement signed in counterparts is deemed to be an original, and all
315/316 identical copies shall together constitute one and the same instrument.

318 **31. REPRESENTATION CONFIRMATION:** Check one (1) box in Section 1 and one (1) box in section 2 below to confirm that in this transaction, the
319 brokerage(s) involved had the following relationship(s) with the BUYER(S) and SELLER(S).

321 Section 1:

322 ☐ A. **The brokerage working with the BUYER(S) is acting as an AGENT for the BUYER(S).**

323 ☐ B. **The brokerage working with the BUYER(S) is acting as a LIMITED DUAL AGENT for the BUYER(S), without an ASSIGNED AGENT.**

324 ☐ C. **The brokerage working with the BUYER(S) is acting as a LIMITED DUAL AGENT for the BUYER(S) and has an ASSIGNED AGENT**
325   **acting solely on behalf of the BUYER(S).**

326 ☒ D. **The brokerage working with the BUYER(S) is acting as a NONAGENT for the BUYER(S).**

327 Section 2:

328 ☒ A. **The brokerage working with the SELLER(S) is acting as an AGENT for the SELLER(S).**

329 ☐ B. **The brokerage working with the SELLER(S) is acting as a LIMITED DUAL AGENT for the SELLER(S), without an ASSIGNED AGENT.**

330 ☐ C. **The brokerage working with the SELLER(S) is acting as a LIMITED DUAL AGENT for the SELLER(S) and has an ASSIGNED AGENT**
331   **acting solely on behalf of the SELLER(S).**

332 ☐ D. **The brokerage working with the SELLER(S) is acting as a NONAGENT for the SELLER(S).**

334 Each party signing this document confirms that he has received, read and understood the Agency Disclosure Brochure adopted or approved by the Idaho real estate commission and
335 has consented to the relationship confirmed above. In addition, each party confirms that the brokerage's agency office policy was made available for inspection and review. EACH
336 PARTY UNDERSTANDS THAT HE IS A "CUSTOMER" AND IS NOT REPRESENTED BY A BROKERAGE UNLESS THERE IS A SIGNED WRITTEN AGREEMENT FOR AGENCY
337 REPRESENTATION.

339 **BUYER'S** Initials (_____)(_____) Date _____   **SELLER'S** Initials (_____)(_____) Date _____

343 RE-21 RESIDENTIAL PURCHASE AND SALE AGREEMENT PAGE 5 of 6 JULY, 2006 EDITION

Completed Real Estate Purchase and Sale Agreement and Receipt for Earnest Money (continued)

344 RE-21 RESIDENTIAL PURCHASE AND SALE AGREEMENT PAGE 6 of 6 <u>JULY, 2006 EDITION</u>
345
346 PROPERTY ADDRESS: _____1313 Honey Locust Drive_____Boise_____ ID#: __41008326____
347

348 **32. ENTIRE AGREEMENT:** This Agreement contains the entire Agreement of the parties respecting the matters herein set forth and supersedes all
349 prior Agreements between the parties respecting such matters. No warranties, including, without limitation, any warranty of habitability, agreements or
350 representations not expressly set forth herein shall be binding upon either party.
351

352 **33. TIME IS OF THE ESSENCE IN THIS AGREEMENT.**
353

354 **34. AUTHORITY OF SIGNATORY:** If BUYER or SELLER is a corporation, partnership, trust, estate, or other entity, the person executing this
355 agreement on its behalf warrants his or her authority to do so and to bind BUYER or SELLER.
356

357 **35. ACCEPTANCE:** BUYER'S offer is made subject to the acceptance of SELLER on or before (Date)___Sept. 2, 2005_____ at (Local Time
358 in which property is located)___5:00_____ ☐ A.M. ☒ P.M. If SELLER does not accept this Agreement within the time specified, the entire Earnest
359 Money shall be refunded to BUYER on demand.
360

361 **36. BUYER'S SIGNATURES:**
362

363 ☐ **SEE ATTACHED BUYER'S ADDENDUM(S):** ___N/A___ (Specify number of BUYER addendum(s) attached.)
364

365 **BUYER Signature**_____   **BUYER (Print Name)**____Mark Swenson_____
366
367 Date ___9/1/05_____ Time ___2:30___ ☐ A.M. ☒ P.M.   Phone # ___377-4198_____ Cell #_____
368
369 Address_____5050 Elmore St._____   City____Boise____ State __Idaho__ Zip __83720__
370
371 E-Mail Address____m&s@hotmail.com_____   Fax #_____
372
373 --
374
375 **BUYER Signature**_____   **BUYER (Print Name)**____Sara Swenson_____
376
377 Date ___9/1/05_____ Time ___2:30___ ☐ A.M. ☒ P.M.   Phone # ___377-4198_____ Cell #_____
378
379 Address____5050 Elmore St._____   City____Boise____ State __Idaho__ Zip __83720__
380
381 E-Mail Address____m&s@hotmail.com_____   Fax #_____
382

383 **37. SELLER'S SIGNATURES:**
384 On this date, I/We hereby approve and accept the transaction set forth in the above Agreement and agree to carry out all the terms thereof on
385 the part of the SELLER.
386

387 ☐**SIGNATURE(S) SUBJECT TO ATTACHED COUNTER OFFER**
388

389 ☐ **SIGNATURE(S) SUBJECT TO ATTACHED ADDENDUM(S) #** ___N/A___
390
391
392 **SELLER Signature**_____   **SELLER (Print Name)**____Jeff Graham_____
393
394 Date ___9/1/05___ Time __8:15___ ☐ A.M. ☒ P.M.   Phone #____388-0000_____ Cell #_____
395
396 Address____1313 Honey Locust Drive_____   City____Boise____ State __Idaho__ Zip __83720__
397
398 E-Mail Address____graham@quack.net_____   Fax #_____
399
400 --
401
402 **SELLER Signature**_____   **SELLER (Print Name)**____Ronna Graham_____
403
404 Date ___9/1/05___ Time __8:15___ ☐ A.M. ☒ P.M.   Phone #____388-0000_____ Cell #_____
405
406 Address_____1313 Honey Locust Drive_____   City____Boise____ State __Idaho__ Zip __83720__
407
408 E-Mail Address_____graham@quack.net_____   Fax #_____
409
410
411 **CONTRACTOR REGISTRATION # (if applicable)**_____
412

416
417 RE-21 RESIDENTIAL PURCHASE AND SALE AGREEMENT PAGE 6 of 6 <u>JULY, 2006 EDITION</u>

INDEX